THE
OLD SONGS
OF
SKYE

1   Frances Tolmie

THE
OLD SONGS
OF
SKYE

FRANCES TOLMIE
AND HER CIRCLE

ETHEL BASSIN

EDITED BY DEREK BOWMAN

ROUTLEDGE & KEGAN PAUL
LONDON AND HENLEY

First published in 1977
by Routledge & Kegan Paul Ltd
39 Store Street,
London WC1E 7DD and
Broadway House,
Newtown Road,
Henley-on-Thames,
Oxon RG9 1EN
Set in 12 on 13 pt Monotype Centaur
and printed and bound in Great Britain by
Morrison & Gibb Ltd, London and Edinburgh
© *The Estate of the late Ethel Bassin 1977*

ISBN 0 7100 8546 X

'I am no Politician nor a Theologian—but a Spectator on the Field of Life, especially in our Island Principality.'

Frances Tolmie

CONTENTS

PLATES

HISTORICAL FOREWORD

I am so proud to have known Miss Tolmie and am glad to know that Miss Bassin's book, which has long been in preparation, is now to be published.

Miss Tolmie was, in every sense of the word, a great lady. I knew her only in old age and superficially but she was a very impressive human being with very considerable charm and I think her work as a collector of the real, true, basic music of the Highlands is precious indeed.

The story we were always told was of the years when my great-aunt Emily Sarah MacLeod lived in Kilchoan Cottage, Dunvegan, where she later died. She was deeply devoted to the people and the people to her and even now the legend of 'Miss Emily' has hardly vanished. Poverty in those days was extreme. Many families lived through those grim winters on a few sacks of potatoes and barrels of salt herring and perhaps a cow slaughtered and salted down. There was very little employment and the little cash there was would have bought tea and little else. Clothes were woven from wool from their own sheep and of course peats were dug to provide winter fuel. In those days each child was expected to carry a peat to school and once a week two peats to feed the Dominie's fire on the Sabbath.

Old-age pensions were not even dreamed of but the community spirit was profound and the devotion and sacrifice of its members an integral part of the philosophy of the last half of the nineteenth century. 'Miss Emily' devoted her efforts to securing orders for knitted goods from different Highland Regiments—and she was thankful to secure orders for a thousand pair of stockings and the wool with which to knit them.

Miss Tolmie was the daughter of the factor and the helper and handmaid of Miss Emily in distributing orders to scattered homesteads over a large area. In this way she learned in its very purity the music of a music-loving people and as they walked with her on her homeward way they sang their songs which she had the talent to translate into musical notation.

This in no way conflicts with Miss Bassin's statement that Lucy Broadwood and Anne Gilchrist played an important part in co-ordinating Miss Tolmie's work. I have merely recorded the simple and charming story of Miss Tolmie's visits as told to me.

Flora MacLeod of MacLeod

MUSICAL FOREWORD

Who am I, a Saxon and a Southerner, to write an introduction to a book by a Scot about a Gael? Well, I can at least bear independent testimony to the value of the subject and the scholarship of the author. I succeeded Lucy Broadwood as editor of the *Journal of the Folk-Song Society* in 1927, though I had not then much knowledge of folk song beyond what I had picked up from playing piano accompaniments for people who sang them, notably my sister who got them from her singing teacher, Walter Ford, an early member of the committee of the Folk-Song Society. Lucy Broadwood figures prominently in Miss Bassin's narrative as the midwife who brought the Tolmie collection to birth. The reader will learn all about this remarkable corpus of Gaelic folk song, which constituted an outstanding volume of the Folk-Song Society *Journal* a dozen years before English people discovered, chiefly from the singing of the Kennedy-Fraser ladies, that there was such a thing as Hebridean folk song.

The debt of the twentieth century to the maiden aunts of independent means is now being computed—it is certainly recognized even in these egalitarian times. Miss Bassin, engaged in this very task of computing what one of these Victorian ladies, Frances Tolmie of Skye, did for Scottish music, in fact anticipating what the School of Scottish Studies is doing today, has found much biographical material that contributes to our knowledge of a vanished society—the formal courtesy of the letters exchanged in these pages, for example, conveys a slower tempo of living, a world in which, whatever its problems and troubles, the savageries of our century find no place. To Scottish readers the accounts of life in Skye, in Oban and in Edinburgh will evoke pleasantly familiar recollections, to Southerners like me the no less pleasant discovery of the different culture of Scotland. The time of Miss Tolmie's work on folk song coincided with the recovery of national folk song in England, where there had been no precursors like Allan Ramsay, George Thomson and William Motherwell, and Lucy Broadwood, who herself collected Gaelic songs at Arisaig, Cecil Sharp and Ralph Vaughan

Williams were making their contribution not only to English culture but to the movement for the regeneration of musical life in Britain.

Miss Bassin has been well placed for this work of making more widely known the remarkable personality and valuable work of Frances Tolmie, since she herself is a Scottish musician of great enterprise and experience not limited to one field. She has, moreover, not being born a Gaelic speaker, made herself one. When I was writing my book, *Folk Music of Britain—and Beyond*, I discovered for myself not only the value of the Tolmie collection but also how valuable her close study will be to scholars, and I have read enough of her book to appreciate its less specialist, more general, social interest in a world that has now greatly changed.

Frank Howes

INTRODUCTION AND ACKNOWLEDGMENTS

A little over a century ago, when university education for women was still a long way off, Frances Tolmie from the Isle of Skye spent a first winter in Edinburgh for the purpose of study. Newly seventeen when she first arrived, she attended classes in English language and literature and had private lessons in French, German, Italian and music.

During the 1860s she was governess for some years to two young daughters of the printer and publisher Thomas Constable; the sympathetic friendship of Mr and Mrs Constable, the social life she enjoyed in their household and the wide range of reading available to her were an influence to which she always looked back with warmth. There it was that she first encountered the newly published *West Highland Tales* of John Francis Campbell of Islay in which she found to her surprise and delight 'the fireside tales known to us all'.

She came from a bilingual environment, being descended on both sides from families notable for centuries in Skye, the Outer Isles and the western mainland as tacksmen,[1] farmers, ministers, doctors and soldiers; like them she was equally fluent in Gaelic and in English. Interested from an early age in Gaelic traditional song, particularly the lesser-known and the half-forgotten, she began in her late teens to write down tunes as well as words that she learned or remembered. In this she was encouraged by the famous folklorist, Alexander Carmichael,[2] at that time a young Inland Revenue officer in the Highlands and Islands.

All this remained in the background for more than twenty years. In 1873 she became one of the earliest women students at Cambridge, at Merton Hall while Newnham College was being built. Thereafter she lived for many years with Miss Harriette Rigbye, an amateur artist of independent means, who was one of Ruskin's circle at Coniston in the Lake District. In 1895, after Miss Rigbye's death, she returned to Scotland and lived with her sister Mary first in Oban and then in Edinburgh, renewing enthusiastically her Gaelic interests and studies. In 1915, after her sister's death, she returned to Skye, to spend her last days in Dunvegan, separated only by a narrow sea-loch from Uiginish, where she was born.

In London in 1911 a double number of the *Journal of the Folk-Song Society* (founded in 1898) was given over to 'one hundred and five Songs of Occupation from the Western Isles of Scotland'. The editor, Lucy Broadwood, in her introduction described this as 'one of the most important contributions yet made towards the preservation of the purely traditional music and poetry of our British Isles in general and of Scotland in particular'.[3]

Its importance is now recognized in the world of Gaelic scholarship and musical studies in general. The School of Scottish Studies of the University of Edinburgh for instance, is well aware of its worth, while Professor Derick Thomson of the Celtic Department of Glasgow University has defined it neatly as 'the first fully significant collection of Gaelic song'.[4]

Frances Tolmie gave generously of her store of folklore and song to those who asked—too generously, said some of those nearest to her. Dr Keith Norman MacDonald in his *Gesto Collection of Highland Music*[5] acknowledged her contribution in a general way; precise documentation was not looked for in the early years of the twentieth century. The famous collection, *Songs of the Hebrides*,[6] of Mrs Marjory Kennedy-Fraser owes to Miss Tolmie's collection twenty-one songs out of a total of 212.

In 1925 I had the privilege of meeting Miss Tolmie and hearing her sing. When I was at Portree, Miss J. C. MacDonald ('Miss Toonie') kindly lent me a well-worn copy of the *Journal*, containing Miss Tolmie's songs. I was pleased to learn that Frances Tolmie was now living in Dunvegan, where my work took me occasionally. I therefore wrote and asked if I might call. A charming and formal little note [Plate 19] invited me to tea on a November afternoon.

She told me how, when she was twenty, living with her mother and sister in her brother's manse at Bracadale, she had been asked by Miss Emily MacLeod of MacLeod to supervise a knitting scheme for women in the hamlets around. Her mother gave permission but insisted that she must always have an escort on the long walks over the moors that this would entail. In preference to a girl of her own age, however, she chose one or other of two elderly women, who whiled away the time by talking of the old lore of the district, or by singing old songs and teaching them to her.

Of the songs she sang to me that day I remember clearly *Òran mu'n Ghruagaich*, 'A Song about the *Gruagach*' and the story associated with it. She sang a couple of others but unfortunately I did not take note at the time of what they were. She turned them up in the *Journal* so that I might follow the tunes transcribed there, but I found these a little bewildering, for what I read appeared to be only the skeleton of what she sang. The Gaelic traditional style of singing was still a mystery to me as I was only a beginner in the language.

I have often wished that I might have had the opportunity of paying further visits to her in order to learn even one or two of her songs as she actually sang them; but I met her only casually a couple of times after that. She died at the end of the following year, at the age of eighty-six.

Her personality remained a vivid memory, and I willingly agreed when I was asked by the then editor of the *Journal of the English Folk Dance and Song Society*, Miss M. Dean-Smith, to write about her for the issue of 1948, the jubilee of the founding of the Folk-Song Society. A little later inquiries in the press as to the whereabouts of her MSS[7] brought these to light in the possession of her grand-niece Miss Morag MacDonald,[8] Edinburgh, and I was asked to examine and write about them.

While working on the manuscripts I came upon little notes here and there that brought her charm and temperament to life again. These came as a substantial and interesting addition to Lucy Broadwood's biographical notes in the original *Journal*, although discarded at the time as not entirely relevant. It was possible, however, that this unique West Highland gentlewoman, a personality of the period in which she lived, a source of information for Gaelic folklorists, genealogists and other scholars of her day and since, merited a biography a little fuller and more easily accessible than a brief account in a specialized journal.[9]

From that point this book began.

I could, however, never have carried the task through without the help and encouragement of very many people, only a few of whom I can name here.

My first thanks are due to the English Folk Dance and Song Society for access to and permission to quote from MS and other material in Cecil Sharp House, in particular Frances Tolmie's letters, notes, the 'Reminiscences' addressed to Miss Broadwood, letters to Miss Gilchrist and other letters connected with Miss Tolmie's work. I have made considerable use of this material throughout the book, and especially of the *Journal of the Folk-Song Society*, no. 16 of 1911, reproducing a number of the songs printed in it. I have also incorporated material from journals of the English Folk Dance and Song Society of 1948 and 1951, where my articles on Frances Tolmie and Marjory Kennedy-Fraser first appeared. All along the Society has been most generous and helpful. A succession of editors and librarians has unstintingly assisted and encouraged me in my researches: I owe more than I can readily express to Frank Howes, S. A. Mathews, Margaret Dean-Smith, Sally Jackson, Ruth Noyes, Mary Dunkley and Barbara Newlin.

I am similarly indebted to members, past and present, of the Tolmie family and their 'near cousins', the Mackenzies in Dunvegan, all of whom have been most courteous and kind to me in my inquiries. Margaret Skene was very helpful—more than this, during the few years that I was privileged to know her, she became a dear friend. Morag MacDonald of Kiltarlity, who through the kindness of her sister, Mrs Flora Stuart, entrusted to me her grand-aunt's invaluable MSS, her commonplace book and letters to Marjory Kennedy-Fraser—all now in the National Library of Scotland—was another courteous 'Tolmie'. Like her great forbear, she shared what she knew and possessed with the utmost generosity. I am also very grateful to Mrs Osbaldeston-Mitford for so kindly letting me use Frances Tolmie's letters to her father, Canon Roderick MacLeod.

The Constable and Cowan families have willingly assisted me, as have done so many correspondents and informants, especially the custodians of the library of the Ladies' Highland Association, housed in the Church of Scotland offices in Edinburgh, and the members of the Cambridge secretariat of the Newnham College Roll. May I also take this opportunity of thanking the Rev. John Macintyre, Miss J. F. Mackinnon and Mr Donald MacPhail who freely allowed me access to the Minutes of the Celtic Union. For the Coniston chapter in Miss Tolmie's life I am especially grateful for the expert assistance I received from Mrs Barbara Gnosspelius and her family.

My researches led me to the School of Scottish Studies, Edinburgh, where I was made very welcome and afforded every assistance by Anna Belfourd, Mary MacDonald, Morag MacLeod, Ailie Munro, Alan Bruford, John MacInnes, Basil Megaw and the Director, Professor John MacQueen. I am deeply grateful for their detailed criticism and practical help with the layout of the book. The Rev. William Matheson of the Department of Celtic, Edinburgh University, also generously gave me the benefit of his historical and Gaelic expertise. William Gillies, also of the Department of Celtic, Edinburgh University, and Francis Collinson of the School of Scottish Studies, with exemplary conscientiousness checked the whole text at a later stage in its progress and suggested various improvements to it. Catherine Dickson and Phyllis Hamilton of the Edinburgh Central Library diligently found for me books I needed, and Mrs M. MacLean, Mrs T. Laing, Mrs M. Bowman and Mrs M. Flanagan provided efficient secretarial help. I also wish to express my gratitude to Professor William Beattie, Director of the Institute for Advanced Studies in the Humanities, Edinburgh University, and David M. Lloyd of the National Library of Scotland for their support so liberally given.

The large circle of Frances Tolmie's relatives and friends, folklorists, musicians, scholars, ministers and lay people, have given me so much, often of inestimable value. I am most grateful to them all, and have sincerely tried to name each one as occasion arises in the course of the story. If the index is rather long it is because I wished to record them all. I apologize if I have inadvertently left anyone out.

ACKNOWLEDGMENTS

Music examples 25 and 27 are reproduced from *Songs of the Hebrides* by permission of the Trustees of the Estate of Marjory Kennedy-Fraser and Boosey and Hawkes Music Publishers Ltd. Examples and extracts from *Journal of the Folk-Song Society*, no. 16 (vol. iv, part 3), 1911, are reproduced by kind permission of the English Folk Dance and Song Society. The endpaper maps are reproduced by permission of the Trustees of the National Library of Scotland.

EDITOR'S NOTE

Ethel Bassin died on 29 April 1974, having providentially completed with me the text of this book, the fruit of many years of research.

CHAPTER I

UIGINISH, SKYE, 1840-4

Na daoine o'n tàinig thu.[1]
The people from whom you are descended.

Frances Tolmie first saw the light of day on 13 October 1840, at Uiginish Farm across the loch from Dunvegan Castle, in country with which her kindred had been associated for generations.

Sliochd nan Tolmach mór, the 'Tribe of the big Tolmes', came to Dunvegan in the sixteenth century. A sept of the ancient MacLeods of Gairloch, senior cadet branch of the MacLeods of Lewis, they had been driven from Gairloch by the Mackenzies. They sought and received protection from MacLeod of Dunvegan to whom they were distantly related. The name Tolmie is said to derive from the Norse *holm*, 'island' or 'islet'. In Gaelic this word could give, with the definite article, *an Tolm*, 'the Isle', and thence *Tolmach*, 'man of the Isle', eventually being spelt Tolm, Tolmach, Tolme or Tolmie.

According to tradition the Tolmies were descendants of John Tolmach or Tolm, son of Roderick, son of Allan, last head of the MacLeods of Gairloch, who flourished in the fifteenth and sixteenth centuries. John Holmach, 'near cousin of the Laird of Raasay', mentioned in an old account of 'some troubles in the island of Raasay in the year 1611', was probably the same John Holmach (or Tolmach) MacRorie MacAllan of Gairloch.

For generations the Tolmes held positions of responsibility under the chiefs of Dunvegan. One is known to have been a gentleman-at-arms in the retinue of Sir Roderick MacLeod (Rory Mór). This great chief lived on a grand scale at Dunvegan Castle, with pipers, harpers, bards and jesters, and was seldom without some important guest. His pipers were the renowned MacCrimmons; the bardess, Mary MacLeod, *Màiri nighean Alasdair Ruaidh*, 'Mary, daughter of red-haired Alexander', states that she was reared in his court.

Before Rory Mór died in 1626 the last of the fierce clan battles was over, and the Highlands were settling down to more peaceable ways. Towards the end of his life he took up residence at Fortrose, in Easter Ross, and a Tolme was among those who accompanied him. Certain prosperous merchants in Fortrose and Inverness were Tolme descendants. So, in the eighteenth century, we come to Frances Tolmie's great-grandfather, William Tolme, known in Gaelic as *Uilleam Mór*, 'Big William', on account of his height and generous build. He for a time extended his business to Stornoway, this island town, and Fortrose on the mainland, being at that time the commercial centres of Ross-shire.

Rory Mór's grandson, Norman, twenty-second of the MacLeod chiefs, was born after his father's death, spent his minority in Fortrose, and on coming of age in 1727 returned to Dunvegan. Uilleam Mór also removed to Dunvegan at this time, leased from MacLeod the farms of Kilmuir and Creagachlachan, and set up a mercantile business. He became postmaster for the whole of the island and factor for the MacLeod estates in Harris, Skye and Glenelg. It was on a mission for MacLeod to Glenelg in 1732 that he and other gentlemen visited the unfortunate Lady Grange,[2] who was being conveyed by ship to Heiskir, a small island to the west of North Uist. The sloop lay at anchor in Loch Hourn, awaiting a favourable breeze for crossing the Minch. In a sad letter from Lady Grange which later reached her friends in Edinburgh she said that the only kindness she had been shown since her abduction was by William Tolme. He seems to have expressed sympathy in conversation, but it was apparently beyond his power to give her tangible help.

Uilleam Mór was twice married, and three of his large family may be mentioned. His eldest son, William, is tragically commemorated in the name of a cliff at Fiadhard, near Dunvegan, known as *Creag an Tolmaich*, 'Tolme's rock', over which the boy, aged only fifteen, fell and was killed. Elizabeth, the youngest daughter, became aunt by marriage of Alexander Mackenzie, the Canadian explorer, whose name is given to the Mackenzie River. John, another son of Uilleam Mór, was known as *Seoc Tolm*, 'Jock Tolme'. When the leases of his father's farms expired in 1773 he did not renew them but instead became tacksman of several properties, including 'the three Uiginishes'. That same autumn saw the visit to Skye of Johnson and Boswell. MacLeod's factor, Seoc Tolm, undoubtedly must have met and talked with them.

It was the young (twenty-third) chief of this period, Norman,[3] whom Boswell praised as being a most promising youth, and whom Dr Johnson also admired for the courage with which he was facing his financial difficulties. Nineteen years of age, he had the previous year succeeded to an estate heavily burdened with debt owing to the extravagance of his predecessor and namesake.[4] He, however, so much endeared himself to his people that in 1777 we find thirty-six of his tacksmen and tenants voluntarily assessing themselves to the amount of 1s. 6d., additional to every pound of rent, Seoc Tolm's signature among them.

Seoc Tolm's son, John, succeeded to the Uiginish farms on the death of his father in 1823. Three years later, at the age of twenty-nine, he married Margaret Hope MacAskill of the island of Eigg branch of the family of MacAskills of Rudha an Dùnain. She was barely eighteen. Of their family of nine, Frances (Fanny) was the eighth child and youngest daughter.

Margaret Tolmie would sing to her babies in the soft Gaelic tongue, using recollections of lullabies and dandling tunes that her own mother and nurses had sung in the island of Eigg, her birthplace, and others with a Skye background. Of the latter, Fanny's earliest memories were to be of the fragments from the story of the piper who daringly entered the 'Cave of Gold', Uamh 'n Òir, at Harlosh, near Dunvegan, hoping to find an exit at a cave of the same name at Trotternish, on the opposite coast. Some hours later, runs the story, a woman sitting at a nearby well heard from below the ground the despairing voice of the piper, lamenting that he had not three hands, two to play the pipes and one to fight the dread monster of the cave who was overpowering him. Four short songs relating to Uamh 'n Òir were sung in the Tolmie nursery, each with its own scrap of tune; there were four distinct tunes, but only two themes. One theme is the cry of despair already mentioned, the other the piper's lament that nevermore will he return (Example 1).

3

Example 1[5]

Uamh'n Òir (i)
(The Cave of Gold)

An early nursery memory,
Skye.—F.T.

1. Mu'n till mis - e, mu'n ruig mis - e; Mu'n till mis - e a Uamh'n Òir.

TRANSLATION

1. Ere I return, ere I attain, ere I return from Uamh'n Òir. 2. the young of the goats will be goats of the crags, and the little calves become great kine. 3. Creel-bearing horses will be riding-steeds, and babes, borne in the bosom, men, bearing arms. But never more shall I return.

1. Mu'n till mise,
   Mu'n ruig mise,
   Mu'n till mise,
   A Uaimh an Òir.

2. Bidh na minn bheaga
   'N an gobhair chreagan,
   'S na laoigh bheaga
   'N an crodh mòr.

3. Bidh na h-eich chliabhta
   'N an eich dhìollaid,
   Mu'n till mise,
   A Uaimh an Òir.

4. Bidh 'chlann uchda,
   'N am fir fheachda,
   'S cha till mise
   Ri mo bheò!

In her 'Reminiscences' (1911)[6] Frances Tolmie was to write:

Some of the Lullabies [*Marginal note*, Uiginish] I remembered from the grand era when I was a wandering and wondering spirit between Heaven and Earth, and my brother Alan was in his cradle. I remember one day, it was in early Summer, when I was in our nursery, he being fed with a spoon, and I with a large egg before me, and a 'piece'. In a complaining voice I exclaimed that I did not like a Duck's egg. O! said the nurse, What! not like the egg which thy own pretty Cock laid! I was then bound in honour to do what was respectful, and ate the egg, which however, tasted very like that of a duck.

Alan (or Allan) was born in April 1842, so this incident may be dated in the early spring of the following year, when Fanny was two-and-a-half.

A glimpse of her father and of the period is to be found in *A Voyage round the Coasts of Scotland and the Isles* by James Wilson, the Edinburgh naturalist, who tells of an evening the previous summer on the Board of Fisheries cutter, the *Princess Royal*, anchored in Loch Dunvegan, below the Castle.[7] The party on board the cutter were visited by Mr Tolmie, 'an extensive farmer of the neighbourhood'. Wilson tells how, later, the big generous farmer sent them the gift of a whole sheep—a large black-faced wether—and a brace of Skye terriers from his noted kennels. There had been conversation about farming conditions in Skye, and Wilson quotes Tolmie's opinion that the island was admirably suited for grazing, but that little should be attempted in the way of agriculture except for potatoes, as the crops were liable to be destroyed by high winds and rain.

In only too short a time the potato crop itself was to be devastated.[8] Another early incident is recalled in the 'Reminiscences'.
I remember my first Prayer perfectly when a very little creature, and believe that it has stood as my sole spiritual action through all these years, though saying words many a time. My Mother was undressing me, and speaking in a whisper, as my Father was lying asleep, and dying, behind the curtain on which was a gay pattern of birds in a tree, much admired by me. It was a great uplift to me to hear that I was now to kneel, at her knee, and to repeat a Prayer. I was in real earnest, and am not wiser or better today than I was at that moment.

That was in May 1844. Mrs Tolmie, not yet thirty-six, was left with a family of five sons and four daughters, from seventeen-year-old Jane (Jeanie) down to baby Allan. Uiginish was given up. Donald Allan, the eldest son, emigrated to New Zealand. Mrs Tolmie and the younger children then made their home with her brother, Hugh MacAskill, at Talisker House in Minginish. Two years later they removed to Rudha an Dùnain, Hugh receiving the tack in succession to his second cousin, Donald, who was also his brother-in-law.
There had been a continuous line of MacAskills at Rudha an Dùnain, reaching back into the Middle Ages. For generations they served the MacLeods of Dunvegan in various important capacities. One later descendant, Malcolm (1723–87), became first Presbyterian minister of the island of Eigg; he, in turn, was the great-grandfather of Frances Tolmie. He was previously parish minister of Kilmallie, Inverness-shire, where he was nicknamed *Am Ministear Làidir*, 'The Strong Minister',[9] and it is recorded that he always wore a kilt of

shepherd's tartan,[10] an appropriate garb for the pastor of a Highland flock.

Miss Tolmie's great-grandmother, his second wife, was 'Mary MacLean of the Coll family, a charming and gifted woman, whose poetic gifts Miss Tolmie inherited to a marked degree'.[11]

Miss Tolmie's grandfather was Dr Donald MacAskill, the eldest surviving son of the Rev. Malcolm and his wife, Mary MacLean. He practised for a time in Fort William, and married Jane, daughter of Duncan Roy Campbell of Edinample, Perthshire, factor to MacLean of Ardgour. Many of the old Scottish families claim royal descent; Frances Tolmie was 'thus descended through her grandmother from the Campbells of Edinample, who through the knightly house of Glenorchy, were descended from Margaret, the sainted Queen of Malcolm Canmore, King of Scotland'.[12]

In 1804 Donald MacAskill became tacksman of Kildonan in Eigg and doctor for Arisaig and the Small Isles. Three of his family had been born in Fort William and seven followed in Eigg. The youngest, a daughter, Colina, was born in August 1816. Little more than a year later, on the night of 28 October 1817, Dr Donald was drowned. He and the parish minister, the Rev. William Fraser, were returning from Arisaig in an open boat in which some cattle were being ferried. A heavy sea was running from the southwest. As the boat was nearing the island a sudden squall caused the cattle to become restive, and the boat capsized. The doctor was a strong swimmer but he and the minister became entangled in their cloaks, and were drowned. The only survivor was a tailor, who clung to a cow's tail and got safely to shore.[13]

Mrs MacAskill and her ten children moved to Borline, near Talisker, in Skye. Hugh, the eldest, was barely eighteen, but apparently shouldered his responsibilities in a most manly way. In 1820, when the MacLeods of Talisker gave up the lands they had held on lease since the days of Rory Mór, Hugh received the tack and proceeded to make improvements, repairing Talisker House and enlarging it.

It was either at Borline or Talisker that Duncan Roy Campbell paid a visit to his daughter in his old age. Making the acquaintance of her MacAskill relatives, he became so greatly attached to them that he made his grandson, Hugh, promise that when he died he would bury him 'in the bosom of the MacAskills'.[14] '*Cuir mi ann an uchd chlann Asgaill*', he said; and so he was buried, not in his native Perthshire, but in the old graveyard at Eynort.

Hugh MacAskill farmed in Mull as well as in Skye. His uncle, Allan MacAskill, captain of an East Indiaman, had built Calgary castle on retiring from sea. Hugh succeeded him as laird of Calgary and tacksman of Mornish. Twenty-seven years had passed since the drowning of his father. Now, for a second time, he assumed the care of a fatherless family.

CHAPTER 2

RUDHA AN DÙNAIN, STRONTIAN, BRACADALE, 1845-57

At Rudh'n-dùnain, over in Minginish, there used to be waulkings at intervals, accompanied by loud singing of many voices in Chorus.

'Reminiscences'

Fanny Tolmie was barely four years old when the family moved to Talisker House in Minginish. She retained a memory of a long drive from Uiginish to Roag or Harlosh[1]—probably over a road of which only traces remain today[2]—and thence by boat to Talisker Bay, where women were waiting at the landing place to carry the smaller children to the house. She recalled her own carrier who, being rather stout, sat down to rest on the way, and how she—impatient little girl that she was—trotted restlessly around her. Considering that she grew up to be a striking example of the 'Big Tolmies', she was probably no light weight even then.

Two years later Hugh MacAskill moved his household to Rudha an Dùnain. This south-westerly point of Skye, at the end of the four-mile-long Glen Brittle and with peaks of the Cuillin towering above it, is bounded on the north-west by Loch Brittle, and on the south-east by the Sound of Soay, with the small island of Soay lying opposite. The farmhouse, a century and more ago when the lively Tolmie children were growing up there, was the centre of a busy village life; today its

8

ruins are one with those of the ancient fort or *dùn* which gave the place its name, *Rudha an Dùnain*, the 'headland of the fort'.[3] Among the ruins and over the surrounding land graze sheep and hill-cattle, and red deer roam down from the hills.

Beyond the Sound of Soay is Loch Scavaig, at the head of which a climb of a hundred yards or so leads to Loch Coruisk [Plate 2], 'Coriskin dark and Coolin high' of Scott's *Lord of the Isles*, and a magnet to many artists.[4]

Hugh MacAskill, tacksman of Rudha an Dùnain, who became guardian of his sister's family, was a man of culture and wide interests. Many years later the background of his niece's upbringing was to be described as follows:[5]

> Hugh MacAskill and his wife took a leading part in the social life of Skye and their hospitality was enjoyed by a large circle of literary and other friends from all parts of the kingdom. It was in that atmosphere that Miss Tolmie grew up, and the contact with these literati made a profound impression, and at an early age she commenced that collection of folklore that charmed so many hearts of the present generation.

Miss Tolmie may hardly have been so precocious a 'collector' as this might suggest, but among the songs and folklore that she was to write down later there was much that was stored in her mind from childhood.

Outstanding among her memories was 'a loving singer', Margaret MacNeill, known as *Peigidh Bhanachaig*, 'Peggy Dairymaid', who sang 'on wild nights, with whirring wheel . . . of incomprehensible, "old, unhappy, far-off things" . . . in deep croaking tones—by the bedside of a favourite little friend in Minginish, Skye, in 1845'.[6]

In contrast to long winter nights were long days of summer, although these might be broken by storms descending upon the peaks of the Cuillin, when 'lightning flashed and darted through every crevice, followed by terrifying peals of thunder'.[7] There were memories, however, of calmer days.

> A great event was to be led up the grassy slopes of the Coolin range to see Eigg far off where our Mother was born. Our tutor would take us for a ramble and tell us the names of the flowers.

9

If he stood and had a chat with the 'grieve'[8] I remember that I did not like his Gaelic which was eastern mainland, too nasal.[9]

Conversation in Gaelic between tutor and grieve, in contrast to the English of the schoolroom, underlined the bilingual structure of the children's environment. Always there was the interlacing of the two tongues. Gaelic was supreme in the nursery, where nurses invariably spoke no other language; their bilingual mother would speak mainly Gaelic to the smaller children.[10] Workers in the kitchen, the byre, the stable and the fields were Gaelic speakers; in Uncle Hugh's office either language would be used, according to convenience; in the dining-room, drawing-room and schoolroom English prevailed.

The tutor, Mr Fraser,[11] had been with the family since Fanny was very young, possibly from Uiginish days, as the following would suggest:[12]

But I remember my first prayer well enough and am certain have not done a better one since. It stands at the beginning of my awaking mind—but the songs were earlier than that, for was not Allan just after me, cradle-lulled, while I was reaching out my hand to the tutor who was seven years with us—and then became a minister—until the older boys were big.

Mr Fraser provided education on sound classical lines, but there was one omission:

He had no voice, so did not encourage singing. But I had Peggy MacNeill and her singing to listen to, as she sat spinning at nights; and then Iain Portear, 'John the Portear' [i.e. 'tunesman'] played on his fiddle to us, and I on one occasion lost my shoes in my activity. But I had demeaned myself by doing what was most reprehensible, going over the sides of my shoes which was therefore basely 'cuagach'.[13]

Puirt a beul,[14] 'mouth-music', those gay tunes mainly in reel, strathspey or jig time with repetitive and nonsensical words as merry as the tunes, was also heard and sung: '"Domhnull Cìbeir" ("Donald the Shepherd"), who married our nurse, Kate M'Swein, used to sing "puirt-a-beul" to us little ones.'[15]

Singing on a larger and louder scale was to be heard when a number

10

of women assembled for the waulking, or fulling (Gaelic, *luadh*) of the home-woven cloth.[16] Apart from tailoring, this was the last of the several wool processes from the back of the sheep to the back of the wearer. All were to be seen in and around the homestead.

The first stage, the sheep-shearing, was a merry occasion in summer. Scouring and dyeing of the wool followed—the latter almost entirely with dyes extracted from the plants and lichens that abounded—after which the coloured fleeces were spread over fences to dry. Carding and spinning occupied long winter hours indoors. Much of the wool after spinning had to be knitted into hose and outer and under garments, and women's hands were seldom idle. From time to time an itinerant weaver arrived, set up his loom—probably in the large farm kitchen—and remained in the house until the work was finished.

The web cut down from the loom, the waulking followed [Plate 3].[17] Waulking or fulling was an arduous task, the time it took depending upon the length of the cloth and the amount of shrinkage it required. For ordinary wear the thirty-inch cloth would be given three inches of shrinkage; blanketing and heavier cloth would receive more. Singing lightened the work and also provided entertainment for the onlookers. An invitation to a waulking, whether as spectator or participator, was almost as highly esteemed as an invitation to a wedding.

When the day arrived, the waulking table—'a long board, about three feet in width, grooved lengthways and resting on trestles'—had been set up in a barn or shed or, occasionally, in the open. On the ground at one end stood a vat in which the cloth was soaking in a 'special liquid', urine diluted with hot water. This simple domestic ammonia served as a mordant to fix the dye, and also gave the wool its softness.

Suitably dressed, with stout aprons and bare arms, the 'obliging guests' took their places at the waulking table, 'six to ten on each side, leaving elbow room'. Over the vat presided 'the good wife of the house or some other person of experience'. The cloth, partially wrung, was dealt out and laid on the table, up one side and down the other. Each pair of hands grasped a portion; with forward and backward beating and rubbing the work began.

After every few beats each woman tossed the cloth to her neighbour on the left; the entire web, its ends joined, thus made a continuous round of the table. Several beats passed in silence, as the workers established a slow rhythm.

Presently the leader, seated in the middle of one of the sides, sang a phrase or two of a song of slow and solemn character—possibly a lament—matching her beat to the pounding of the wet and heavy cloth. She was not expected to touch the cloth, her function in this way resembling that of the shanty-man on a sailing-ship; waulking songs have the same antiphonal features as sea shanties.

The basic pattern of a waulking song was described by Miss Tolmie as follows:[18]

> its solo verse-part, consisting usually of but one line, though some-times of two, was often (though not invariably) followed by a little refrain in meaningless syllables, and was succeeded by the chorus, in which all present—both workers and audience—joined. . . . There seems to have been no fixed rule as to the point at which the waulking-songs began, whether with the solo or the chorus. . . . A continuous round was kept up of the three parts (solo verse, solo refrain, and chorus) with no very marked ending.

As the moisture evaporated and the cloth grew lighter, quicker and merrier songs succeeded the opening slow ones. The singers warmed to their work, rocking their bodies forward and backward in time with the pounding on the board which was growing 'as exciting as an African drum beat'.[19] The onlookers joined in the chorus refrains, which were usually equal in length to the solo verse line and refrain together, or even longer. Where the 'verse' consisted of two lines, the second usually became the first of the following couplet, thus doubling the length of the song.[20] The first line in this case might be repeated at the end, bringing the song full circle.

From time to time there was a halt to let the singers draw breath, or to let the mistress of the proceedings judge how the shrinkage was going, by measuring the cloth over the middle finger of her left hand: *h-aon, 's a dhà, 's a trì, 's a ceithir*, etc. 'one and two and three and four', before asking for a few more songs, or having it plunged again into the vat, 'to get a drink'.

Songs giving scope for improvisation brought teasing and laughter. Then there came a point when the cloth was pronounced to be suffi-ciently shrunk and thickened; an *òran teannachaidh*, 'tightening song', followed as the web was wrung or tightened, the tempo of such a song varying with the action. Finally the cloth was carefully wound round a piece of wood called a *coinneal* in preparation for pressing.

The song, *Chaidh na fir a Sgathabhaig*, 'The men have gone to Scavaig' (Example 2), bears a note in the MS: 'Always sung at the waulkings at Rudha 'n Dùnain with a great energy by Catriona Mhòr.' Miss Tolmie adds, on the MS, 'There must be more of this song'.

Example 2   *Journal, 63*

Chaidh na Fir a Sgathabhaig
(The Men have gone to Scavaig)

Remembered from childhood
in Minginish, Skye, 1852.—F.T.

2. Chaidh fear mo thighe-s' ann;   3. Sealgair 'an ròin teillich thu;
    Caol mhala gun ghruaman;   Is na h-eilide ruaidhe;

4. Is na circeige duinne thu,
    Nì a nead's a luachair.

TRANSLATION
1. The men have gone to Scavaig; (*R.*: Fà ill, etc.) for them this day is cold. (*R.*: O hi; *Ch.*: Hi ri.) 2. The goodman of my house went there; he of the slender eyebrows, showing no frown. 3. Hunter of the blub-cheeked seal art thou, and of the red hind, 4. and of the little brown hen that makes her nest among the rushes.

The ballad of *A' Bhean Eudach*,[21] 'The Jealous Woman', was current from end to end of the Outer Isles and West Highlands both as a waulking song and a lullaby. The text of some thirty or more couplets was essentially the same throughout, but there were (and are) several tunes, each with its own refrain syllables. In her MS of the text Miss Tolmie outlined the story as follows:[22]

The envious woman enticed the victim of her evil thoughts and purposes to the shore at low water as if to gather dulse and, tying her by her long hair to the rocks, left her to drown at the return of the tide—regardless of her cries and entreaties. After that, the bad woman married the husband. Overhearing her repeating to herself the lamentations of his first wife, he was filled with horror and put her away.

Of the many visitors to the farmhouse of Rudha an Dùnain one of the most welcome was the parish minister, 'Mr Neil', the Rev. Neil Mackinnon. 1843 had seen the great church upheaval, the 'Disruption', when a large breakaway from the Church of Scotland resulted in the formation of the Free Church. Hugh MacAskill and his household remained among the 'Moderates' of the Established Church; the parish church, however, was at Bracadale, seventeen miles away, so they could count upon only an occasional pastoral visit.

Mr Neil has been described as a handsome young man of fine physique, with 'hearty buoyancy of spirits together with many qualities of sterling friendship'.[23] From his father, Dr Farquhar Mackinnon of Kyle, he had acquired some knowledge of medicine. Often, when no doctor was available, he was concerned not only with the cure of souls, but of bodies as well.

Mr Neil was but one of many cultural influences upon the young Fanny Tolmie: all fed her growing musical and poetic imagination.[24]

At *Rudha 'n Dùnain*, over in Minginish, there used to be waulkings at intervals, accompanied by loud singing of many voices in Chorus; and we children used to listen with pleasure; acting the scene afterwards in our own playground, a hollow near the river, and outside the garden wall. We had a series of plays for the 'Slochd' or in the nursery and Staircase, on long winter evenings— such as Macleod of Macleod and his party riding down the glen; Johnny's dead; a lamentation on our brother John, after his departure for College at Aberdeen; a waulking; a preaching, after a visit from our minister Mr Neil Mackinnon. (*Marginal note:* Deep groaning among the audience—exclamations of *Och*—Ochan —Ochan.) The expulsion of Adam and Eve from Eden was also a favourite and very noisy performance.

In the early evening hours before candles were lighted, our

eldest sister Jeanie, well instructed ere I began to go around, used to sing, and play on our table-shaped Piano, and I would often go and sit beneath it to hear the wonderful vibration. But the finest musical strains were from an iron gate on which we swung when waiting to welcome home members of the family & friends riding in a cavalcade down the glen. These musical sounds were afterwards recalled when I heard the Sonatas of Beethoven in Edinburgh.

The years went by. John, the eldest of the four brothers at home, went to Aberdeen University to study for the ministry. In the early 1850s William emigrated to New Zealand where he took up sheep-farming, played his part in public life and became a Member of Parliament. Malcolm, next in age, became a banker in Geelong, Victoria, Australia.[25] Jane (Jeanie) the eldest of the family, in 1855 married Laurence Skene from Aberdeenshire, banker and tweed mill owner in Portree; Normanna in the previous year at the age of nineteen had married Donald MacLellan, tacksman of Vatersay, Barra. Only Mary, Fanny and Allan were still at home.

One of Fanny's interests was botany. Her uncle had a copy of Sir William Jackson Hooker's *British Flora* (2nd ed., 1831) in which, from time to time, he added his own annotations. It later came into Fanny's possession and she did the same. It is interesting to note their identification of some seventy varieties of wild flowers found in their part of Skye.[26]

The *Illustrated London News* arrived at the house every week. Fanny and Allan would study the descriptions and drawings of scenes in the Crimean War. Sixty years later, during the First World War, Aunt Fanny was to amaze a younger generation by her familiarity with place names that to them were novel tongue-twisters, and to quote to them passages about a war long ago that had remained in her memory from her childhood reading.[27]

Song no. 105 in the *Journal, Oran an t-Saighdeir*, 'The Soldier's Song', became popular in Skye the year before the Crimean War, through the singing of a young shepherd, Patrick MacLeod. The words were written by Major Neil MacLeod, R.A., Waternish, in his youth (d. 1879). 'For several months every one in our glen sang and hummed this song, whilst at work'[28] (Example 3).

Example 3   *Journal*, 105

Oran an t-Saighdeir
(The Soldier's Song)

Sung by Patrick Macleod (young shepherd),
at Rudh an Dùnain, Skye, 1853

'N uair bhios mo chàird - ean   'nan   cad - al,   Air   an   leab - aidh   gu

sàmh - ach, 'S ann bhios mis' anns   an   oidh - che   fó an choill' aig   mo

nàmh - aid.   Fo an choill' aig   mo nàmh - aid; Feadh mhach-raich-ean còmhn-ard; Feadh

bheannt - an - an   àrd - a,   Ag - us   fàs - aich - ean   ceòth-ach.

TRANSLATION

When my kindred are slumbering peacefully in bed, I shall be at night in hiding from
my enemy. In hiding from my enemy, amid level plains, lofty mountains, and wilder-
nesses enveloped in mist.

In the autumn of 1854 the Rev. John Tolmie became minister of
Strontian in Ardnamurchan. As he was still a bachelor his mother went
to keep house for him, taking with her Mary, Fanny and Allan, aged
sixteen, fourteen and twelve respectively. There arose the question of
schooling for Fanny and Allan. 'A young lady [Miss Whyte] came from
Edinburgh to finish my education while Alan attended the parish
school.'[29]

The finishing process included music lessons. A Collard and Collard
piano had been bought from John's predecessor. 'I was hearing all sorts
of "pieces" of music; but no more Gaelic singing was heard in the

house; though a Gaelic-speaking parish. There were several Lowlanders in the community.'[30]

The nature of these pieces can perhaps be imagined, for this was the era of 'The Maiden's Prayer', 'Warblings at Eve' and Thalberg's Variations on 'Home, sweet Home'. Or is it possible that Miss Whyte introduced Mary and Fanny to Clementi, Haydn and Mozart? Mendelssohn, not long dead, had become popular among amateur pianists through his 'Songs without Words', but some decades were to pass before Bach—whom he had done so much to re-discover—reached the schoolroom.

Fanny's own playing at this stage cannot have been more than elementary. It may be assumed, however, that she practised diligently, learned the rudiments of music and acquired some finger facility. In later years, when all the womenfolk of her family played the piano to a greater or less extent, she confined herself almost exclusively to Highland music. Her sisters, Jane and Mary, and certain of her nieces were considered to be more accomplished pianists.

After two years in Strontian, in 1856 the family returned to Skye, John succeeding the beloved Mr Neil as parish minister of Bracadale. His mother and two young sisters again made up his household. Allan in due course followed his brothers to New Zealand. Miss Whyte remained at the manse for a time as Fanny's governess, but her mother died, and she had to leave. 'Utterly un-Gaelic', wrote her one-time pupil when living in Edinburgh many years later, 'she is my good friend to this day.'[31]

Fanny was now sixteen, grown tall and erect of carriage, blue-eyed and with long hair described by some as 'sandy', by others as 'red' or 'red-gold'. She was by nature studious, in contrast to her sister Mary, who was domesticated and practical. With Miss Whyte's departure her education appeared to be interrupted, if not formally 'finished'; just then, however, she found a new field of study open to her.

A frequent visitor at the manse was Mr Macintyre, the parish schoolmaster, in whom her brother John discovered a kindred spirit in a love for Gaelic poetry and song. Of an evening a favourite book would be reached down from the shelf, John Mackenzie's *Sar-Obair Nam Bard Gaelach* or 'The Beauties of Gaelic Poetry and Lives of the Highland Bards', and the young minister would read aloud or sing to his friend the compositions of Alexander MacDonald (*Mac Mhaighstir Alasdair*), Duncan Bàn Macintyre and others.

Fanny listened, but her delight was clouded by the realization that she had very little facility in reading Gaelic, in spite of speaking and understanding it equally with English. Both languages had been familiar to her from babyhood, but she had been taught to read and write only one of them. She worked hard at reading the Gaelic Bible to make up for this deficiency. The church services offered good practice, as did family prayers. English was never heard at family or public worship, unless occasionally out of courtesy to a visitor.

There was plenty of Gaelic around the manse. It was the language of workers inside and out, of those concerned with cooking, milking or butter-making, ploughing and reaping, currying the minister's horse or looking after the hens. The crofters and cottars in the vicinity spoke no other language. The professional people and the lesser gentry spoke Gaelic in addition to English, although younger members of a family were apt to be less fluent in Gaelic than those older.

Since even before the Union of the Crowns of England and Scotland it had been government policy, whether in Edinburgh or London, to cultivate English as the language of the whole of Scotland. A Privy Council Order of 1616 desiderated the suppression of the Gaelic language as a cause of 'barbaritie and incivilitie'. Times were still too troublous to allow for the consideration for minority languages that is found today. To ensure that at least a proportion of the inhabitants of the Highland area knew English well it was required that the chiefs should have their children sent to the Lowlands to be instructed in English. These early enactments may have had little practical effect, but they reveal their framers' state of mind accurately enough. The eighteenth-century Jacobite insurrections gave renewed strength to Lowland fears and especially after the '45, the goals of 'religious improvement' and 'education' in the Highlands were associated consistently with the extirpation of the Gaelic language. Even before the beginning of the nineteenth century these efforts had clearly begun to take effect. Gaelic might remain the daily language of the Gaels at home, but in the south at school or university, in social intercourse among friends and relations furth of the Highland line, and in visits from these friends to them in their Highland homes, English became more and more the everyday language.[32] As patrons they turned their attention away from the Gaelic arts to more 'civilized' ways, and so the traditional Gaelic learning—so much a part of upper-class Highland life in mediaeval times—was in the last three centuries or so either eliminated or transformed. Since then the various departments of Gaelic culture flourished—or else subsisted—in a non-literate ambiance, as an oral, popular tradition. Although the first printed collections of Gaelic poetry and the first Gaelic dictionaries and grammars were in print well before 1800, the writing and reading of the language was virtually confined to the ministers and scholars.

Thus without formal studies in Gaelic Frances Tolmie turned her mind to the Gaelic language and its old songs and traditions. She was at the source. Her mother was a sweet singer with a repertory of older songs she had learned in her youth, and Fanny begged her to teach them to her. The waulkings that had been such an outstanding feature of life in Minginish were now, however, only a memory in Bracadale, and she realized that with their passing the songs were also disappearing.

CHAPTER 3

EDINBURGH, 1857-8

Then came Miss Matilda Wrench to our parish, who knew Miss MacLeod of MacLeod in London. She invited me to spend a winter with her in Edinburgh, and with my Mother's consent, I went away with her in Oct. 1857.

'Reminiscences'

On a summer afternoon, more than a year after the Tolmies went to Bracadale, Fanny sat reading on the moor. There it was that Miss Matilda Wrench came upon her, and expressed interest in the book in her hands. Fanny had naturally heard of the Englishwoman who was staying at the Free Church manse with the Rev. John Fletcher and his wife, and the Englishwoman in turn was aware of the new young minister in the Parish Church manse, with his mother and two young sisters making up his household. Miss Wrench was working for the furthering of education in the Highlands, and just then was visiting schools set up and administered by the Ladies' Highland Association.

The Association for the Religious Improvement of the Remote Highlands and Islands, known as the 'Ladies' Highland Association' was founded in Edinburgh in 1850.[1] It followed upon the first wave of spontaneous help sent from Lowland congregations of the Free Church to the districts stricken by the failure of the potato harvests of 1846–8. The potato blight, however, was only the climax to a series of misfortunes. The kelp industry, risen to its peak in a short fifty years, had collapsed in face of new chemical discoveries;[2] severe storms had wasted the small crops of oats and barley and, worse still, had broken up boats and fishing gear, which there was no cash to replace.

To relieve actual want was the first objective of the Ladies' Highland Association. It was quickly found, however, that clothing was urgently needed as well as food, while a startling discovery was the widespread illiteracy. Schools there were, in Skye as elsewhere—parish schools, Gaelic Society schools, General Assembly schools and others—but the geography of the island was such that there were many districts that had no school at all. In such a district a school existing previously might have been closed many years before, so that half a generation or more had grown up unable to read or write. The Association applied itself energetically to the setting up of schools where they were most needed.

It was found expedient to link the schools with the training of ministers for the new Gaelic charges. There was therefore an arrangement whereby divinity students served as teachers in the Ladies' Schools during their long vacation. As their college classes lasted for only two winter terms they were free to teach for nearly seven months in the year. During their absence there was usually one of their summers' pupils sufficiently advanced to act as substitute. Not that there can have been much schooling in winter: long distances over trackless moors made journeys to school too perilous for children on many stormy short days between November and February.

Education in the Ladies' Schools did not stop at religious instruction and the ordinary three R's. Clothing was so badly needed that sewing schools were established:[3]

> Some far-seeing member of the Ladies' Highland Association suggested that instead of sending city clothes and materials to the Isles it would be cheaper and wiser to help these schools to make outfits for boys from local materials—'They are very strong and most ingeniously dyed with herbs and seaweed prepared by the people themselves . . . a boy's dress can be got of these home-made stuffs for six or eight shillings.'

The Ladies' Schools were visited at intervals by members of the Edinburgh committee and other subscribers. Travelling conditions were by no means easy. There were arms of the sea to be crossed, bad roads—or none—to be faced, and the weather was uncertain. It should be remembered also how heavy, tight and cumbersome women's clothes were in those days.

Matilda Wrench from London was one who braved these journeys, and the early reports contain several full and informative letters about her visits; in committee she made recommendations that were listened to and acted upon. Born in 1804, she was a gifted linguist, evangelical in religion, a practical philanthropist, a brilliant organizer—and an indefatigable writer. She came of a family that numbered men of standing in the City of London, her father and a cousin having occupied the position of Master of the Ancient Drapers' Company, and one of her brothers being a Liveryman; among clergymen in the family one or two had been 'Lord Mayor's Chaplain'.

In the British Museum Library catalogue seven titles appear under her name. Some are translations from German, either of religious tracts or of children's stories with a moral. There is also a report, entitled *Visits to Female Prisoners at Home and Abroad*,[4] which links her with a ladies' association, begun in the days of Elizabeth Fry. An earlier book of hers is a translation from the German of J. A. W. Neander's *Life and Times of St Bernard*,[5] which, dedicated to her Liveryman brother, an Army chaplain, was published with a view to helping a fund for the parish church of her native place, Boughton-under-Blean in Kent. In relation to the costs of printing and publishing today it sounds fantastic that the sale of such a book could be profitable to any fund! Was it just that this lengthy and scholarly work provided the translator with an interesting ploy, its charitable object being an afterthought?

She was known in Scotland, however, for a pamphlet entitled *The Highland Glen; or, Plenty and Famine*.[6] Dedicated to H.M. Queen Adelaide, it appeared in a fourth edition in 1858, and its profits were to be given to 'the Suffering Highlanders'. The author, having travelled extensively in the Highlands, drew a vivid, if somewhat fanciful, picture of the distress of the time, as opposed to former prosperity. Her appeal was to Londoners who, like herself, had enjoyed Highland kindness and hospitality.[7]

> The Highlander . . . has a peculiar claim on our bounty, for he has ever been ready to minister to the wants of the stranger and the traveller. During a tour of some weeks among the mountains and glens, we very frequently closed an evening ramble by a visit to their cottages. And never in one single instance, though we were a party of five, were we allowed to depart without partaking of their hospitality; nor would they receive remuneration in return. Their hospitality they can no longer offer . . . and is it not time for us to render back what we so fully received?

In contrast to the scarcity that had come about she drew a picture of a 'house of refreshment' in previous times, when there was to be found 'the table spread with freshly-made oat-cake, still hot and crisp, a large bowl of rich cream, fresh butter, a bottle of whisky and a drinking horn'.[8]

From the moment the Ladies' Highland Association was formed the London Auxiliary contributed generously. Help of every kind—money, clothing and books—was given, and certain subscribers visited the schools, some making themselves responsible for the teacher's salary. £20 was the usual amount paid to a general teacher, £5 to a sewing teacher. Lists of subscriptions 'collected by Miss Wrench' included for several successive years the names of residents at Denmark Hill, where she herself lived, and at nearby Herne Hill. The name of John Ruskin's mother occurs more than once as a subscriber.

Miss Wrench now lived in Edinburgh; with this gifted and purposeful woman Fanny was invited to spend the winter. A new world was opening out to her. She was to recall her first impressions when, in old age in Skye, her own travelling days over, she wrote to two lady teachers in Dunvegan, as they left for the winter term in Glasgow, 'the great city':[9]

> I would gladly travel along with you by the grand way at this season . . . as you arrive from sunshine into the shades of night, and the wondrous lines of lamplight which impressed myself as a sort of mystery and symbol of some great blessing in my first arrival into city life.

She tells that she attended an English class every day and that she had music lessons.[10] She appears to have studied French and Italian also, possibly with Miss Wrench herself. The most lasting impression, however, of that winter in Edinburgh was the beginning of a friendship with the family of the printer and publisher, Thomas Constable: 'Mr C. was friendly with Miss Wrench,—and arranged that I should go to church with his family on Sunday—my dear friend having a seat in a Church where the ministers would certainly be beyond a young girl's comprehension.'[11]

Her Sunday host was the son of Sir Walter Scott's publisher, Archibald Constable. He was an elder in Pilrig Free Church, Edinburgh (now known as Pilrig and Dalmeny Street Church), whose minister at that time was the Rev. (afterwards Dr) W. G. Blaikie, who later became Principal of the New College.

Except for the language the services in her brother's church in Bracadale, Skye and in Pilrig Free Church were much alike. Both observed the custom of standing to pray and sitting to sing. At Pilrig, however, there may well have been a choir singing in harmony, for the Free Church in its earliest years issued books of harmonized psalm tunes.

Bracadale, where the service was in Gaelic, retained the early seventeenth-century custom of 'lining out',[12] whereby a precentor chanted each line of the words, which was repeated by the congregation to the appropriate phrase of the tune, and so on to the end. This method—except that originally the precentor may have read rather than sung his line—had received parliamentary approval in 1644 in order to foster the singing of the new metrical psalms of the Reformed Church. It was intended as a temporary expedient only, until everyone should have a psalm book and be able to read it. More than two centuries later, however, the custom still lingered in a few Anglican and Nonconformist churches in England.

Because so few in the Highlands could read their native language, 'lining out' took a firm hold and in a generation or two became a pious tradition. It may also be said to have satisfied a natural instinct for antiphonal singing. Deprived of the plainsong of pre-Reformation worship, the Gael proceeded to make the new metrical version of the psalms non-metrical. The precentor 'gave out the line' on a reciting note surrounded by certain fluctuations in pitch; the congregational phrases in course of time developed into florid passages which, through constant repetition, became familiar to the singers. This singing survives today as a feature of Gaelic Presbyterian services. In spite of the harshness of voice in which it is sometimes expressed, it has a power and a beauty of its own, and may be regarded as an example of folk music at its sturdiest and most authentic.

Edinburgh, however, was to provide Fanny with more conventional music. The Constables were musical, Mrs Constable a good pianist, and they recommended a teacher for her. Miss Mary Yaniewicz who lived with her widowed mother in Great King Street, was the daughter of Feliks Yaniewicz (or Janiewicz), a Polish violinist and composer. He had known Mozart and Haydn in Vienna, and had studied composition with the latter for a time. After living in Italy for some years he had eventually reached Edinburgh via Paris, London and Liverpool,

and had married a Liverpool lady. One or two of his works are occasionally heard today.[13]

Miss Yaniewicz, with her cosmopolitan background and the high
standard of performance which obtained in her home, must have found
the Skye girl an original pupil but not a great success as an executant.
Music to Fanny meant sounds which called forth an emotional response
—the songs of Peggy the Dairymaid heard through the whirring of the
spinning wheel and the roar of the storm on winter nights, the mouth
music or fiddle playing for dancing, the antiphon of the waulking
women, or of precentor and congregation. She could not at that stage
have expressed this in words, but years later she wrote: 'Miss Y. should
have played herself, and awaked my enthusiasm, which would then
rise like a tide over all difficulties. I was not equal to my music lessons,
& had no gladness in them.'[14]

CHAPTER 4

BRACADALE, 1858-62

On returning home to Bracadale, my spirit was always going behind
the present day, and then when walking over the moors escorted by
Effie Ross, I learned her songs, as the music I ought to have.

'Reminiscences'

After her busy and stimulating winter in Edinburgh, Fanny returned
to Skye in the summer of 1858. She was not yet eighteen. At home in
the manse at Bracadale her sister Mary, domesticated and practical, was
her mother's right hand, and household duties that fell to Fanny were
of the slightest. In December their brother John married Christina
Mary, daughter of Captain Alexander MacDonald of Vallay, North
Uist. The Tolmie household was, however, not much changed by this:
John's mother and sisters seem to have made their home with him and
his wife for a little longer.

Fanny continued her studies in a somewhat desultory way. Miss
Wrench corresponded with her, and sent exercises for her to write in
French and Italian. On her own she worked to improve the reading and
writing of her native Gaelic. She tells in the *Journal*[1] that 'from a
mistaken notion on the part of teachers' this had not been part of her
education, and that now she was 'but slowly advancing' in her general
knowledge by reading the Gaelic Bible. She was nearly twenty, however,
when an occupation turned up which, in an unforeseen way, led to
what became her lifelong interest and the work for which she is
remembered.

The ploy that came her way was the supervision of some knitting by
women in the hamlets around. Miss Emily MacLeod of MacLeod,
sister of the chief, who spent her time between Dunvegan and London,
had obtained a contract for 1000 pairs of socks to be knitted for a

Highland regiment. This would involve distribution of the wool, collection of the finished work and payment of the knitters. Fanny Tolmie at the manse appeared to have some time on her hands; she would surely be the very person to do it.

The district was wide, however, the dwellings scattered, and there would be long walks over the moors. Fanny's mother consented to her doing this work, with one stipulation—she must always have an escort.

Who was her escort to be? There might well have been some girl of her own age nearby who would be willing and pleased to go. Instead, Fanny chose the company of Oighrig Ross. Oighrig ('Effie' in English) was elderly and somewhat eccentric. Fanny was to describe her[2] many years later as

> rather feeble-minded in practical life, but with a poetical soul . . .
> a kind creature, but wild-looking, and apt to turn crazy if unduly
> provoked; she had immense front teeth, tawny locks of hair strayed
> from beneath her cap over a high and peaked forehead, and her old
> skirts hung in fringed tatters over her bare feet.

She lived alone in a bothy on the glebe.[3] It was possibly one of a few dwellings whose traces can still be seen on the hillside above the former manse, near where a streamlet breaks into a 'pretty waterfall known as "Am Forsan" '.[4]

The tall red-haired girl and her elderly companion might have been seen on some warm summer's day setting out from the manse on one of their long walks. The scene is very little changed today; bent, rushes and colourful wild flowers must have grown among the grass then as now. The old Bracadale church, now rather dilapidated and no longer in use, stands back from the angle where the short moor road to Portree leaves the main road at Struan. The manse, now named 'Balgown House', is higher up the hill. From time to time it has been enlarged and altered, and is now partly concealed by more than a century's growth of trees. The road below manse and church skirts Loch Beag, an arm of Loch Bracadale, and across the loch rise undulating hills, above which peep one or two peaks of the Cuillin. Between the church and the road are old humped grave mounds and, not inappropriately, the hillock facing them—between the road and the loch—is still known as *Cnoc a' Ghuil*, 'Knoll of Weeping'.

Over the moors they walked and climbed, Effie delighting Fanny with her talk about old lore of the district. Talk led to song, song to story. Effie knew waulking songs no longer current; Fanny, at any rate, had never heard them, even in her childhood at Rudha an Dùnain, when the pounding and shrinking of the wet home-made cloth, accompanied by long and loud chorus, was still a frequent occupation. She was to obtain various waulking songs in Bracadale, but they appear from her accounts to have been sung to her by individuals only, and not at actual waulkings. Meanwhile Oighrig carefully taught her the refrains, and they sang together as they went.

They must often have talked of the *Gruagach*, the unseen guardian of the cattle; the song about him was to remain a lifelong favourite of Fanny's. In a MS version[5] by Frances Tolmie the story is told as follows:

> This song is the lamentation of a Mother over the dead body of her daughter, who having incurred the displeasure of the Gruagach, received a tap of his wand, of which she immediately died.
>
> This incident took place in Glen MacAskill, Bracadale, when the woman and her daughter were one evening gathering the cattle into the fold—and one of the cows becoming intractable, the girl impatiently made use of opprobrious words to the distracted creature—whose spiritual Guardian the Gruagach, with long golden hair and a shining white bosom, was standing invisibly there—and smote the girl for committing such a sin—for the Gruagach would not tolerate rough words any more than blows, to the objects of his care. The Mother was lamenting all night—while the Gruagach stood gazing at her—and leaning against the rafters of the shieling till daybreak—when he vanished.

Eight lines of the song not quoted here appear in *The Gesto Collection*, Appendix, p. 19 and in the *Journal*, p. 198. The *Journal* version differs from the *Gesto* one in so far as it appears to have 'benefited' from the scholarly hand of George Henderson. Oighrig and Fanny must have sung it in the usual waulking-song pattern as they crossed the moor, the second line of each couplet becoming the first of the next. The *Journal* gives the following translation of the remainder:

> 2. swift-footed herdsman on the slopes of the glen, on whose head the hair has grown in curling locks! 3. Oh, a sorrowful woman am I, mourning solitary in this glen; 4. sorely afflicted, and in anguish, laying thee out, thou darling of thy mother.

The last couplet, in Gaelic, runs:

5. 'S mi gun phiuthar! 'S mi gun bhràthair. Rìgh nan dùl! bi teachd làimh rium.

Translation

5. Having no sister nor a brother, King of Nature, be thou near me!

What a shapely tune it is; and how perfectly suited to antiphonal singing. The first verse line and solo refrain move only a third away in each direction from the keynote; the second line moves cautiously a little higher, rises to the sixth degree and descends to the second. So far, verse line, solo refrain and second verse line have each taken up two bars; the four-bar chorus is an excellent 'development' of the two-bar solo refrain, with its leap to the octave (high *doh*) and its drop to the fourth below the keynote (low *soh*) before achieving its cadence. Note also the stresses of the three *hi ri*'s.

Example 4   *Journal*, 42

Oran mu'n Ghruagaich
(A Song about the Gruagach)

Sung by Oighrig [Effie] Ross (cottar),
Bracadale, Skye, 1861

1. Chaor - ain nash deän thu sol - us dhomh! E-hò hi ri,

rith ibh ò hó.   Gus am faic mi fear àrd a bhroill-ich ghil!

E-hò hì ri, rith ibh ò hò, Hi rì, hò - rionn ò.

TRANSLATION

1. O ember, do thou give me light, (*Refrain:* Ehò, etc.) so that I may behold him who is of lofty stature, and white bosom; (*Chorus:* Ehò, etc.).

Là Millegàraidh, 'The day (or battle) of Millegàraidh', or 'The Battle of the Spoilt Dyke' was a fine song of Oighrig's.[6] It commemorated a fierce sixteenth-century battle at Trumpan, Waternish in Skye, when the MacLeods inflicted heavy losses on the invading MacDonalds of Clan Ranald.

Example 5   *Journal, 45*

Là Millegàraidh
(The Day [i.e. Battle] of Millegàraidh)

Sung by Oighrig Ross (cottar),
Bracadale, Skye, 1861

TRANSLATION OF VERSES I AND 2
1. Remember ye (Chorus: O-hi, etc.) the day of the Aird, (Refrain) 2. or that other of Millegàraidh?

> 3. Bha fir an sin
>   Air dhroch càradh,
>
> 4. An druim fòdh',
>   'S am buinn bhàn ris.
>
> 12. 'S ioma bean bhochd
>   Bha gu cràidhteach,
>
> 13. 'S i gun mhac ann,
>   'S i gun bhràthair,
>
> 14. Gun duin' ann a
>   Ghabhadh bàigh dhi.
>
> 15. 'S mo mhollachd sin
>   Aig Clann-Rànuill!

Translation

3. Men were there in sad condition, 4. lying prone, showing the white soles of their feet. 12. Many a woman was sorely grieving, 13. missing her son there, having no brother, 14. and no man left to delight in her. 15. May my malediction be with Clan-Ranald!

Effie's conversation and songs Fanny found very satisfying. Songs, as exemplified in the two just quoted, were, in a sense, comment upon the stories. Despite the contrast in age, intellect and formal education between the old woman and the girl, they had a common bond in their fluent and expressive Gaelic, their love of song, their need for poetry. A couple of centuries earlier, Effie, with her wild appearance and quickness to resent being 'provoked', might have been in danger of being dubbed a witch, particularly if it had got about that, as she confessed to Fanny, she had one day gone down on her knees to a beautiful cloud overhead, and was convinced that in so doing she had not committed a sin. Coming from a woman supposed to be 'not very practical in everyday things', this was a very independent opinion indeed, especially in face of some of the theological thunderings of that day.

Fanny had already begun to write down the words of songs that she fancied, especially those that appeared to be older and little known. She also tried her hand at putting down the tunes. Her piano lessons, intermittent though they had been, had given her a reasonable knowledge of musical notation for her purpose. She had a good ear, and somewhere en route she learned enough tonic sol-fa to be of use to her. A few of Frances Tolmie's earliest attempts in staff notation are to be found in Donald Campbell's *Treatise on the Language, Poetry and Music of the Highland Clans*, published in Edinburgh in 1862. The theoretical part of this book is better than its musical illustrations. One or two songs from Frances Tolmie can be identified by their resemblance to songs of the same title in the *Journal*.

In this matter of writing down tunes she received much encouragement from a young Inland Revenue officer, Alexander Carmichael, whom she met now and then either in the manse at Bracadale or at her uncle Hugh MacAskill's at Rudha an Dùnain, over in Minginish. He himself was already gathering traditional material that was to build up into his famous *Carmina Gadelica*, the first two volumes of which were published in Edinburgh, 1900. Impressed by Fanny's growing ability to write down tunes, a skill rare enough in women at that time but rarer still in men, he urged her to write the tunes as well as the words of the old songs. Carmichael's advice supplied the stimulus she needed, and from that time forward she became a conscious collector.

The chronological list of songs (appendix A in this book) shows twenty songs noted in 1861, eleven of them being nursery songs. By this time there were two babies in the manse and they were provided with plenty of lullabies and dandling songs by their mother (from North Uist), their grandmother (from Eigg), their two young aunts and the nurse, Janet Anderson (Seònaid in Gaelic) who belonged to Strath in Skye. Example 6 shows one of these nursery songs.

Example 6   *Journal*, 103

Fàill ill o-ho-ro

A memory from Eigg,
revived at Bracadale Manse, Skye, in 1860

Fàill ill o - ho - ro, fàill ill ó! Hù ill o - ho - ro, hù ill ó.

Fàill ill éil - e hù ho - ró. O! 'si rùn mo chéill a bh'ann.

1. Là dhomh bhi 'sa' choill' ud thall, Chunn-ac - as gruag-ach nan rosg mall;

Slat-ag 'na làimh 'si cuall - ach mheang. O 'si rùn mo chéill a bh'ann.

2. Dh'innsinn dreach mo leannain duit:
    Dà ghruaidh dhearg cho dearg ri subh;
    Beul gun lochd nach aithris sgeul;
    O! 'si rùn mo chéill'a bh'ann.
    (Chorus)

TRANSLATION

(*Chorus*: Fàill ill, etc. Hu ill, etc. Oh, the joy of my heart was she!) 1. When going over one day to yonder grove, a maiden I met, of soft-moving eyes, holding a twig in her hand while tending kids. Oh, the joy of my heart was she! (Chorus). 2. Fain would I describe the aspect of her I love: two red cheeks as the raspberries red, and an innocent mouth that repeats no tale. Oh, the joy, etc. (Chorus).

By 1861 Mary and Fanny and their mother were living at Ebost Farm, three miles from the manse. Fanny continued her knitting rounds but her escort was now Margaret Gillies, known in Gaelic as

Mairearad bheag, nigh'n Domhnuill 'ic Ruairidh, 'Little Margaret, daughter of Donald-son-of-Roderick'. Little Margaret was an elderly woman, living alone. A less colourful character than Effie, she also took pleasure in singing and in teaching her songs to Fanny. Among these songs were three composed by the seventeenth-century poetess, Mary MacLeod; all three are in the *Journal.* Little Margaret herself sang two of these for Fanny's notation, *Fuaim an taibh,* 'The sound of the ocean', (*Journal,* 98) and *An crònan,* 'The croon', (*Journal,* 99); for the third she brought to the house Rory MacLeod, a very old man, 'who bent low when singing the last low note of the song'. On the MS of the text Fanny wrote:

From old Rory MacLeod, Ebost 1861—with the tune. Rory said he would sit near 'am piana'—and I would sound each note after him, and it was with much effort that he produced the last low notes, owing to the weakness of extreme old age. I admired this song very much—and thanked old Rory and thanked Little Margaret nigh'n Domhnuill 'ic Ruaraidh for their kindness.

In this lament of four short stanzas to a fine flowing tune of wide range (Example 7), the mourner, at the thought of MacLeod in a fine woollen shroud and no covering to his side but boards, sings of her 'acute suffering' and 'the lashes worn away from my eyes'.

Example 7   *Journal,* 43

Cumha Mhic-Leòid
(Lament for MacLeod)

Sung by Roderick Macleod (cottar),
Bracadale, Skye, 1862

2. 'S mi gun sunnd air stà;
Gun mo dhùil ri bhi slàn;
Tha mo shùgradh gu bràth air chùl.
(Repeat as chorus.)

3. 'S ann tha Leòdach mo ghaoil,
'S an oll-anart chaol,
'S gun chòmhdach ri thaobh, ach bùird.
(Ch.)

4. 'Sè bhi smaointinn ort,
So-chràidh mi'm chorp,
'Sa chnàmh na ruisg bho m'shùil.
(Ch.)

[Màiri Nigh'n Alasdair Ruaidh, 17th century]

TRANSLATION

1. In the state in which I am this night, I am satiated with sore weeping; without rest, without peace or joy. 2. With health uncertain, and of recovery there being no hope, my gladness is for ever gone. 3. For Macleod, beloved, is in a fine woollen shroud, with no covering to his side but boards. 4. It is with thinking on thee that my body has been in acute suffering, and the lashes worn away from my eyes.

[By Mary Macleod, 17th century]

From another singer, *Oighrig Pheutan* (Effie Beaton, aunt to Effie Ross) one song only was obtained (Example 8), but that was a fine *iorram*, or rowing song.[7] 'Many a time', said Oighrig, 'I have heard our people sing this *iorram* when returning home with a heavy load of fish —The more sad the strain, the more glad would I be—as I knew that the boat would be full.'

Example 8   *Journal*, 75

Iùraibh o-hì, iùraibh o-hù

Sung by Oighrig Beaton (cottar),
Bracadale, Skye, 1863

I-ùr - aibh o - hì, iùr - aibh o - hù. 1. Chì mi'n t-àit' 's an robh mi'n

uir - idh, hó rò ho - ì, O - ho eil - e.

TRANSLATION

(*Chorus*: Iùraibh, etc.) 1. The place I behold, where last year I was staying, (*R.*: Hórò, etc.) 2. though this year I no longer there abide; 3. the slopes of Lochiel and of Kinloch-Luinnard, 4. Kinloch of the vessels and of fleets. 5. On Saturday I was seized with sorrow, 6. and never have been so overcome; 7. sitting solitary on the knoll, 8. where I could not hear the voice of any other person; 9. hearing the sound of the waves; 10. the rustle of the hazel against the holly, 11. of the sand-drift over the sea-bent, 12. of the nut-trees against the moss, 13. the stir of the foreigners and their ships, 14. the noise of the ropes against the blocks, 15. and the sound of oars rending the waves. 16. How sorrowful I am! 17. No boat can I behold, nor skiff 18. sailing from the land of the bent-grass, 19. returning from the land of the billows [Uist]. 20. I see the deer on the moor, 21. and the geese lingering on the strand. 22. They may remain there safe from harm; 23. my hunts-man will not shed their blood. 24. My brown-haired sportsman lies enfolded, 25. and the chest of boards is fastened. 26. When I see the men passing along 27. I make no choice among them. 28. Beloved by me was the genial hero, 29. who grew not up sluggish, weak, nor indolent; 30. was never drunken at the beer-house. 31. A greatly afflicted woman am I; 32. John have I buried, 33. and Ruairi, the brown-haired youth, his locks in curls, 34. at the temple on the hill.

Oighrig was over eighty years of age. Her mother, as a young girl, had been a maid at Ullinish when Johnson and Boswell stayed there in 1773, and she enjoyed telling of how *an Dr Shanstan* at breakfast one morning drank eighteen cups of tea.

Fanny went over to Rudha an Dùnain from time to time, happily renewing old friendships there. On one of these visits she noted some additional lines to the *Bean Eudach* song. Her MS bears the following note:

Archibald MacDiarmid's wife Anne at Rudha 'n Dunain, when singing the above song, which I asked her to sing in remembrance of my childhood, said 'Many a time have I wept when our mother used to be lulling one of us to sleep with this song. It was so sad.' I was then living in Bracadale—1861.

From Kate MacDiarmid (*Catriona Mhòr*), who had led the singing with much gusto at the waulkings, Fanny learned and noted *Cumha an eich-uisge* (Example 9).[8]

The *each-uisge* (water-horse) is a familiar figure in Gaelic folklore. In the guise of a man he might lay his head in the lap of a girl and invite her to 'dress' his hair. The tales vary between the girl who does, or does not, discover in time from the sand in his hair and on his breast what he really is. Mórag, in this instance, does not make the discovery until after she has borne him a child. In terror she flees, leaving the baby with him. This song—a lullaby still current in oral tradition—is the *each-uisge*'s entreaty to Mórag to return, alternating with his affectionate lulling of the child.

In the *Journal* Miss Tolmie remarks that her pleasure in these old wives' songs was considered very odd by her contemporaries, 'for they were not deemed "poetry" or worthy of notice by song-collectors of that period'.[9] Some of her elders, fortunately, were of her own way of thinking, notably her aunt, Mrs Hector Mackenzie (Annabella Tolmie), whose only son, John Tolmie Mackenzie, was postmaster, merchant and harbour-master at Dunvegan as well as being factor to MacLeod of MacLeod.

Example 9   *Journal, 7*

Cumha an Eich-Uisge
(Lamentation of the Water-Horse)

Sung by Kate Macdiarmid (cottar),
Minginish, Skye, 1862

1. A Mhór-ag dhonn! A   Mhór-ag dhonn! Till gud'mhac-an;'Sgheibh thu'm brad-an

breac o'n loch.   A - hó hì.   A - hó hì.   A - hó   hó - an.

A-hó   hó - an,   A-hó   hó - an,   A - hó hì.   A - hó - hì.

2. Tha 'n oidhch' an nochd
    Gu fliuch frasach,
    Aig mo mhac-sa ri sgàth cnocain. (R.)

3. Gun teine, gun tuar,
    Gun fhasgadh,
    'S tu sìor chonràn. (R.)

4. Mo shean-a chab liath.
    Ri d 'bheul beag baoth.
    'S mi seinn phort duit am Beinn Frochdai. (R.)

TRANSLATION
1. O brown-haired Morag, come back to thy little son, and thou shalt get a speckled salmon from the loch. (R). 2. The night is wet and showery for my son in the shelter of a knoll; (R.) 3. without fire, pale, forlorn, and wailing without cease. (R.) 4. My unsightly old grey mouth, against thy silly little mouth, while I sing dandling songs to thee in Ben Frochdai. (R.) [(R.)=refrain.]

Before Mrs Mackenzie's death in 1862 Fanny had noted four songs from her, of which two may be mentioned here. Both are waulking songs, and both have the shortest solo 'verse' found in such songs, only four syllables. The first, *Oran mu' n Ghruagaich-mhara* ('A Song about the Mermaid', *Journal*, 61), diminutive though it is, has interesting features. The octave-leaping chorus is in bold contrast to the solo verse-line confined to three adjoining notes, the solo refrain rising only to the fifth (Example 10).[10]

Example 10   *Journal,* 61

Oran mu'n Ghruagaich-mhara
(A Song about the Mermaid)

Sung by Mrs Hector M'Kenzie,
Dunvegan, Skye, 1862

Hill   o   ho,   Hùill o   ho. 1.'S mis 'a chunn-aic!   Hill   o   ho.

TRANSLATION

(*Ch.*: Hill o ho, etc.) 1. What a wonderful sight (*R.*: Hill o, etc.) 2. I beheld to-day, 3. in the early morning when 4. I was searching for sheep! 5. A maiden I saw, 6. sitting on a rock alone, 7. and she had a grey robe 8. on for clothing. 9. It was not long ere 10. this changed; 11. raising her head she stretched herself, 12. and assuming the appearance 13. of an animal without horns, 14. she went cleaving the sea on every side; 15. through the Sound of Mull; 16. through the Sound of Islay; 17. through the Sound of Orasa 18. of Mac-Phee, 19. toward the spacious region 20. of the bountiful ones.

The *Gruagach* here is female. Although a 'maid of the sea', she must not be pictured as the conventional golden-haired nude terminating in a fish's tail. The spectator, while searching for sheep, sees a grey-robed maiden sitting on a distant rock. Raising her head, she stretches herself and assumes the form of the 'animal without horns'. Then 'she went cleaving the sea on every side . . . toward the spacious region of the bountiful ones'. Although the literal word 'seal' is not used, 'the hornless animal' whose form the mermaid took, one may suppose to be a seal. The 'grey robe' of the maiden further points to her seal character, the seal being often described as 'grey'. 'In the superstitious belief of the North,' says Mr W. T. Dennison in his *Orcadian Sketch-book*,[11]

the seal held a far higher place than any of the lower animals, and had the power of assuming the human form and faculties. . . . Every true descendant of the Norsemen looks upon the seal as a kind of second-cousin in disgrace.

The words are known traditionally today, some twenty 'verses' of them, but to another tune. The tune above, a chant-like solo alternating with a plunging chorus, to beats on the waulking board grouped into threes and sixes (rather than the more commonplace twos and fours) must have been exhilarating to sing and mesmeric to listen to. Fanny, hearing it sung by her aunt, could visualize it at such waulkings as she herself had known.

The second song of Mrs Mackenzie's to be mentioned here is another tune to the *Bean Eudach*, with thirty couplets. In the *Journal*, 50 (ii) the song is entitled *Bean Mhic a' Mhaoir* ('The Wife of the son of the Maor [or Bailiff]'). The one title, *Bean Eudach*, names the murderess; the other, the victim.[12]

Miss Wrench was in Skye again in the summer of 1860, staying in the Free Church manse in Bracadale, visiting and examining schools set up by the Ladies' Highland Association. Two years later she was back on a larger errand, establishing a school, eligible for the Privy Council grant, at Braes, near Portree. The L.H.A., already supporting two schools in the district, had not the funds to provide another so near. She had her own list of subscribers mainly in London and now decided to apply her funds to this new school at Braes. The school and dwelling-house were ready, the former to provide accommodation for upwards of a hundred children and also to serve as a meeting place for Sunday services. Much as the people of the district desired a school it was impossible for them to raise the salary required by the Privy Council to be paid to the teacher. That year both herring and potatoes were again a failure. Miss Wrench, therefore, but in friendly and even affectionate terms, notified the Association that she was obliged to withdraw her list of subscriptions. She had made herself responsible for the teacher's salary and for payment of the sewing mistress, and this would absorb all her resources.

Matters settled at Braes, Miss Wrench was ready to return to Edinburgh for the winter and invited Fanny to accompany her a second time. The next few years were to bring changes. John Tolmie became minister of Contin in Ross-shire in 1863, and his mother and sisters went to live in Portree. That same year Hugh MacAskill died. For the first time for centuries there was no longer a MacAskill at Rudha an Dùnain.

CHAPTER 5

EDINBURGH,
1862-6

It was then that Mrs Thomas Constable asked me to come by-&-
by to stay with her, when two young daughters would be under my
care.

'Reminiscences'

In the autumn of 1862 Fanny again went to Edinburgh with Miss
Wrench. As before, her studies were encouraged and guided by Mr
and Mrs Constable. After a short interval, however, she became
governess to their daughters, Maimie and Katie, aged twelve and ten.
She herself, only a year older than the eldest of the family, Elizabeth,
was to remain in the household for nearly four years.

Those years established a friendship that was to last throughout her
long life, not only with the Constables and their descendants but with
their relations, the Cowans. Mrs Lucy Constable was one of the younger
members of the first family of Alexander Cowan (1775–1859), founder
of the paper-making firm at Valleyfield, Penicuik.[1] Twice married, he
had had a family of twenty and at his death left sixty-one descendants.[2]

In 1826 he had been trustee for the creditors in the bankruptcy involving Archibald Constable, James Ballantyne and Sir Walter Scott.
Many stories are told of his private kindnesses and public benefaction.
Among the latter was his active participation in and generosity towards
the educational side of the Ladies' Highland Association, and this
tradition was continued by his sons. A daughter, Charlotte, was for
many years joint secretary with Miss Christina Rainy.

In the unpublished diaries of Sir John Cowan of Beeslack[3] the names
of Miss Wrench and Fanny Tolmie figure from time to time between
1862 and 1866. There were many visits to Beeslack, by carriage and
pair or by public coach over the eight-mile road. The first entries
(October 1862), however, concern a longer journey:

Saturday 28. Papa [the diarist], Mr Stuart, Dr Thin and F. Tolmie to London.
Monday 30. Papa and party at the Exhibition all day. Tea at Aunt Jessie's and Christy Minstrels.
Wednesday, 1 November. The Crystal Palace and 4000 children singing.

December entries show Fanny and others frequently visiting Beeslack:

Wednesday 10. Papa and girls[4] to town. Bring out Miss Wrench, Fanny Tolmie and W. J. Wilson who lectures.
Thursday 11. Aunt E.[5] takes Miss Wrench and Fanny T. to town.
Wednesday 17. Bring out F. Tolmie and T. Gillespie.
Thursday 18. Aunt E., F. Tolmie and Papa to town. Call on W. Carmichael. W. Scott's funeral.[6] Mrs Thomas' sale. Fearfully windy drive out.

There is much coming and going over Christmas and New Year.

December. Wednesday 24. Papa out by Straiton coach.
Thursday 25. Aunt E., Miss Tolmie, Willie and Joan at Penicuik. Christmas dinner.
Friday 26. Uncle James' Christmas tree.[7] Drove in to it. Miss G. brought her sister and Miss Wrench. Mr MacDonald juggling. R. Ballantyne singing.[8] Left at 10.30.
Saturday 27. Wet day. Plum puddings given. Ed Madden at dinner. Dance at night in hall.
Tuesday 30. Christmas Tree made magnificent a delightful evening. Presents to servants, dancing, etc. 46 present.
Wednesday 31. All at Auchendinny Sabbath School Treat. Christmas Tree, Magic Lantern, 370 big and little presents.
1863
Thursday, January 1. Began Dr Chalmers' daily Bible reading.[9] At Valleyfield charming women's party. Songs, Tom's stories, Christy Minstrels, Magic Lantern, Scissors designs.
Friday 2. Volunteer Presentation at Eskmills and Ball. Aunt E., F. Tolmie, Papa, Miss G., Janie and W. Maxwell there.
Saturday 3. Papa, Miss G., F. Tolmie and Janie at Valleyfield School fete, a very pretty sight. New school-room beautiful.
Sunday 4. All walked to church.

Monday 5. Malcolm, Murdo, Jamie, F. Tolmie, M. and K. Constable leave.

The last entry suggests that Fanny Tolmie had already joined the Constable household, or would shortly do so. Her feelings, returning from Skye to Edinburgh when she was newly twenty-two, were vividly recalled in the 'Reminiscences' she was to send to Lucy Broadwood nearly fifty years later.

> And then Miss Wrench came again and I accompanied her a second time to Edinburgh—suffering much mentally. I am now a thought-less child compared with what I then was—the music was in dire confusion—the religious opinions of the time difficult to adjust. . . .
> It was then that Mrs Thomas Constable asked me to come by-and-by to stay with her, when two young daughters would be under my care. It was while with this dear family that some kind of order came into my conflicting ideas regarding the Ancient and Modern times. It was an illuminating atmosphere, from rare sympathy, social intercourse, and varied reading.

The Constables lived in Royal Terrace, one of three terraces, Royal, Calton and Regent, almost surrounding the Calton Hill, and designed by the architect Playfair as part of the fifth of Edinburgh's 'New Towns'. To no. 35 Alexander Cowan had moved in 1845, when it was not long built, from the historic Moray House in the Canongate.[10] In the early 1860s the Constables were at no. 34, the second Mrs Cowan and her family at no. 35, Charles Cowan at no. 37 (later acquiring Logan House in the Pentlands) and James at no. 38 (moving into no. 35 after his stepmother's death).

Thomas Constable's library was a joy to Fanny; her reading was serious and wide. She found unexpected pleasure and undoubted stimulus in two newly-published, and important, Gaelic works that she found there. One was the first printed edition (Edinburgh, 1862) of the early sixteenth-century MS known as the *Book of the Dean of Lismore*. Edited by the Rev. Thomas McLauchlan, it contains a transcript of a considerable portion of the Dean's home-made, semi-phonetic text, a transposition of the content into standard spelling and an attempted translation. This archaic material, with an Irish flavour, was new to her; of outstanding interest were the heroic lays which told of *Fionn mac Cumhaill* (Finn MacCoull) and his followers, the Fiann.

41

In the other publication, however, she found herself very much on her own ground. 'In that atmosphere of light and goodness', she wrote to Lucy Broadwood on 20 June 1909, 'I first saw the *West Highland Tales* of Campbell of Islay, and to my wonder found glorified in print many of the fireside tales familiar to us all, and much of which I had only a vague knowledge heretofore.'

The four volumes of *West Highland Tales*, in Gaelic and English, appeared between 1860 and 1862. ' "The Book of the Dean of Lismore" ', she tells in the 'Reminiscences', 'I read aloud to my German Master, Herr Weisse—and with that the West Highland Tales of Campbell of Islay. In German I read Sophocles and Aeschylus —and a beautiful Hindu legend, the story of Savitri.'

Traugott Heinrich Weisse had left Germany in 1848. Settling in Edinburgh, he earned a high reputation as a teacher of his native language, and compiled a German grammar that ran into several editions. In the 1890s he was to be seen, white-haired and blind, going about with his secretary, a devoted young man.[11] His wife was Sophie Marquidorff, a Lithuanian pianist, whose chamber-music concerts were a feature of Edinburgh musical life in her time. A daughter of the Weisses, also Sophie, was to be heard of later as the principal of a fashionable school for girls in the south of England, the lady who directed the early musical education of Donald Francis Tovey.

Meanwhile, in the 1860s, at their flat in Howe Street, Fanny Tolmie had music as well as German lessons, 'to which I was not equal,' she adds in a marginal note in the 'Reminiscences', 'partly from near-sightedness which made reading difficult while the ear was too quick.'

Considering that she became an amateur pianist who derived much pleasure from playing and could communicate pleasure to others, her lessons must have been more successful than she thought. Her quick ear was in the long run to be her great asset. Near-sightedness may have prevented her from reading as easily as she wished, but she learned how to write tunes with facility and accuracy, though this may have been a side result unsuspected by her teachers! Also, it is highly probable that she heard more playing from Frau Weisse than from Miss Yaniewicz.

The day after New Year 1864, a Saturday, Fanny Tolmie turns up again in the Beeslack diary. 'Papa, Miss Irving, Tolmie, George, Janie, Willie, Katie and Egmont to Arniston. Bonfire and tea in the forest.'

It must have been a very mild New Year. On the Monday, Fanny Tolmie and the Constables left.

Towards the end of April 1865 'Papa brought party including Fanny T. From Edinburgh'; next day, 'A large party to Logan House'; and next again, 'A party to see the steeplechase'.

That summer John Cowan sailed his yacht, *Red Deer*, among the Inner and Outer Hebrides, with a large party of relations and friends on board. He combined this holiday with visits to the 'Ladies' Schools' of which there were now a great number.[12]

Fanny Tolmie and the Constable girls joined the yacht in the Firth of Lorne—probably at Oban—on the last day of June. Two days later, being Sunday, they were in church, probably at Tobermory. 'Mr Gray chants beautifully in Gaelic. F. Tolmie there', runs the diary. They embark for Coll, cannot land but get milk, butter and eggs, then set out for the south—'much pitching and discomfort'—and by midnight anchor in Loch Tuadh. They sail slowly past Colonsay and by Islay Sound to Port Askaig, and 'land on Jura for an evening walk'. Twice they visit Iona, the second time 'taking up their quarters partly at the Manse and the rest at the little inn'. They spend the following day 'in the ruined tombs and on the Eastern and Western shores'. Towards the end of the month Dr Livingstone's sons join the party, and on the 28 June 'F. Tolmie goes to Skye'.

On her return in the autumn Fanny was to spend one more season in Edinburgh. Maimie and Katie were older and were soon to outgrow their governess. They all appear in the diary enjoying Hallowe'en junketings at Beeslack.

> *Wednesday, October 25.* E. T. and Ellie to town and bring back Miss Tolmie, Maimie, Katie, Willie and Jamie Simpson.
> *Thursday, 26.* Great doings at the chalet. Russian dance at night.
> *Friday, 27.* Halloween at night. Fanny Tolmie exhibits as a beautiful stork. Miss Urquhart burns nuts with Uncle George.
> *Saturday, 28.* F. Tolmie leaves.

The Hallowe'en entry raises a teasing question—how in the world did Fanny Tolmie 'exhibit as a stork'? The dress of that day—and for many a day later—was discouraging to the exhibition of any long-legged bird. Perhaps—as with a glove puppet—the likeness stopped at the waist.

A glimpse of her, however, in that place and period, and in her own words, comes from her 'Reminiscences': 'It was never forgotten where I came from and occasionally I might be asked to sing a Gaelic song—when my choice usually was the "Lament for young Raasay,"—the Song about the Gruagach; and Ailein, Ailein!'[13]

The *Gruagach* song has already been given (Example 4); the 'Lament for young Raasay' (Example 11), appears, as given in *The Gesto Collection*, and 'Ailein, Ailein' (Example 12), as in the *Journal*.

Example 11   *Gesto*, p. 17

Cumha Mhic Gille-chalum a b'òige
Lament for McLeod, younger of Raasay

S mi nam shuidh air an fhaoghlainn,
Gun fhàilte gun fhuran,
Cha tog mi fonn aotrom,
Bho Dhì-h-Aoine na dunaich.
  Hìll ò, hìll ò hò, hìll ò,
  O ró hù ò rill ò hò, hù ill ò hò, hìll ò.

Cha tog mi fonn aotrom
Bho Dhì-h-Aoine na dunaich.
Ach ri tuireadh 's ri caoineadh,
Tha mo dhaoine 's na grunnaibh.

Gille Calum a b'òige
'S Iain Mór mo sgéul duilich.

Sud na fir a bha làidir
Gus na shàraich a mhuir iad.

Gun siòd air an cluas-aig,
Ach fuarachd na tuinne.

Ann an goirtean na tràthad,
Tha mo ghràdhsa bho'n uiridh.

Gun mhire, gun mhànran,
Gun Tàileasg ga iomairt,

Gun do mhial-choin air iallach,
Gu bhi triall cho'n a mhunaidh,

Gu fireach na seilge.
Na gu garbhlach a Chuilinn. Hill ò, &c.

44

E xample 12   *Journal,* 64

Ailein, Ailein, 'sfhad an cadal
(Alan, Alan, long is thy slumber)

Sung by Oighrig Ross (cottar),
Bracadale, Skye, 1862

(a) Sint 'thug-aibh i,   'n àill   leibh i?   O   hò,   thug-aibh   i   ò.

(b) 1. Ail - ein, Ail - ein,'s fhad   an cad - al!   (c) O   hò,   thug-aibh   i   ò.

2. *Tha'n uiseag 'gairm 's an là air glasadh.
3. Tha'n ceò air sgaoileadh air an leacainn.
4. 'S fhad o'n chàraich mi do leabaidh;
5. S cha b'ann air lic luim a chladaich;
6. Air clàiribh do luinge faide,
7. Tigh mór rùmail, ùrlar farsuinn.
8. Chunnacas bàta seach an rudha;

9. Chrath mi fhein mo bhreacan riuth';
10. Is dh'ordaich mi bhi cuide riutha.
11. Gè nach b'ann air ghaol am fuidheall,
12. Air gaol òg an òr-fhuilt bhuidhe.
13. 'Dhìreadh beann's a theàrnadh bruthach,
14. 'Dh'fhàgadh calp an fhéidh 'na spriùiribh,
15. Is eala bhàn nan spògan dubha.

*The lines come in in position (*b*) always preceded by (*a*) and followed by (*c*).

TRANSLATION
(*Chorus:* †Reached forth, wish ye it? O-ho, give ye it!) 1. Alan, Alan, long has thy slumber been! (*R.:* Oho, etc.; then Ch.) 2. The lark is warbling, day has dawned, 3. and the mist has spread on the hill-side. 4. It is long since I have made thy bed; 5. and not on the bare rocks of the sea-shore, 6. but on the boards of thy galley, 7. a spacious house with wide floor. 8. A boat was seen going round the headland, 9. and, waving my tartan scarf, 10. I wished that I might be with them; 11. and not for love of their refuse [*or* 'rubbish', *i.e.* the mean ones], 12. [but] for that of the youth of the golden hair 13. who climbs the mountain and descends the slope; 14. who would leave the leg of the deer in fragments, 15. and the white swan with the black web-feet.

†Apparently a reference to the handing backwards and forwards of the cloth in waulking.

Miss Wrench was in poor health at this time. A few weeks after the Hallowe'en party John Cowan noted, 'Dear Miss Wrench comes out', with the remark, a few days later, 'We read *Battle of Drumclog* at night. Miss Wrench down to enjoy it.' She appears to have stayed at Beeslack for some time. Fanny went out now and then to visit her, usually staying for a night or two. An entry at the end of May 1866 mentions Fanny's arrival on a Saturday, staying at home with Miss Wrench on the Sunday, and returning to Edinburgh on the Monday.

That may have been their last meeting. Fanny returned to Skye for good that summer, and in October Matilda Wrench died in the Free Church Manse at Bowden in Roxburghshire, where the Rev. James Pirie was minister. She was buried in Edinburgh, in Old Greyfriars' Churchyard, this London woman who had devoted so much of her life to the furthering of education in the Highlands.

Three years after her death a teacher from Braes was to write: 'Six of the Braes boys were engaged as teachers before I left Skye last week, and another is coming to the Normal School this week. This is all owing to Miss Wrench's noble efforts.'[14]

It is perhaps not irrelevant to recognize some of the drive of Matilda Wrench in her twentieth-century not-so-distant cousin, the late Sir Evelyn Wrench,[15] founder of the Over-Seas League and the English Speaking Union.

CHAPTER 6

PORTREE, NAIRN, NORTH UIST, CONTIN, 1866-73

Between the years 1868 and '73 I was at Portree and over in Uist more than once, where I met those nice elderly women who chose from among their ancestral recollections some of the songs of the Ossianic time as the most select and rare to sing. . . .

Letter to Lucy Broadwood, 20 June 1909

When Fanny returned to Skye in 1866 she joined her mother and Mary in Portree. Two years later they removed to Nairn, often revisiting Portree, to stay with the eldest daughter, Jane, Mrs Laurence Skene and her family.[1] It was on such a visit in 1870 that Fanny found a fresh opportunity to learn and note old songs—an opportunity again associated with knitting.

Margaret MacLeod (*Mairearad Mhór*, 'Tall Margaret') did much of the necessary knitting for the Skene household. She was about eighty years of age and lived by herself in a little bothy near the Great Moss, a few miles to the north of Portree. On days that she made an expedition to Mrs Skene's she would sometimes remain for the evening, delighting the maids in the kitchen with her witty and amusing stories.

Not only the maids but their mistress and Miss Fanny enjoyed those evenings with Mairearad. Conversation, gay or serious, was in Gaelic. Mairearad, for one, knew no other language. Maids who had been in the house for any length of time had, of necessity, picked up some English, but it was easily discarded when they talked among themselves. Mrs Skene, herself bilingual, encouraged them to read both their native language and English.

47

In the warm kitchen, with its oil lamp and shadowy corners, Fanny sat listening. Mairearad, in a mesmeric kind of chant, was unfolding the story of a tragedy a thousand years ago and more—if it had ever happened at all. To Mairearad it was as real and vivid as any occurrence in her own lifetime.

Example 13   *Journal, 85*

Laoidh Dhiarmad
(The Lay of Diarmid)

Sung by Margaret Macleod (cottar),
Portree, Skye, 1870

1. 'S ann an raoir bu ghorm an tul - ach, Gè dearg an diu   e   le fuil Dhiar-mad;

'S gur h-ann leis an Fheinn bu duil-ich.   Mur   a bith-eadh Fionn 'ga iarr - aidh.

2. 'Fhinn, nach toir thu dhomh-sa
        deoch,
    Dhearbh mhic a righ is mo
        chobhair,
    Tighearn mo bhiadh, agus
        m'aodaich?'
    'Och-òin-a-rì! 's mi nach tabhair!

3. Cha toir mise dhuit-sa deoch,

    Ni mò a chaisgeas mi t'ìotadh,

    'S beag a rinn thu riamh dha
        m'leas,
    Is mór a rinn thu dha m'aimhleas.'
    Canar gun fhonn:
        An sìn bhàsaich Diarmaid air an
            tom.

TRANSLATION
1. Green last night was the knoll, though it be red to-day with the blood of Diarmid; and grievous were this to the Feinn, had it not been the desire of Fionn. 2. (*Diarmid*) 'Fionn, wilt thou not give me to drink, thou true son of a king, and my succour; lord over my food and my clothing?' (*Fionn*) 'Och oin-a-ree! that will not I! 3. I will not give a drink to thee, and neither shall I quench thy thirst; help thou didst never offer me, nor didst render but to my ruin.' (Spoken) Then died Diarmid upon the knoll.

The *Laoidh Dhiarmad* (Example 13) Fanny recalled from the *Book of the Dean of Lismore*. She had read it in English to her German master, but had never heard it sung before. Mairearad knew only a few verses of the lay, but she knew all the details of the story. Not only did she discuss the incidents as she had heard them told, but she knew where they had

48

happened, actually in or near Portree. She sang as if she herself had seen it happen.

Yes, the Fiann had hunted in these parts. Diarmad was one of the strongest of the band, invulnerable except for a certain spot on his foot, and certainly the handsomest! He possessed a *ball seirc* or love spot which women found irresistible. He had to be careful to keep his bonnet well over his face when women were about: one glance at his *ball seirc* and a woman would be ready to follow him to the ends of the earth. The misfortune was that the woman who caught sight of the *ball seirc* was Gràinne, the wife of Fionn—and Fionn was not only his superior, but his uncle. Thus it came about that in the last scene of the story Fionn challenged Diarmad to arm himself and kill the magic boar that no man yet had overcome:

> The enormous beast lay dead on the ground. 'Measure the boar, Diarmad!' cried Fionn.
>
> Diarmad paced its length from snout to tail—twenty paces, perhaps more, perhaps less.
>
> 'Measure it again! And this time against the pile!' Fionn demanded. He knew that the boar had a poisoned bristle.
>
> Diarmad turned, this time pacing from tail to snout. A prick on his heel—and he dropped to the ground, bleeding to death.
>
> He called to Fionn for water to drink. There was a spring close by, whether with special healing powers or not. Fionn, instinctively kind and humane, ran to the spring and filled his cupped hands.
>
> Carefully nursing the precious water he moved towards the dying man.
>
> His thoughts turned back to Gràinne and her flight with Diarmad. His fingers fell apart, and the water trickled on to the grass.

The last phrase of the song was not sung, but spoken: *An sìn bhàsaich Diarmaid air an tom*, 'Then died Diarmad on the knoll'.

Mairearad also sang *Laoidh Fhraoich*, 'The Lay of Fraoch' (Example 14), the story of another of the heroes. As for Maibh, or Maive, who brought about his death, Mairearad declared she was a *baobh*, 'witch', 'the worst woman that ever was in the world'. Jealous of the love between Fraoch and her own daughter Fionnabhair, and maddened by his rejection of her advances, she planned his ruin. Feigning severe sickness, she insisted that nothing would cure her but a handful of rowan berries

49

from the tree across the 'little cold pool', and that none but Fraoch should gather them.

Fraoch, 'of keen-edged weapons', agreed to go, though remarking that he had never done 'a fruit-gathering like that'. 'Gracefully he swam the loch.' Beneath the tree a monster lay asleep, 'her great mouth up near the cluster of fruit'. Eluding her, he returned with his hands full. Maibh, foiled, invented another errand for him, that he should bring back to her a branch from the tree.

This time the monster awoke and Fraoch was mauled to death.

Example 14   *Journal*, 86

Laoidh Fhraoich
(The Lay of Fraoch)

Sung by Margaret Macleod (cottar),
Portree, Skye, 1870

1. Thàin - ig ea - slaint - e throm, throm, Air nigh - ean [?]nan

corn fial, Ag-us chuir i fios gu Fraoch,'Sdh'fhid-ir an laoch ciod è a

miann. 2. Thubh - airt i nach biodh i slàn,. Mur faigh'dh i làn a

bas mhaoth, De chaorr- ann an lod - ain fhuair,O'sgunabhith 'g am buain ach Fraoch.

3. 'Cnuasach sud nach d'rinn mi
        riamh,'
    Arsa Fionn mac-Idhaidh nan arm
        geur,
    ''S ged nach d'rinn mi'n
        cnuasach s'riamh,
    Thèid mise bhuain chaorann do
        Mhaidhbh.'

4. Dh'fhalbh è, 's cha b'è turus àigh;

    Shnàmh è gu grinn air an loch,

    Is fhuair è bhéist na sior-throm
        suain,
    'S a craos suas ris an dos.

TRANSLATION

1. There came an overpowering illness to the daughter [?   ]* of the generous drinking-horns, who sent a message to Fraoch, and the hero asked what was her desire. 2. She declared that she would never be well unless she were to receive the full of her tender palms of rowan-berries from the little cold pool (or lake), but that no other was to pluck them than Fraoch. 3. 'A fruit-gathering like that have I never done,' said Fraoch Mac Idhaidh (son of Idad) of keen-edged weapons, 'and though I have never done the same, I will go and gather the rowan-berries for Maive.' 4. He went on his unpropitious way, and gracefully he swam the loch, and found the monster fast asleep, with her great mouth up near the cluster of fruit.

* Name forgotten here. It was no doubt some form of 'Eochaidh', the sick woman's father.

Laoidh Oscair, 'The Lay of Oscar' (*Journal*, 87) is also in straightforward narrative form, in quatrains. Two more from Mairearad were adapted for communal singing round the waulking board, the lines interspersed with choruses and solo refrains.

Comhairl' Oisein dha 'Mhàthair, 'Ossian's Warning to his Mother', shows this construction (Example 15).

Example 15   *Journal*, 89

Comhairl' Oisein dha 'Mhàthair
(Ossian's Warning to his Mother)

Sung by Margaret Macleod (cottar),
Portree, Skye, 1871, and Mrs M'Vicar, N. Uist, 1871

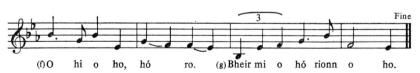

1. If thou be my mother, who art a deer,* be up before the rising of the sun. 2. Go over the hill ere heat come on, and beware of the action of dogs. 3. If thou go upon the mountains high, beware of the clan of the 'cairds', the sons of the artificers and their dogs. 4. Two dogs and ten on a leash they have, and his own dog in each man's hand. 5. If thou reach the low glens, guard thee against the forest clan, the sons of the forest and their dogs. 6. Two dogs and ten on a leash they have, and his own dog in each man's hand. 7. If thou go into the deep glens, beware of the children of the smith.

† The lines marked (a) and (c) form the verse couplets in this song. The other lines are refrain and are repeated with every verse.

* Legend told of the transformation of Ossian's mother into a deer. His father was Fionn, the leader of the Fiann. Ossian was said to have outlived the rest of the band and to have conversed with Saint Patrick. (Mar Oisein an déidh na Féinne, 'Like Ossian after the Fiann', is a popular description of a man who has outlived his contemporaries.)

From Portree Fanny went on to visit cousins in the west. At Dunvegan she stayed with John Tolmie Mackenzie (only son of her aunt Anabella), postmaster among other offices, and owning a couple of smacks with which he fulfilled his mail contract between Skye and North Uist. The crossing from Dunvegan to Lochmaddy could be very rough. There were occasions when the mail-bags were lashed to the mast to prevent them from being washed overboard;[2] but there were wonderful evenings when the boat headed straight for a calm sunset before turning into harbour between the two rocks called the 'Maddies' (Gaelic madadh, 'dog').

From Lochmaddy there would follow a drive of ten miles or so to Newton Farm, the home of her cousins John MacDonald and Mrs Margaret MacNeil. Newton lies to the north of the island, facing Obbe (now called Leverburgh) in south Harris.

John MacDonald, tacksman of Scolpaig, had succeeded to the tack of Newton on the death of his brother-in-law, Captain William MacNeil. A bachelor, he now lived there with his sister.[3] He was factor to Sir John Powlett Orde, who had purchased the island in 1855 from the trustees of Lord MacDonald. Six feet four inches in height, he had inherited the build of the 'Big Tolmies' and was popularly known as am bàillidh mór, 'the big factor'.[4]

At Newton Fanny met Mrs Harriet—or 'Herrot'—MacVicar. A note on the MS of Òran do Dhòmhnull Gorm, 'A Song to Donald Gorm' (Journal, 78) describes their first meeting. A weaver had arrived that day, set up his loom, and was getting on with the warping.[5]

I learned this song from 'Herot' in N. Uist—1870—and thought it a beautiful Chant. There was a great stir at Newton—N. Uist one day in my cousin's kitchen—spinning—carding and warping going on, as well as cooking. 'Herot' was spinning, and was asked to sing to me—as I admired the song we both [went] up to a quiet garret—where I learned it from her—and marked the music in sol-fa—lest I should forget.

Herrot was elderly, tall and grey. '[She] sang in the same manner [as Margaret MacLeod] with great reverence as about a sacred subject' (*Journal*, p. 146). She knew the lays that Mairearad had sung and she contributed another, *Cumha Dhiarmad*, 'Lament for Diarmid' (*Journal*, 88). Three of her songs were eulogies of chiefs or lairds, detailing their appearance, virtues and prowess in battle, concluding with blessings upon them and good wishes for their future. Donald Gorm, of the song already mentioned, was chief of Clan Donald in the reign of James VI, 1603, and a contemporary of Rory Mór MacLeod. A second song praises *Fear Bhàlai*, 'MacDonald of Vallay' (*Journal*, 92), a small island off the north-west of North Uist. The third of these eulogies, *Oran do Mhac-Iain-'ic-Sheumais*, 'A song to the Son of John-son-of-James' (Example 16) is still widely known. It refers to an able warrior of Clan Donald, who fought at Càrinish, North Uist, about the year 1601, one of the last clan battles.

The story associated with the song is that Donald MacDonald, *Domhnall mac Iain 'ic Sheumais*, heard the lamentations of his foster-mother as her only cow was being driven away by the invading MacLeods of Harris. Hastening to the rescue, he drove them off, slaying their leader, Donald Glas, whose head he buried in a knoll. (This knoll, on a croft near the old Temple of Càrinish, is pointed out to this day.) Donald himself, however, was badly wounded, his back and limbs being pierced by arrows. The story goes that while the arrows were being extracted and his wounds dressed, his foster-mother set women to waulk a web of cloth, and to sing as loudly as possible, to prevent his followers from hearing his groans.

Each of the three eulogies is said to have been composed by a nurse or foster-mother. Fosterage was for centuries an important feature of clan life. Between foster-parents and children there were close bonds, as also between foster-brothers and sisters.

53

Example 16

Oran do Mhac-Iain-ic-Sheumais
(A Song to the Son of John-son-of-James)

Sung by Harriet M'Vicar (spinner),
North Uist, 1870

1. A Mhic-Iain-'ic-Sheum-ais, Tha do sgeul air m'air - e.

Air fair a lail ó, Air fair a lail ó! Bho'n là thug thu'n cuan d'i Bha gruaim air na beann - aibh. Hi ó.· Hi ri rith-ibh ò hi eil - e Hi ó, Hi rith-ibh ò rò ao ò! Chall eil - ibh hò ró, Hao ri o ho i ò.

2. *Solo:* *Bho'n là thug thu'n cuan d'i,
   Bha gruaim air na beannaibh,
   Refrain: Air faire lail ó, air faire lail ó.
   Bha smal air na speuran
   'S bha na reultan 'gam falach.
   Chorus: Hi ó, hi-ri, etc.

3. 'S è Mac-Iain-'ic-Sheumais
   Duine treubhach smiorail.

4. Gruaidh ruiteach na féile
   Mar éibhleag 'ga garadh.

5. Bu cheannard roimh shluagh thu
   Dol suas troimh thir ain-iùil.

6. Le claidheamh geur cruadhach,
   'S dé! cha d'fhuaireadh sgann' air.

7. Cha'n iarradh tu cluasag
   Ach cluain am bi gaineamh.

8. Nam biodh agam curach,
   Gu'n cuirinn air chuan i,

9. Is gille maith turuis
   Bhitheadh furachail uaithe

10. Feuch am faighinn naigheachd,
    Air mac an duin 'uasail.
    [Le Mhuime.]

* Two couplets are sung as a verse, the last couplet of one verse forming the first couplet of the next.

TRANSLATION

1. O thou son of John-son-of-James, for tidings of thee I am writing. (*Ref.*: Air, etc.) Since the day on which thou didst turn thy galley towards the open sea, the mountains have been in gloom, (*Ch.*: Hi, etc.) 2. darkness has overspread the skies, and the stars have been hiding. 3. John's son, the son of James, is a valorous and vigorous man; 4. ruddy, of the generous countenance, like an ember enkindling. 5. Going through a strange land, a true leader of men art thou. 6. with a sharp sword of steel, in which most certainly no fault might be found. 7. No pillow wouldst thou desire but a meadow, where there should be sand. 8. If I had a skiff I should launch her on the sea, 9. with an excellent emissary who should look well around him, 10. so that I might gain tidings of the son of him who was of good descent.

[By his foster-mother.]

Between 1870 and 1872 Fanny stayed for a time at her brother's manse at Contin and taught his children. She played an active part in the whole life of the family. A story has come down to us from that time. Aunt Fanny, who was known as a keen walker, occasionally slept heavily in the morning and would come downstairs rather late. She then appeared at the breakfast-table with a hat on in order supposedly to give the impression of having been out for a brisk walk. The Tolmie children had increased in number since the Bracadale days—eventually there were ten—but the nurse, *Seònaid*, Janet Anderson, from the parish of Strath in Skye, was still there to sing lullabies and *puirt a beul*. From her was noted a poignantly beautiful lament in waulking-song form

Example 17   *Iournal*, 46

Cumha Bhraithrean
(Lament for Brothers)

Sung by Janet Anderson (nurse),
Manse of Contin, Ross-shire, 1870

Hù ò - rò, hù ò. Rò-hò ù - ò hì ò. Hù ò - rò,

hù ò. 1. Gur h-è mis - e tha' fo mhul - ad, Tha leann-dubh air mo ghruaidh.

2. *Cha b'è cumha mo leannain
   Ged a dh'fhanadh è bhuam,
3. Ach a cumha mo bhràithrean
   Tha cnàmh anns a' chuan.
4. Cumha Eachainn is Lachlainn
   Dh'fhàg tana mo ghruag.
5. 'S oil leam diol'ur cùl clannach
   'S an fheamainn'ga luadh.
6. 'S tric mo shùil air an rudha,
   Fodh'n bhruthaich ud shuas,
7. Ach am faic mi seòl bréid-gheal
   Là gréine 'sa'chuan.
8. Cha'n 'eil long thig o'n rudha,
   Nach toir snidh air mo ghruaidh.

9. Cha'n 'eil bàt thig'sa' chaolas,
   Nach caochail mo shnuadh.
10. Cha dhìrich mi bruthach,
    'S cha shiubhail mi uair,
11. Cha dhean mi céum idir,
    Gus an tig na bheil bhuam.
12. Cha chaidil mi còmhnard
    A Dhòmhnach no Luain.
13. Tha bhur leabaidh na h-ònar,
    Anns an t-seòmar ud shuas;
14. Cha teid mi 'ga càradh
    Sibhs'a ghràidhean fad bhuam.
15. Gur h-è mis'tha fo mhulad
    Air an tulaich luim fhuair!
    [Le'm piuthar.] [By their sister.]

TRANSLATION

(S.R. and Ch.) 1. Under what sorrow am I! and tears are on my cheek! 2. It is not because of mourning for my lover, though he were to stay away, 3. but lamenting for my brothers, who are lying dead in the sea. 4. Grieving for Hector and Lachlan has thinned my hair. 5. The state of your locks, being waulked in the sea-ware, distresses me sore! 6. My gaze is often towards the promontory below yonder hill-side, 7. in the hope that I may descry a white sail, on a day of sunshine, out at sea. 8. There is no ship coming round the headland that brings not tears upon my cheek; 9. and no boat appears in the Sound without causing my colour to change. 10. I cannot climb the slope, nor walk for an hour; 11. I cannot move a step, till they return whom I mourn. 12. In peace I am unable to sleep either on Sunday or Monday! 13. Your bed is forsaken in the chamber above, 14. and I cannot arrange it, while ye, beloved, are away. 15. Most mournful am I, on the bare, chilly knoll!

* The S. and Ch. refrains come before every verse, and after the last.

(Example 17). 'Locks' (in stanza 5) is only an approximation to the meaning of *cùl clannach*, which is really the ringleted back of the head. Stanza 5 implies that their heads of hair are beaten and tossed by the waves together with the seaweed on the bed of the sea, as cloth is beaten and tossed by the hands on the board at a waulking (*luadh*).

Fanny's pencil was ready to note any song of uncommon interest that came her way. The bardess Mrs Mary MacPherson (Mary MacDonald) from Trotternish, Skye, who was at that time living in Inverness, came to Contin manse some twenty miles away '. . . in great trouble to be comforted. The poetic power came to her afterwards when 50 years of age,'[6] writes Miss Tolmie. The latter noted from her on that occasion a song with the curious title *Colann gun Cheann*, 'The Headless Body' (*Journal*, 32). It is a little startling to find this song in the *Journal* under the heading 'Nurse's Songs,' particularly as *Colann gun Cheann* was a creature who had the nasty habit of floating in the air above a certain narrow pass in Arisaig in Inverness-shire, throwing down his head upon passers-by and killing them. Eventually a courageous young man caught the head on the point of his sword and refused to give it back until the creature promised to return to Trotternish, where he originally belonged. The song is not a forerunner of the horror comic, but the creature's lament at being sent packing, with a jingle of the names of places through which he must travel.

It has a cheerful tune, as shown in Example 18.

Example 18   *Journal, 32*

Colann gun cheann
(The Headless Body)

Sung by Mrs Macpherson (Mary Macdonald),
poetess, at Contin Manse, Ross-shire, 1870

'S fhad - a bhuam fhéin,   bonn Beinn Ead-orr - a; 'S fhad-a bhuam fhéin

Beal-ach a Mhòr - bheinn;'S fhad-a bhuam fhéin   bonn   Beinn Ead-orr - a

'S fhad-a gun teag-amh bhuam Beal-ach a Mhòr - bheinn O bhonn, gu   bonn,

bonn Beinn Ead-orr', O Bhonn gu bonn,   Beal-ach a Mhòr-bheinn. O bhonn gu bonn,

bonn Beinn Ead-orr - a, 'S fhad-a gun teag-amh bhuam Beal-ach a Mhòr - bheinn.

TRANSLATION
Far from me is the base of Ben-Edar, and far from me is the pass of Morven, etc.
From base to base, the base of Ben-Edar, from base to base, the pass of Morven, etc.

There are many versions of this legend. In certain districts the song was taboo to men, *Colann gun Cheann* being a female monster.[7]

At that time there was nothing Fanny could do with her songs except preserve her notes. She had a feeling all along that some day she might meet a sympathetic musician who would understand their value. Meanwhile she willingly gave copies of certain of them to Miss MacLeod of MacLeod[8] who, in turn, passed them on to John Francis Campbell of Islay.

Campbell, with the assistance of other collectors, among them Fanny's old friend, Alexander Carmichael, was at this time putting together his *Leabhar na Féinne*, 'Book of the Fiann', published in London, 1872. He included variants of each of several lays and in two places quotes versions from Fanny Tolmie. He gives her version (words only) of 'Ossian's Counsel to his Mother' with the following note (p. 31):

October 6, 1871. Copied at Dunvegan, a version lent by Miss MacLeod of MacLeod, written this year in North Uist by Miss Tolmie from the repetition of women who used to sing this song at their work, but who have been forbidden to sing any secular music, and have given up the practice as wicked.

Similarly, as a comment upon the lay, there occurs this

Extract from a Letter

addressed to Miss MacLeod of MacLeod, by a lady, sent April 18, 1872, from Dunvegan. This shows that Heroic Ballads are known to the very poorest classes in the Highlands, and that they are localised everywhere.

'Beinn Ianabheig, a peaked hill above the Bay of Portree, was once called *Beinn Gulban*, where Diarmad, the friend of Fionn, was wounded when measuring the boar. At Sgor is the grave of Diarmad; and at Benmore is *Tobar an Tuirc* ('Well of the Boar'), from which, when dying, he besought Fionn to fetch him a drink. Margaret MacLeod, a poor forlorn woman at Portree, knows these places and can sing the songs about them.'

After Fanny returned to Nairn, Miss MacLeod wrote to her (from Gesto in Bracadale), saying that Campbell of Islay meant to call on her about a tune to one of her songs noted in Uist; 'but affairs hurried him to the south, and I never heard again of the matter'.[9]

Circumstances were such that she saw neither the book nor its references to herself and her songs until more than twenty years later.

About 1870 three little cousins, Mary Skene, Margaret Tolmie and Menie (Marion) MacLellan, all aged seven, were sent to their grand-mother in Nairn to attend school there. Menie MacLellan later plays an important part in our story. It was not for very long, for the MacLellans went to live in Dollar, allowing Menie to attend the Academy there, as also did Mary Skene and later her younger sister Margaret, while Margaret Tolmie went to the Ministers' Daughters' College in Edinburgh.[10]

The only item in the *Journal* marked as from Nairn is a nonsense song, 'A' big lees frae the head to the tail',[11] sung by Jessie MacDougall from Moidart, Inverness-shire, who, aged twenty-five, was maid in the house. The story attached to it is that it was composed in one night by a girl who was promised a reprieve for her brother under sentence of death, if by the morning she could produce a song in which there was not a word of truth.

> The cuckoo is calling, cuckoo! cuckoo!
> while picking out the eyes of the sheep

runs its chorus (Example 19).

Example 19   *Journal*, 37

Tha chu'ag is 'gug-gug' ·aice
(The Cuckoo Calls)

Sung by Jessie Macdougal, servant at Nairn,
from Moidart, Inverness-shire, 1870

Tha Chu'-ag is 'gug-gùg' aic - e, 'Gug - gùg' aic - e, 'gug - gùg' aic - e. Tha

chu' - ag is 'gug - gùg' aic - e, 'Si pioc - adh sùil nan caor - ach.

1. Chunna mi, s gu'm b'fhiosrach mi,
   Na ròin a falbh le litrichean,
   Màileid is pailios orra,
   Is iad cho glic ri daoine.
       (Ch.)

2. Chunna mi na partanan
   A danns' air ùrlar charbadan
   A chorra-ghritheach is bat aice,
   'S i'cur a steach nan caorach.
       (Ch.)

3. Fhuair mi nead an tàrmachain
   Ann talamh-toll's an àrd-dhorus;

   An dreathan-donn's dà ràmh aige
   'Cur bàt' an aghaidh gaoithe.
       (Ch.)

4. Chunna mi na cudaigean
   A sniomh air an cuid chuigealan,
   An iolair(e) mhór is buideal aic
   A falbh an cuideachd dhaoine.
       (Ch.)

5. Chunna mi na donnagan
   Is cuailtean móra chonnaidh orr';
   An fhaochag bheag's an donnalaich
   A falbh le dronnaig fhraoich oirr'.
       (Ch.)

TRANSLATION

(*Chorus*: The cuckoo is calling cuckoo! cuckoo! while picking out the eyes of the sheep.)
1. I beheld, being well-informed, the seals going about delivering letters, dressed in a pelisse with a wallet, and looking as wise as men. 2. I have seen crabs on the floor of chariots, and the heron with a staff driving home the sheep. 3. I saw the ptarmigan in an earth-hole in the door-lintel, and the wren with a pair of oars pulling a boat against the wind. 4. And I saw young 'saithe' spinning off their distaffs, and the grand eagle carrying a cask in the company of men. 5. Cockles I have seen bearing heavy loads of fuel, and the little whelk howling under a burden of heather.

I cannot help thinking that the three children with their Gaelic background—even in an increasingly English environment—understood and enjoyed this song.

An incident that occurred at that time was related in 1954 by a Tolmie relative visiting Scotland from New Zealand. In the early 1870s the wife of Donald Allan Tolmie (Frances's eldest brother) was in Scotland, and one day she and Fanny and another were negotiating a narrow country gate. The other two ladies had some difficulty on account of their voluminous dresses, but Fanny, 'who disliked the crinoline and never would wear one', slipped through easily, 'looking like a tall daffodil with golden hair on top', and a woman passing was heard to exclaim, 'Siccan a tall lass!'[12]

A photograph of Miss Tolmie taken in Nairn about this time shows her large build and erect carriage [Plate 4]. She has blue eyes and a light complexion, masses of red-gold hair, and large hands and feet. She was dreamy and studious rather than practical. Soon she was to find in England and further afield scope for the dreamy side of her nature.

CHAPTER 7

CAMBRIDGE, 1873-4

In 1873 I went to England, and remained there for many years.
Journal, p. 146

The seven years that Fanny Tolmie spent at home, first at Portree and then at Nairn, were pleasant enough. Yet time was passing. Her taste for study, nourished during her stay in Edinburgh, found little food in a round of small domestic duties and visits to relations. Her learning and noting of lesser-known traditional songs, interesting and unusual hobby that it was, hardly occupied her fully.

She kept in touch with her friends in Edinburgh and was well aware of the movement there and elsewhere towards higher education for women.[1] While she was still at the Constables' she had undoubtedly heard of the 'Essay Society', a group of intellectual young women who met on a Saturday morning once a month for discussion and debate. This society, shortly afterwards to be renamed the 'Ladies' Edinburgh Debating Society', was to last for seventy years, the presiding genius throughout its existence being Miss (afterwards Dame) Sarah Elizabeth Siddons Mair, great-granddaughter of the famous tragedy actress, after whom she was named.[2]

The Saturday morning meetings were held round the mahogany dining-table in the Mairs' house in Abercromby Place. The members were young, Miss Mair herself only nineteen when the society took shape in 1865. In a very short time there stemmed from these meetings the Edinburgh Ladies' Educational Association, founded not to provide intermittent courses of lectures for ladies on all sorts of subjects, but to set up in Edinburgh an equivalent for ladies to the Faculty of Arts in the University.

The doors of the University were to remain closed to women until the 1880s, full membership and the granting of degrees to be withheld until the 1890s. While Fanny Tolmie was collecting songs from Mairearad and Herrot in Skye and Uist, however, women in Edinburgh were already attending lectures by university professors on the subjects of their professorships, such as English Literature, Mental Philosophy, Experimental Physics and Botany. Enrolments ran into the hundreds, and the classes continued until the day that the University class-rooms were opened to women. Except for the first year or two they were held in rooms in Shandwick Place.

David Masson, Professor of English Literature, was the first to give a series of lectures, for which two hundred and sixty-five women enrolled. Over the years he continued to be the champion of university education for women, and it is appropriate that today a residence, Masson Hall, bears his name.[3]

Out-of-town students in the early 1870s, however, had to live in lodgings, and classes were held only twice a week. This may have been part of the reason why Fanny Tolmie, in search of higher education, went not to Edinburgh but to Cambridge.

In Cambridge at this same time there were the beginnings of the women's colleges, Newnham and Girton. Both sprang from extra-mural lectures given by visiting Cambridge dons. Girton, under Miss Emily Davies, began with classes for a few students at Hitchin, Herts, thirty miles away. Newnham sprang from a more widespread movement in Liverpool and several north of England cities, initiated by Miss Anne Jemima Clough and Mrs Josephine Butler.

Miss Clough was invited to accommodate in Cambridge itself a few young women to study seriously under university professors and lecturers. Through Professor Henry Sidgwick—the women's champion in Cambridge, as Professor Masson was in Edinburgh—a town house was secured, and there in 1871 Miss Clough enrolled five students. The house was drab and inconvenient, however, with no garden and no facilities for games, so in 1872 this embryo college moved to Merton Hall, and the building of Newnham College was begun. Merton Hall was a rambling old house with a large garden and orchard, situated on the reputed site of the ancient School of Pythagoras. A ghost was said to haunt its corridors.

In those early days at Newnham (under which name Merton Hall is included) two types of student were to be found:[4]

There were the brilliant intellectual girls reading for the various Triposes, who more than held their own with the men in the final examinations; and there were the well-read and serious girls who only took Higher Locals, either because they could not stay longer, or because the shape and bent of their minds was different.

Of the second type Mrs Mary Agnes Hamilton in her book, *Newnham. An Informal Biography*, mentions three. There was one who later won fame as a poet.[5] Another, Alix von Cotta, with the aid of the Empress Frederick, founded and became principal of the Victoria Lyceum, one of the first colleges for women in Germany. The third was Frances Tolmie, at Newnham earlier than the other two, 'a West Highlander with a rare knowledge of Gaelic songs, of which she later published a unique collection'.[6]

In October 1873 there were about a dozen names on Miss Clough's register, among them, 'Frances Tolmie, from the Island of Skye'.[7] A fellow student, one of the original five, was Mary Paley, later to be Mrs Alfred Marshall, Hon. D. Litt. of the University of Bristol, of which her husband was first principal. Many years later, in January 1928, she contributed the following description to an obituary of Frances Tolmie:

> Frances Tolmie was only at Merton Hall for two terms, but she was not easily forgotten. I can recall clearly a tall rather gaunt figure (she must have been over six feet)[8] and a fine strong serious face. She was older than the rest of us and all we knew about her was that she was a Highlander from some remote island and that she was supposed to be gifted with second sight. On All Hallows E'en she held us entranced with weird Highland stories and offered to tell our fortunes. She mixed the white of eggs with water and watched the figures that were formed and according to these she described our characters and our futures. My walks with her were generally to the Old Windmill on Madingley Hill—even then bereft of some of its sails. She would stand gazing at it as if fascinated and would wake with a start when I suggested returning home. She inhabited a small room adjoining the School of Pythagoras which was called the Nun's Cell, and my most vivid recollection of her is when she sat reading there under the gas lamps with the light shining on her red hair let down and reaching the ground.[9]

The 'weird Highland stories' on Hallowe'en may well have included 'The Bleeding Bone', 'The Headless Body' or her favourite story of the *Gruagach*. Her natural gift as a story-teller had certainly been influenced by Oighrig Ross, Mairearad Bheag and the rest.

Another student, Annie Armitage, remained her friend for life. Miss Armitage's niece by marriage[10] wrote me on 24 August 1952:

> I remember Miss Tolmie very well, since I met her twice when I was staying for my school holidays with my uncle Marshall Bulley at Hindhead: his wife, Annie Armitage, had been at Newnham with Miss Tolmie and my mother (Caroline Bulley) in the '70s. Miss Tolmie was older than the rest of the students, my aunt always called her 'The Great One' & I remember her telling me how Miss Tolmie sat combing her wonderful red gold hair, which fell round her in a cloak, & singing Gaelic songs: a figure straight out of a ballad which much impressed them.

In the Newnham obituary Mrs Bulley is quoted as writing, 'She left her mark on those who had anything to do with her. She had the remoteness and greatness and simplicity of a dedicated spirit.'[11]

How did it come about that Frances Tolmie, just short of her thirty-third birthday when she enrolled, found her way to Cambridge at all? True, in those pioneer days of women's university education students were often of necessity much older than the girls of today. Sophie Jex-Blake, born in the same year as Frances Tolmie, was twenty-nine when she began to batter at the doors of the Edinburgh Medical School; and Louisa Lumsden, also an exact contemporary, had left school ten years before she went south from Aberdeen to Edinburgh, to live in lodgings and attend the Shandwick Place classes, eventually —via Girton—becoming the first Head Mistress of St Leonard's School for Girls, St Andrews.

Nor was Frances Tolmie at all well-off. Her mother's means were moderate; it must have been hardly possible for a widow with two unmarried daughters to support one of them at university. An answer seems to lie in a legacy from Matilda Wrench, who had died in 1866: 'To Frances Tolmie, Portree in the Isle of Skye, Spinster, free from legacy duty all my books in Scotland and my writing table and further to the said Frances Tolmie the sum of one hundred pounds sterling.'[12] It may be only surmise but it is tempting to think that Fanny Tolmie set this sum aside for some future educational purpose that might occur; the beginnings of the women's college at Cambridge in 1871 and what she must have heard of it may well have led to her going there two years later. Residence at Merton Hall at that time cost £20 a term (£15 for girls preparing to teach). Lectures, given only twice weekly, cost a guinea a term (10s. 6d. for prospective teachers).[13]

Although she remained for only two terms and took no examinations, Fanny was by disposition serious, intellectual and industrious. After all, her gifts had impressed both Miss Wrench and the Constables. Lessons with her brothers' tutor at Rudha an Dùnain, with her governess in Argyll, at the English classes and with the Weisses in Edinburgh, as well as the wide range of reading available to her at the Constables'—cultural and pleasant though it all was—had perhaps not been calculated to prepare her for the swifter pace of reading for examinations. One can, however, benefit from higher education without taking examinations, and Frances Tolmie was undoubtedly the type to do so.

Gun sireadh, gun iarraidh, 'without seeking, without asking', (a Gaelic phrase she was fond of) came the next stage in her story. It began with her acceptance of an invitation to spend a fortnight at Coniston in the Lake District with a friend of some years' standing, Miss Harriette Rigbye. They had met in Edinburgh 'either through Miss "Rennie" or the Cowans of Beeslack'.[14]

Fanny's mother provided her with two new dresses, one of them brown, with lots of velvet bows. Was this visit perhaps an experiment, with a longer stay in view?

A longer stay it proved to be.

CHAPTER 8

CONISTON, 1874-95

...a dream, a wonderland of beauty & kindness ...
Frances Tolmie to Lucy Broadwood[1]

In her 'notes and reminiscences' in the *Journal*[2] Frances Tolmie dismissed in a single sentence the period of more than twenty years that she spent in England. The biographical details she supplied to Lucy Broadwood were naturally only such as had bearing upon the songs. Once or twice, however, she refers in letters to her long absence from Scotland and things Highland, 'all the years of my stay in England . . . a deep slumber fell on my spirit. I lived in a dream, a wonderland of beauty & kindness, for twenty years.'

That wonderland was the Lake District. The dream is reflected today in a row of headstones in Coniston churchyard. There John Ruskin lies among his friends, his own grave marked by a cross nine feet high, carved in the hard greenstone or volcanic ash of the fells. Beside him lie his cousin Joan Agnew ('Joanie')[3] and her artist husband, Arthur Severn, who was the youngest son of Joseph, the friend of Keats in Rome. Beyond them are W. G. Collingwood—Ruskin's friend, secretary and first biographer—and his wife. Collingwood, author of a monograph on Northumbrian crosses, designed the towering cross with its allusion to Ruskin's life and works.

On the opposite side of Ruskin are four small crosses. Nearest to him is Susanna Beever, the favourite friend and correspondent of his later years. Then come Margaret and Mary Beever and finally— Harriette Susan Rigbye.

Rigby is the name of many families in Lancashire and Westmorland, although it is unusual to find it spelt with an 'e'. Harriette's father appears in military and municipal records as Major Edmund Winstanley Rigby of the Lancashire Militia, a Free Burgess of the county borough of Lancaster. He was her mother's second husband, her first having been the Rev. Alan Chambré of Kendal, who was killed in a carriage accident in 1800, the year after their marriage. Was it Harriette's mother—Mary Russell—who, having for a short time borne a name of Norman-French origin, gave to Rigby's third daughter (her own fourth) a French form of first name, and tacked on to the surname a romantic and decorative 'e'? If so, the middle name must surely have been overlooked, for it remained plainly English.

Mary Alan, the one child of the Chambré marriage, inherited from her grandfather, John Russell, the property of Low Bank Ground in Monk Coniston. This property, on the east side of Coniston Water, passed eventually to Harriette Rigbye. Nearby is Brantwood, where Ruskin took up residence in 1873.

Miss Rigbye was over sixty when Frances Tolmie went to visit her [Plate 5]. A cultured woman of private means, she found her chief interest in landscape painting, mostly in water-colour. Some of her pictures are still to be found in the house in Dunvegan, belonging to the present generation of Miss Tolmie's relatives. She lived, however, not at Low Bank Ground but on the opposite side of the lake at Thwaite Cottage, and that during the summer months only. Every winter she left for Italy or the south of France, sometimes visiting Switzerland, where one of her sisters was married in Lausanne.

For twenty years she was accompanied in this migratory life by Miss Tolmie.

Thwaite Cottage [Plate 6] is a comfortable-looking, longish, two-storey building, adjoining a farmhouse, and was occupied at that time by the family of Edward Redhead, plumber and house decorator. The ladies returned there summer after summer. The national census return of 1891 names Miss Rigbye as head of the household.

The small garden of Thwaite Cottage adjoined the extensive grounds of The Thwaite, a large, square-built, family house. Forty years previously it had been acquired by a Manchester merchant, William Beever, retired and a widower. A son, John, (1795–1854), a keen sportsman, was the author of *Practical Fly-Fishing*, first published in 1849, a book valued in its day, considered worthy of a new edition in 1893 (London), with a memoir by W. G. Collingwood, and still cherished by certain anglers today. There were four daughters, two of whom came to be recognized as authorities on the botany of the Lake District. References to them are to be found in William Baxter's *British Flowering Plants* (vols 1–6, Oxford, 1834–43) and J. G. Baker's *A Flora of the English Lake District* (London, 1885).

They had various ties with Scotland. It was not only that the brother had been acquainted with certain salmon streams, but the sisters, as well as visiting Edinburgh and elsewhere for pleasure, were active and generous in Scottish social betterment schemes of the day. For many years their names figured in the subscription lists of the Ladies' Highland Association. Their naturalist tastes seem to have been profitable, for more than one entry reads, 'Miss Beever, for a collection of algae, one guinea'. Susanna, the youngest, wrote two small pamphlets appealing for funds for Dr Guthrie's 'Ragged Schools' in Edinburgh. The titles are typical of the period, the first, *A Pocket Plea for Ragged and Industrial Schools; or, A Word for the Outcasts* (Edinburgh, 1852), and the second, *Foodless, Friendless in our Streets, being a Letter about Ragged Schools addressed to Boys and Girls* (Edinburgh, 1853).

None of them married. By the time Frances Tolmie went to Coniston only the two younger sisters, Mary and Susanna, were left. It was in order to be near them that their old friend, Harriette Rigbye, had come to Thwaite Cottage.

One day in September 1873 John Ruskin, newly settled at Brantwood, called on the Victor Marshalls of Monk Coniston Hall and on Miss Rigbye at Thwaite Cottage. A fortnight later he called at The Thwaite. 'Yesterday called on the Miss Bevers (sic)', runs his diary, 'and delighted with them.'[4] Between him and Susanna a friendship quickly sprang up, a friendship which was to express itself over many years by a continuous exchange of playful little notes and gifts, and by his frequently rowing across the lake to visit The Thwaite. Already he was addressing her as 'Dear Susie' and signing himself her 'loving J.R.' From this large body of letters a selection came to be published in the late 1880s, entitled *Hortus Inclusus*.[5]

At this time, in 1874, Ruskin was fifty-five years of age, Susanna sixty-eight, while Frances Tolmie was not yet thirty-four. At Newnham Fanny had been older than her fellow-students; here she found herself in the company of people similarly cultured but older than herself. One is tempted to feel that this curious pattern, observable at other stages in her life, of being more frequently among younger or older people than among contemporaries may not have been entirely fortuitous.

There are in the letters two small references to Miss Rigbye. Slight as they are, they indicate her as one of Ruskin's immediate circle. From Paris on 4 September 1880 he writes[6]

> and today at the Louvre we saw the Cassette of St Louis, the Coffre of Anne of Austria, the porphyry case, made into an eagle, of an old Abbé Ségur, or some such name. All these you can also see, you know, in those lovely photographs of Miss Rigbye's. . . .

A note from Brantwood on 16 February 1881 concludes, 'Love to Mary, to Miss Rigbye, and my own St Ursula, and mind you give the messages *to all three, heartily*'.[7]

Did Susanna show her friend Harriette the drawing Ruskin made of a pair of peacock's feathers she sent him, the first little gift to pass between them? If so, Fanny Tolmie probably saw the drawing also, and heard that he had spent a whole day over it. And what of his letter in which he declined the offer of one of the penwipers Susanna had made of peacock's feathers, protesting that he always wiped his pen on his left coat-tail?

Strutting peacocks were a feature of the terraces of the Thwaite garden, a show-place in its day. A detailed description of what it was like may be found in a book on famous gardens of the period, *Tongues in Trees and Sermons in Stones* (London, 1891), by the Rev. William Tuckwell, where Susanna Beever is one of two to whom the book is dedicated. The garden then was laid out in four terraces on a steep hill, divided centrally by flights of steps, displaying old-fashioned flowers, anemone, narcissus, blue gentians, creeping phloxes, sweet-scented lavender and rosemary, as well as old rose-trees and all kinds of rock plants. The many fruit trees were maintained for Susanna's friends, the birds, rather than for the household. The earliest flowers were sent from 'The Garden' (The Thwaite) to 'The Wood' (Brantwood), and in the reverse direction came favourite stones and minerals for the younger of the 'Sister Ladies of the Thwaite'.

In all likelihood—in the earlier years at least—the Beevers and Miss Rigbye met almost daily. They were somewhat elderly company for Fanny Tolmie, but she was given to admiring and respecting older people and those whose gifts she considered superior to her own. It was natural that she should admire Miss Rigbye's painting ability, although the Beevers' botanical knowledge was not necessarily greater than her own. Nearer in age to her was Joan Severn. They were good friends and remained so for life, long after Ruskin, the Misses Beever and Miss Rigbye were gone.

Her position with Miss Rigbye may well have been the envy of many. Governessing was usually the only occupation open at that time to a young woman of good family but slender means—whether she had intellect and education or not. The life that Miss Rigbye offered her was an accidental piece of good fortune. Her duties appear to have been entirely social; in any case, she was quite undomesticated. The life with Miss Rigbye, always in rooms, whether at home or abroad, left her entirely free of domestic obligations—which suited her admirably. It has been said of 'Aunt Fanny' that it is doubtful whether in all her life she 'ever as much as dusted the drawing-room'. During those years with Miss Rigbye there was no permanent household life that would have involved a drawing-room or its dusting. All that was asked was that she should be 'in attendance' rather after the manner of a lady-in-waiting in more exalted circles.

She thus became Miss Rigbye's lifetime companion. It was a simple friendly arrangement and remained so because she received no salary. All expenses were paid and she had the opportunity of foreign travel that would scarcely otherwise have come her way. At Coniston she shared Miss Rigbye's friendships with Ruskin, the Severns, the Beevers, the Collingwoods and others. From her mother in Nairn, and later in Oban, she received replenishment of her purse and her wardrobe from time to time.

It would be interesting today if during this period she had kept and preserved a dairy; but no such record survives. In after years she spoke often of Ruskin and valued the privilege of having known him personally. Her contemporaries, however, who might have remembered what she had to say of him, are gone.

As drowsy summer was followed each year by shorter, sharper days the two ladies left for the south. The years slipped by in a rhythm alternating between the English Lakes and the Mediterranean.

Failing a diary, there is a commonplace book of Frances Tolmie's with dates from 1886 to 1890, but it gives only the barest hint of her travels: 'Castellamare, Dec. 1886' and 'Capri, Jan. 1887', beside the little German lyric, *Aus der Jugendzeit* by F. Rückert. Those are all.[8]

If places visited are not named there is more than a hint, however, as to her reading. The titles are distinctly heavier than one would expect to find on the library list of the usual Victorian 'companion'. Frances Tolmie was attracted to the spiritual realm, showing a marked predilection for books of poetry, magic, metaphysics, comparative religion and especially mysticism. Two quotations that she singles out may show the discrimination of her mind. The first is from Dr Faber: 'I am satisfied that fitting the mind for the reception of truth rather than filling it with knowledge is the proper object of education.' The second is a Chinese saying, quoted by the Japanese patriot Yoshida Torajira (A.D. 186):

> 'Better the crystal that breaks
> Than the tile that is safe on the housetop.'

A 'List of books read since May, 89—to Feb., 90' includes, among over twenty titles, Arnold's *Essays in Criticism*, Roden Noel's *Essays on Literature*, Newman's *Apologia pro Vita Sua*, Henry Drummond's *Natural Law in the Spiritual World* and *Tropical Africa*, as well as biographies of Boehme, Swedenborg, Fichte and Hume. For lighter reading there were Barrie's *Window in Thrums*, *Horace in Homespun* by 'Hugh Halliburton', and novels by Mrs Oliphant. Further titles up to April 1890 are rounded off with the note, 'Last of Mudie'.[9] *Buddhism in Christianity* by A. Lillie, and a popular *Life of Buddha* rub shoulders with a gift of Thoreau's *Walden* from her Newnham friend, Annie Armitage, and the first of the eventual five volumes (1889-95) of Lord Archibald Campbell's *Waifs and Strays of Celtic Tradition*.

Back in the Lakes a glimpse of Miss Rigbye and Miss Tolmie in the late 1870s and early 1880s comes from Mr Fred R. Forsyth, Carlisle, who was born in Coniston in 1874. His father, one of the gardeners at Monk Coniston Hall, kept poultry, and it fell to the small son to deliver chickens and eggs to Mrs Redhead at Thwaite Cottage while the ladies were there. Chickens, he comments, were then 1s. 6d. to 2s. each, and eggs sixteen, eighteen or twenty for 1s.

Mr Forsyth's recollections are naturally those of a very small boy— of the peppermint given to him by Miss Tolmie, so hot that he hastily escaped in order to spit it out; of the tangerine orange she gave him, and he, not having seen one so small before, politely asked her if she had grown it herself. He was observant enough for a youngster, however, to remember that Miss Tolmie was very tall, Miss Rigbye short and stockily built, that both ladies wore some sort of suspender to keep their long skirts from trailing on the ground, that one wore a 'chatelaine' and the other used a lorgnette, and that he remembered Miss Tolmie in a brown dress with a black lace scarf over her shoulders. He went away to school when he was eight and seldom saw them after that.

The two ladies are to be met again in the diaries of George Holt,[10] the Liverpool shipowner who, in 1886, leased Tent Lodge from Victor Marshall. Tent Lodge, like Brantwood and Low Bank Ground, is on the east side of Coniston Water. Mr Holt had the pleasant habit of noting in his diary his daily walks and the people he met, and there are several references to Miss Rigbye and Miss Tolmie, though his spelling of the name varies.

On a June day in 1887 he goes for a walk 'through Miss Rigbye's wood to the hill above Brantwood'. In November 1888 we find the ladies at tea at Tent Lodge, presumably to take leave before going abroad for the winter.

In May 1889 they are back again, and Mr Holt 'called on Miss Rigbye and Miss Tolme, and then on Miss Beever in her garden'. Susanna was now the only one of her family left. In summer she moved about the garden in a wheel-chair, but in winter had to remain indoors, viewing her garden and its birds from the windows.

An entry in May 1890 reads, 'walked along footpath to gaze upon Miss Rigby's notice boards which she has lately and as generally thought improperly caused to be set up'. Miss Rigbye, it seems, was tampering with an ancient right-of-way. On an afternoon in August 'Miss Rigbye and Miss Tolme came to tea. Interesting conversation with the former about false ear drums, she being very deaf and finding advantage therefrom. Miss Tolme, native of Skye, also interesting about her native land.'

In 1882 a favourite niece of Miss Tolmie's became governess to the Severn children in London. This was Menie MacLellan [Plate 7], who had been one of the three little cousins at Nairn.[11] When her family left Skye for Dollar she had continued her education at the Academy there, after which, wanting to specialize in music, she became a pupil-governess at a boarding-school in Leicester. She, however, joined the Severn family at Herne Hill when she was nineteen. Her cousin, Margaret Skene, described her as tall and slim, with dark hair and brown eyes, very calm in manner and very pretty. A portrait of her, by

Arthur Severn, dated 1881, shows a lovely young girl. Mrs Severn took her to theatres and concerts, and the children gave her the pet name 'Clennie'.

Ruskin found her attractive and restful. There are many references to 'Clennie' in his diaries between 1884 and 1886 [Plate 8], her name frequently associated with 'Joanie' (Mrs Severn) and 'Diddie'. The last-named was Sara Anderson, one of his secretaries, afterwards secretary to Burne-Jones and to Kipling. Of the afternoon of 4 October 1886 Ruskin writes:[12]

Find Arthur playing lawn tennis with Agnes [Greig] and Clennie. I pause to contemplate the game with the eye of a philosopher, upon which Arthur warns me off my own tennis ground on the plea that the girls will be shy. I advise the girls to conquer that remarkable weakness of the girls of the period, and proceed to enquire why all the balls are catching in what I suppose to be a salmon-trout net. . . .

More teasing follows, countered by good-humoured retort from the girls, and Ruskin concludes 'I leave them to "serve" each other in their own way and go home to my own tea'.[13]

A reflection of this incident turns up in his diary eleven days later:

Made Rhyme, dressing:
In the Isle of Skye
The girls are shy
And out of tune
At the Crook of Lune,
And—they can't tell why—
But balls go awry,
And they can't play tennis—
Not Aggies, nor Clennies—
With the Stones of Venice
A-standin' by.[14]

Menie remained as governess with the Severns for many years, until the last of the sons went to school. Ruskin's difficult spells grew more frequent and time and again his manservant, Baxter, would appear at the schoolroom door. 'I wish you'd come and talk to the master for a little,' he would say. Sitting beside the old man, Menie's presence and quiet manner acted as balm. Gradually the bad mood passed. He would then send Baxter for his cabinet of precious stones and minerals and, after handling one and another, would select the most beautiful of them all, a large sapphire, and ask her to accept it. Menie told in after years of how it was usually back in the cabinet within the hour. Sometimes, however, she carried it about in her pocket for a few days, for the delight of handling it and looking at its loveliness—before returning it to the cabinet, ready for its next ceremonial presentation.[15]

The years were running on, the dream almost over. From the Holt diary come a few more glimpses. In July 1891: 'Called at the Thwaite —did not see Miss Beever—afterwards on Miss Rigbye and Miss Tolmie.' In April of the following year: 'Walked to village . . . met Miss Rigbye and Miss Tolmie.' In 1893, towards the end of April, Mr Holt walks to the village, meets Mr Evennett (Mr Victor Marshall's agent), 'with whom a friendly chat touching local affairs and persons, of no great importance'. The two men continue round the head of the lake to call on Miss Rigbye, 'Just returned from her usual visit to the south of France—quite a wonderful bright little old lady, not yet quite 90 but getting on.' She was actually nowhere near ninety—a mere eighty-one.

That year Harriette Rigbye's dear friend Susanna Beever died, reading at the last a note from Ruskin, a few lines that had cost him three painful hours to trace, and one of the last letters he was to write with his own hand. With the approach of winter Miss Rigbye and Miss Tolmie left again for the Riviera. They were back again in 1894, Mr Holt recording a call upon them in June. The summer passed and they made preparations to winter abroad as usual, but at the end of September, after only a day's illness, Miss Rigbye died. Her two friends gone, Miss Tolmie no longer had the same ties with Coniston.

There are still a couple of references in Mr Holt's diary. On an October afternoon he rows across the lake to leave partridges with Miss Tolmie, but finds she is in bed with a bad cold. The illness must have been a little more serious than a cold, for a week later he meets Mrs Severn coming from the train with Miss Mary Tolmie, who had left Oban at five that morning to visit her sick sister.

With the exception of a couple of legacies—to her widowed brother-in-law and to the daughter of a friend, both in Lausanne—Miss Rigbye named Frances Tolmie her heir and executrix. The estate amounted to some £4000, a sum that, coupled with Miss Tolmies' own means, was sufficiently unencumbered in those days to provide her with a tidy income for the rest of her life.

In 1895 Fanny joined her sister Mary in Oban, where their mother had died six years before.

CHAPTER 9

OBAN,
1895-1900

I . . . began . . . to note down tunes when friends wanted any.

'Reminiscences'

The Misses Tolmie were contrasted both in appearance and temperament. Mary, the elder, of medium height, was bustling and practical, with a gift for nursing; in earlier days it had been a family tradition in times of emergency to 'send for Aunt Mary'. Once, indeed, she had spent a year in New Zealand, helping the wife of one of her brothers to cope with life on a distant sheep farm. Fanny was of the build of the 'Big Tolmies', slower in her movements, studious and not at all domesticated. Both had the Tolmie colouring, with reddish-gold hair, although now, in their fifties, they were going grey.

After Fanny's return they moved to no. 2 Dalriach Terrace, Oban. A key figure in the household was the maid, a little younger than her mistresses, Mary Ross from Trotternish, Skye [Plate 9], who had been with Mrs Skene in Portree for ten years before joining the household of Mrs Tolmie and Mary in 1882. Tall and alert-featured, she was highly capable, quick with her tongue and an excellent cook. Her English was sketchy, but in Gaelic with Miss Mary and Miss Fanny her conversation was witty and intelligent; with the younger generation and other visitors her exchanges were perforce in English.

One day, at the kitchen table preparing a fowl for the pot, she was chatting with Margaret Skene—a nurse probationer on leave from Edinburgh Royal Infirmary. 'You'll know the names of all the bones in the body, Miss Margaret,' she suggested. The young probationer replied that she did— whereupon Mary proceeded to dismember the fowl, naming each bone in Gaelic as she did so.

With English in the parlour and Gaelic in the kitchen, this household of three had something of the atmosphere of former days of farmhouse and manse in Skye. For Fanny it was a congenial background for a re-awakening after 'the deep slumber in England'. There had from time to time, however, been stirrings in the slumbering Gaelic side of her, as at Hallowe'en at Newnham and at later tea-times in the Lakes. Her songs had lain dormant, but some time in the 1890s she noted what must have been her first tune since the early 1870s. This tune is in *The Gesto Collection*, p. 52, but bears no date. There is no date on the MS either, but a clue is given by a note that it was sung to her at Sierre in the Rhône valley of Switzerland by Mrs Boog Watson (Mrs Thomas Constable's half-sister, Janet Cowan) who remembered it from the singing of boatmen at Ballachulish in her youth. The tune and chorus syllables are complete, but only one verse line was remembered, 'I see the boat pass the headland' (Example 20).

Example 20   *Gesto*, p. 52

O Rionnn o, hó-ró 'm bàta!
(Rowing song)

Fanny's first concern was to acquire books dealing with Gaelic language and lore:[1]

It is only in these later times that one has been buying Gaelic books that were very expensive in my youth. When I returned from England, in 1895, I began to gather about me all that had been published in my absence—since 1872. . . . I was in London, & bought up Campbell of Islay's West Highland Tales, with the signature of Palgrave heightening the price on the Fly-leaf. I having a profound reverence for good English—took the books—4.vols. for the double associations—& on the same day, I bore off Lord A. Campbell's Waifs and Strays. Years before—I had for Auld Lang Syne—purchased Mackenzie's Beauties, which I never liked —calling it a 'man's book', merely, and not congenial to me as the simple strains of my old waulking women always were.

Much had happened in the world of Gaelic since the 1860s and 1870s. The Crofters' Commission of the 1880s, concerned primarily with bringing improvement and security to agriculture and land tenure, had not been unmindful of social and educational questions, including the status of Gaelic. An important landmark in the field of learning was the establishment in the University of Edinburgh in 1882 of the first Chair of Celtic in Scotland, the moving spirit in the raising of funds for its endowment having been that vivid personality, John Stuart Blackie, Professor of Greek.

He it was who, at Kinlochleven many years before, had asked the boy holding his horse what was the Gaelic name for the animal.

'*Each*,' was the reply.

'*Equus!*' was the professor's surprised reaction; and that little spark it was that set fire to his enthusiasm for the language. His subsequent study of Gaelic, with 'its beauty, its poetic capabilities, its kinship to Sanscrit, Greek and Latin, convinced him of the recklessness of letting the language perish'.[2]

A lead was given to Gaelic scholarship by the formation in 1871 of the Gaelic Society of Inverness, which attracted a large membership in Scotland, England and overseas. The standard of scholarship in those early days, and the quality of the lectures given and recorded in its published *Transactions*, caused it to be described as almost a university of the north. The campaign for the establishment of the Edinburgh Celtic Chair was actually opened by Professor Blackie at one of the meetings. The Society continues to flourish, and its *Transactions* form a valuable library of learned papers on the language, literature, history and social customs of the Highlands.

The reverse of the medal, however, was the Scottish Education Act of 1872. Blackie, for one, regarded the schools to be set up to provide free and compulsory education for the native Gaelic speakers of Scotland as 'sapping the very foundations of their language';[3] yet today, over a century later, spoken Gaelic is by no means dead. Perhaps it achieved renewed viability on the lips of those who, as children, put up a tough—if bewildered—resistance to certain monoglot school-masters who punished them for speaking their mother tongue.

The Inverness Gaelic Society in the 1870s and the Edinburgh Chair of Celtic in the 1880s were expressions of the learned side of Gaelic. The next decade saw a popular development: in 1892 the newly-formed *An Comunn Gàidhealach*, 'The Gaelic Association', held a first *Mòd* at Oban, inspired by the pattern of the Welsh *Eisteddfod*.

There were numerous Highland societies at the time, but 'mainly concerned with social activities and athletic prowess'.[4] The Oban pioneers of *An Comunn* felt that more was wanted than the 'throwing of pine trees and heavy stones and hammers';[5] they were troubled that the folk culture of the Highlands 'lulled by the strains of a thousand pipers, for whom there was no lack of encouragement . . . [should] wilt and die'.[6] The annual National Mòd today, held at different centres from year to year, is a week-long festival of Gaelic music, speech, bardic composition, art and sociability, attracting large numbers of competitors and crowded audiences; but the solid work of *An Comunn* for the preservation of the language—today as in the 1890s—lies in its educational programme, of which literary and musical publication and the work of the branches form an important part.

Miss Fanny, following her bent, bought books and read assiduously. She next discovered, under her very roof, one of similar tastes.[7]

> It was in 1896 that I attempted to read up Alexander Macdonald's works, and those of Duncan Ban with Mary Ross, & it was wonderful how familiar she was with passages that she could only have known when as a 'little bairn' she rambled about her native hamlet, & entered, wherever she had a right to be. . . .

Alexander MacDonald's poems of the sea or of the 'Forty-five' were made to be sung, as were Duncan Bàn's, describing the beauties of the countryside and the thrill of stalking the deer. Mistress and maid sang rather than read them together, and in so doing it came to light that

Mary Ross remembered a number of songs from her youth, some of which Miss Fanny had never heard. As they came from different 'countries' (or parishes) this surprised neither of them; what was surprising was that Mary, never considered a singer, knew so many songs. As she recalled them, Miss Fanny began to note them down. The earliest one noted in the *Journal*[8] as sung by Mary Ross, is the slow waulking song, *Caoidh Màthar*, 'A Mother's Mourning', which Mrs Kennedy-Fraser later used as the basis for her song, *Caristiona* [Plates 12 and 13]: 'I had not touched a piano for more than twenty years on returning to Scotland from England, but began to recall favourite airs then, & to note down tunes when friends wanted any.'[9]

It has been said of Frances Tolmie that she set no great store by her collection and willingly gave away to friends and others any tunes they asked for.[10] She had what appeared to onlookers in her later days an unjustified under-valuation of her own abilities. She loved and treasured her songs in the spirit of the collector of fine porcelain, each a thing of beauty and a pleasure to contemplate. Unlike many a connoisseur of *objets d'art*, however, she had no sense of commercial value, nor of any reputation she might gain through her knowledge of these songs. She had a vague idea that her songs might be interesting to a 'real musician', but so far had met no one who answered to this description.

She was shortly to welcome, however, what promised to provide a focus for her somewhat amorphous Gaelic studies, when—in a casual way—she came into touch with Dr Keith Norman MacDonald, whose *Gesto Collection of Highland Music* was published in Leipzig in 1895, about the time of her return from England. It was suggested that she might contribute songs to a proposed second edition.

'*The Gesto Collection of Highland Music* compiled and arranged by Keith Norman MacDonald and dedicated to the McLeods of Gesto 1895. Price one guinea.' So runs the title page. The compiler was resident physician at the Gesto Hospital, Edinbane, near Dunvegan, which bears its name as a memorial to the founder, Kenneth MacLeod of Gesto.[11]

Dr MacDonald was an enthusiastic exponent of Highland airs which, deaf though he was at this time, he played on the violin. He had a genuine regard for older tunes, and it was a happy thought to combine a collection of these with a compliment to the founder of the hospital and his kin.

Engraving and production were entrusted to a firm in Leipzig, Oscar Brandstetter, and a handsome outsize volume of 154 engraved music pages resulted, bound in vivid red or blue, gilt-edged and gilt-enscrolled. The title page, in colour, showed Gesto House against hills and a loch, and 'MacLeod's Tables' in the background. One can visualize it on the desk of the piano in many a Highland country house.

Of the 260 tunes and over that the volume contained more than half were military marches; the remainder, apart from a sprinkling of dance tunes, were Gaelic songs, with or without words. Part of this edition was left unbound, to be bound up with an appendix or appendices as further material came to hand.

In the course of the next few years two further editions appeared, the first with an appendix of thirty-three pages and the second with an extra thirty-four, bringing the number up to sixty-seven. Dates of publication are not given, but these can be assumed from two known copies presented and autographed by the compiler. In the Glen Collection in the National Library of Scotland there is a copy containing the first appendix only, inscribed to John Glen and dated 1898; in the possession of a member of the Tolmie family there is a copy containing both appendices, inscribed 'To my dear friend and coadjutor Miss Fanny Tolmie June 30th. *1902*'.[12]

> I gave off from my own notes several songs to Dr M. and before I had made his acquaintance, about 1896. He sent me an off-hand message by a friend, and I, pleased to learn that so warm a lover of the music of his country existed, responded [eagerly?] 'for Auld Lang Syne!' 'They must have some sort of Bass' so that he being extremely deaf, might the more easily hear the melodies he loved.

It was not so much on account of the doctor's deafness that 'some sort of Bass' was required, but rather so that the tunes might be played in Highland drawing-rooms. Dancing and music were a tradition in Highland families; Johnson and Boswell both tell of how at Raasay House in 1763, every evening the carpet was rolled back and there was dancing until supper time. 'After supper,' writes Johnson, 'the ladies sung *Erse* songs, to which I listened as an *English* audience to an *Italian* opera, delighted with the sound of words which I did not understand.'[13]

By the 1890s there was perhaps less Gaelic conversation to be heard in Highland drawing-rooms, but the 'Erse' songs still held their own.

Many ladies liked to turn to them from the classics and salon pieces of their earlier music studies, although they had perforce to play them by ear. Some pianists—not necessarily the most brilliant by orthodox standards—played them well, with pleasing touch and a nice sense of rhythm and harmony. Not so many could write down accurately what they played, while there were others who made the attempt but were not very successful either as improvisers or transcribers.

Dr MacDonald felt, and rightly so, that such tunes should have a place in his collection: the intention, unfortunately, was not matched by the achievement. He asked for contributions among his friends and acquaintances and—without any revision—printed what they gave him. The result is that the song tunes in the collection are very mixed, some competently set down, others very inexpertly indeed.

The appendices, on the whole, are better, and here the hand of Fanny Tolmie is evident. Her noting of the melodies themselves was careful and accurate. Her songs were part of her own repertory; she could both sing them and write them down. Though she described them as 'fitted and badly enough, with piano accompaniments',[14] hers show a musicianship absent from many others in the volume. Her harmony equipment was of the slenderest, but she did not go beyond what she understood. Her basses are tentative and discreet, often a mere accompanying octave; she appreciated the use of ties, rests and prolonged notes in the bass, and thus avoided the crude harmonizations that so often bedevilled Scots song collections.

She gave Dr MacDonald some forty-five songs in all, of which approximately nineteen went into the first appendix, and nine into the second. He was grateful for her help, as his inscription to her shows. Her name occurs here and there, but usually in footnotes and not systematically attached to each of her songs. The whole collection, however, is more or less anonymous.

Some of Miss Fanny's songs—seventeen are identifiable—reached the doctor too late for the second appendix and were tossed into a booklet, *Puirt-a-Beul*. 'Mouth-Tunes', or 'Tunes for Dancing', printed in tonic sol-fa at the *Oban Times* in 1901. Now she was really dismayed. These were not *puirt a beul* at all—with the exception of a fragment, 'For a Child'. They comprised some of her most treasured waulking songs, rowing songs and lullabies, among them two out of her three versions of the *Bean Eudach*, the four versions of *Uamh 'n Òir*, the lovely *Iùraibh o-hì, iùraibh o-hù* and the *Gruagach mhara*. Though grateful to Dr MacDonald for his interest, she was critical of his method: 'he hurried the "Puirt a Beul" through the press, huddling all sorts of things together . . . and the Gesto Coll. was not much better'.[15]

Miss Tolmie remarks in the same letter that it was an 'off-hand message by a friend' that had introduced them. Elsewhere Frances Tolmie elaborates: 'It was Bardess Mary Macpherson who told Dr MacDonald that I could give him songs & tunes for his Gesto Coll!— and he put them in the Appendix.'[16] The friend, then, was Mrs Mac-Pherson [Plate 10], who is held in high regard by lovers of Gaelic poetry and whose songs are frequently sung.[17] She it was who at Contin Manse more than twenty years before had given Miss Fanny the song and story of the 'Headless Body'.[18] In her expansive manner she probably felt that she was doing a good turn to both collector and compiler when she told them of each other. In the course of correspondence, however, Miss Fanny, having trustfully sent to the doctor several of her songs, began to realize that here was no skilled musician and competent editor, as she had innocently taken for granted, but an impulsive and vague—though kindly—enthusiast.

Haphazard as these volumes were, they had their merits. Fortunately for Miss Fanny, they were not to be the final repository for her collection.

CHAPTER 10

OBAN, EDINBURGH, 1900-7

These songs come with certain moods to remembrance.
Note on a song, Frances Tolmie MS

Among the many friends with whom Fanny Tolmie renewed contact on her return to Scotland were Dr Alexander Carmichael and his family. Many years had passed since, as a young Inland Revenue officer in Skye and the Outer Hebrides, he had encouraged her in the beginnings of her collecting. Now retired and living at Taynuilt, near Oban, he was putting in order his own collection of folklore. The first two volumes of his *Carmina Gadelica* appeared in Edinburgh in 1900.

On a visit to the Carmichaels one day that same year Fanny met a young minister—already a Celtic scholar of note—the Rev. Dr George Henderson of the parish of Eddrachillis in Sutherland. He was greatly interested not only to hear her sing old unpublished songs, but to learn of the existence of 'a rolled-up bundle of manuscript'[1] that she had cherished for many years: 'both friends expressed a wish that I would write down all the tunes that I remembered; this I promised to do, on condition that they would get the gaps in my verses filled up.'[2]

In Oban she began diligently to transcribe her pencilled notes of the 1860s and 1870s, adding to them memories from her earliest child-hood, such as her mother's songs and the songs of the waulking women at Rudha an Dùnain. The tunes—each underlaid with a single set of words—eventually filled two six-stave manuscript music books. Complete texts, as far as she had heard them sung, went into two exercise books. On the first page of one of these she wrote:

LINGERING MEMORIES

of some of the Waulking Songs of Skye
as remembered after many years of absence
Committed to the kind consideration of Dr George Henderson, in
the hope that he may find a place for them in the general collection
of ancient remains, and supply missing lines and verses.[3]

Tunes and texts were elegantly written and carefully indexed, the
waulking songs in the music notebooks being given a certain panache
by the use of red ink and neat brackets to show clearly the separate
parts of solo verse, solo refrain and chorus. The word books contain
much interesting information relating to the songs and their singers,
and even little sidelights upon the collector herself, as exemplified in
the following note beside the waulking song, *Chaidh na fir a Sgathabhaig*,
'The men have gone to Scavaig'.[4]

> When spending some hours at Rudh 'n Dunain in May 1900 I
> found some of the old folk still living but so full of the 'present
> world' that they had forgotten the old songs. I had not time to tune
> them up—to *gleus* them. These songs come with certain moods to
> remembrance.

Fanny had greater success, however, under her own roof. More and
more she consulted Mary Ross as to this song or that, whether she
knew it and, if so, what was her version of it. Mary belonged to the
'MacDonald country' of Trotternish where traditions were sufficiently
different from her own 'MacLeod countries' of Duirinish and
Mininish.

Mary was born at Kilmaluag in the parish of Trotternish, the north-
eastern peninsula of Skye; she was the eldest child of Ranald Ross, a
crofter of intelligence and industry.[5] He was known in Gaelic as
Raghnall Buidhe, 'Ranald the yellow-haired', and she herself as *Màiri
Raghnaill*, 'Ranald's Mary'. Her mother died when she was only seven
and her father married again. The second wife, a weaveress, spent much
of her time at her loom, and upon Mary fell the care of the younger
children. It was natural to sing to them the well-known lullabies and
puirt a beul. In addition, playing with the children on the *machair*, the
level green areas by the sea, she learned many songs and rhymes from
an old man they met herding cows there.

Her step-mother wove cloth for various purposes—blankets and bed

85

covers, drugget for women's skirts, and what is today called 'tweed' but was then known as 'kelt'. She received the wool already washed, dyed, carded, spun and wound onto spools, and was concerned only with the actual weaving and the subsequent shrinking required. Waulkings, therefore, were frequent, and were great occasions for singing and merriment. The crusade of the dogmatists and bigots against colour, culture and gaiety had not yet succeeded in banishing the old songs.

Mary recalled the first occasion on which she actually took her place at the waulking board, although as a child she had often looked on and listened. She and another girl were placed each side of the elderly woman who was to preside and lead the singing, but not to touch the cloth. This woman had great gifts of imagination and ready wit, and her improvised verses caused gales of laughter. There was, however, another side to her songs. With an amazing memory she sang verse after verse of lengthy panegyrics and elegies, her solo verse lines and refrains answered antiphonally by the chorus of women around her. Young men who had slipped in to watch and listen, blushing perhaps when the singer coupled their names with certain of the girls, were joined by older men who listened admiringly to the poems the gifted leader sang. 'It was believed that her mother, a native of Lewis, and full of lore, had imparted it all to her, together with her skill in certain magical practices for which the people of Lewis were renowned.'[6]

Mary had also listened to her grandfather—an old soldier of the Peninsular War—with her father and their cronies as they punctuated their talk of old battles with the songs that commemorated them. Thus it was that she heard the songs of Alexander MacDonald of Ardnamurchan—*Mac Mhaighstir Alasdair*—especially his songs of the 'Forty-five', which not only praised the Prince, often under the name of 'Mòrag', but eulogized the chiefs and heroes who supported him. Equally popular were the songs of Duncan Bàn Macintyre, descriptive of mountain, moor and stream, and the beauty—as well as the chase—of the deer.

Mary heard songs of still another type, murmured quietly by her father to himself as he sat with busy hands on winter evenings [Plate 11]. Light fell on his work from the peat fire in the centre of the floor, supplemented by a crusie, a small vessel filled with home-made fish oil into which a rush wick was inserted. He might be twisting heather into a rope—and ropes had many uses unknown to the outside world.

86

They were needed in spring to tie down the new thatch on the roof—weighted with stones known as 'anchors'; while the cow put out to graze required its tether, not so much to keep it from straying as to economize on the grass. Mats for various uses were plaited out of grasses, and harness or nets had to be mended. While their father's hands were occupied with one thing or another the children heard him sing half to himself long narrative songs, full of stirring deeds and strange-sounding names.[7]

> [Mary] remembered that she never heard her revered father sing, but when he crooned ancient words to himself, while making heather ropes, and matting which would be his ordinary occupation during the winter evenings—they were songs of grave character such as the death of Oscar, or the Lament for Fraoch.

Before meeting Dr Henderson Miss Fanny had already noted songs from Mary Ross. Two more may be given here. *Eile na hùraibh O-ho* (Example 21), noted in 1898, was a rowing song, though its words are posed as sung by a woman, the sweetheart of one of the rowers. The song was also used for waulking, as is frequently the case with these songs. Blessings are called down upon the builder of the new ship that is putting out to sea this cold wet night. He has made her strong, swift and secure, with not a wet or a damp board in her. She will surely not go off her course: already she has swept close to many a black rock. The singer's beloved, skilful of hand, is on the windward side, fastening and loosening the ropes, and taking his turn at the helm.

Example 21   *Journal, 76*

Eile na hùraibh o-ho

Sung by Mary Ross,
from Killmaluag, Skye, 1898

Eil - e na hùr-aibh o - ho!   ·Eil - e na hùr-aibh o - ho! 1.'S fliuch an oidh-che, o -

hù, a - hó. Eil - e na hùr-aibh o - ho.'Nochd's gur fuar-i! o - hùr-aibh o - ho.

Solo: 2. Thug an iùbhrach, o-hù, a-hó
       Chorus: Eile na hùraibh, o-ho
  Solo: Ùr an cuan oirr', o-hùraibh, o-ho. (Ch.)
    3. Dùrachd slàn dh'an
       T-saor a dh'fhuaigh i.
    4. Dh'fhàg è dionach
       Làidir, luath i.
    5. Acfhuinneach gu
       Siubhal chuanta.
    6. Cha'n eil bòrd fliuch innt',
       No bòrd fuaraidh.
    7. 'S ioma sgeir dhubh
       Ris'na shuath i;

    8. Agus faochag
       Chròm a ghluais i.
    9. Cha'n 'eil cùram
       Orm m'a fuadach;
  10. Tha mo rùn air
       Bòrd a fuaraidh.
  11. Làmb cheangail nam
       Ball's 'gam fuasgladh.
  12. Cha b'è fear cearraig
       Bheireadh bhuat e;
  13. No fear laimhe-
       -Deis' is fuachd air.

TRANSLATION

Solo Ref.: Eile na, etc. (Repeat in Ch.) 1. The night is rainy, (Ch.) and it is also cold. (Ch.) 2. The new ship has turned towards the ocean. 3. My blessing be with him who built her, 4. and left her secure, strong and swift, 5. well-equipped for traversing the seas. 6. There is not a wet nor damp board in her, 7. and she has swept close by many a black rock, 8. moving the lowly whelk. 9. I have no fear lest she be driven out of her course, 10. for my beloved is on her windward side, 11. whose hand fastens the ropes and loosens them. 12. Not a left-handed man is he to take the helm, 13. nor his the right hand of a man benumbed with cold.

'Wet is the night . . . cold it is tonight' run the verse lines, interspersed with chorus and solo refrain.

Ailein duinn, beul a' mhànrain, 'O Alan of the brown hair, mouth of tender tones', dated 1899, is entitled in the *Journal*, 48, *Hó rionn eile*, the opening of the refrain. In contrast to *Eile na hùraibh o-ho*, which expresses confidence and pride in a new ship and its crew, *Ailein duinn* is a grievous lament for a boat overturned, casting into the sea father, three brothers, a son and, bitterest of all, the woman singer's beloved Alan.

Songs from Mary Ross mounted up: eventually they numbered thirty-seven out of the 105 in the *Journal*. Some also went into *The Gesto Collection* and *Puirt-a-Beul*. None of the heroic lays are attributed to her, but this need not prove that she did not know them; with her memory for words she must have remembered fragments at least from the evening crooning of her father. It is quite probable, however, that these may have so closely resembled those that Miss Fanny already had, that they were dismissed as variants and not included in the printed collections.

Mary contributed waulking songs in many moods, also lullabies and other songs for children—all worthy of a study in themselves. Amusing are the waulking songs that opened with a few stock lines, affording scope for the leader to improvise teasing and nonsensical verses. One of these is *An Long Éireannach*, dated 1900 (Example 22). 'Ho!' runs

Example 22   *Journal*, 70

An Long Éireannach
(The Irish Ship)

Sung by Mary Ross,
from Killmaluag, Skye, 1900

Hó, cò bheir mi leam. Air an luing Éir-eann-aich? Hó, cò

bheir mi leam? 1. Gur h-è Domh-null bheir mi leam.'Sfhad a null a sheòl-as sinn.

    2. Ged thuiteadh è 's a' ghrunnd
       Bheir è plumb, 's'éiridh è.
                (Ch.)

TRANSLATION
(*Chorus*: Ho! whom shall I take with me on board the Irish ship? Ho! whom shall I take with me?) 1. It is Donald I will take, and we shall go far under sail. (Ch.) 2. Though he should tumble into the depths of the sea, he will plunge, and rise again.

the chorus, 'Whom shall I take with me on board the Irish ship?' 'It is Donald I will take, and we shall go far under sail.' The leader would continue, coupling the name of Donald—or Peter, Alastair or John, as might be—with that of one of the women, elderly or young, who was eventually supposed to rescue him from a pummelling in the folds of the cloth, or from the tub into which he had fallen—he is being treated as if he were the web of cloth—before bearing him off on the imaginary Irish ship.

Miss Fanny was a slow worker, but eventually she completed the four notebooks—made up of two exercise books with the words and two six-stave MS books containing the tunes—and dispatched them to Dr Henderson. After that a long time was to elapse before anything further came of them.

Meanwhile she enjoyed the renewal of old friendships and the making of new. Twenty years and more had brought the inevitable gaps among her relations and friends; the children she had left were now men and women. Her brother John had died in the 1880s. His eldest daughter, Margaret, was married to the Rev. (afterwards Dr) Archibald Mac-Donald of the parish church of Kiltarlity, near Beauly, Inverness-shire. A Celtic scholar of repute, his best-known work is *The Clan Donald* (Inverness, 1896–1904), a three-volume history of the Clan, of which he was joint author along with a fellow-clansman and minister, the Rev. Angus MacDonald of Killearnan, Ross-shire. Fanny was keenly interested in her nephew's work and particularly in the later *MacDonald Collection of Gaelic Poetry* (Inverness, 1911), in which the two ministers again collaborated and to which she contributed some traditional material.

Her friendship with the Constable and Cowan families endured. Mr and Mrs Thomas Constable and Sir John Cowan were gone, but Maimie Constable was nearby at Quinish in the Isle of Mull, the wife of James Noel Forsyth, Deputy Lieutenant for the county of Argyll. It was only a short sail from Oban to Mull and visits were often exchanged. The Forsyths had a family of seven, at that time in their teens and early twenties; they enjoyed Fanny Tolmie's conversation and amusing stories; she also played reels for them when they danced. Then she would sit tall and very straight at the piano, the candles throwing their light on her large white hands which were always beautifully groomed.

From time to time she visited her Newnham friend, Annie Armitage. Miss Armitage had married S. Marshall Bulley of the Liverpool Cotton Exchange; after his retiral they lived at Hindhead in Surrey. A niece of Mr Bulley's (Mrs Rachel Marshall, Cambridge) recalls Miss Tolmie as she was about 1900:[8]

My own memory of Miss Tolmie is much like the photograph in the Journal you sent me: a tall, full bodied, silver haired woman with a wonderful pink & white complexion & a direct blue eye. She had great dignity of carriage & brought her own atmosphere of calm serenity with her. To a child of 12 she was fascinating, full of tales of her childhood in Skye, told in her soft, leisured voice; she would sit back in her chair, fold her hands, & 'tell' us her songs in a light, soft, true voice. She was dressed, one might say caparisoned in voluminous flowing black robes, with wonderful capes & bonnets trimmed with feathers & jet which my aunt (who herself belonged to the William Morris period & was usually dressed in peacock blue or sage green with embroideries) used smilingly to tie under her chin for her when they went out driving.

I subsequently visited Mrs Marshall, when I was given an insight into Miss Tolmie's manner of singing. The latter declared about herself, 'You know, I don't sing: I just lilt.' She had also stated, when her attention was drawn to it, that she varied her tunes in the traditional manner from verse to verse.

Miss Tolmie on one of her visits to Edinburgh not long after—and through their mutual friends, the Carmichaels—met Kenneth MacLeod, later to become Mrs Kennedy-Fraser's Gaelic collaborator. Steeped in the folklore of his native island of Eigg, Kenneth MacLeod was at that time a young lay missionary of the Church of Scotland for the Highlands and Islands. As Miss Tolmie not only had family ties with Eigg but knew it well, they found much in common. Kenneth MacLeod got his sister, who still lived there, to learn songs from an old nurse, Janet MacLeod, in order to pass them on to Miss Fanny. 'Everyone called her "Miss Fanny",' he once said to me. She noted some seal songs from him and was fond of singing them, but these are still unpublished. He also noticed—as the Bulleys had done—that she varied her tunes.

The Rev. Dr Alfred Brown—latterly minister of Maxwell Church, Glasgow—was the young minister of St Columba's Church in Oban. I met him once or twice and we had tea together. In 1952 he kindly wrote to me:

> The Tolmies were dear friends of mine: when they were in Oban I saw them frequently. Miss Fanny was quite a unique and distinctive character, tremendously interested in everything Gaelic. When she was 'lost' she was always found in McDonald's book shop or the Post Office. Mary was the practical one and managed all household affairs. Mary Ross was indispensable: she was a strict 'Wee Free'.[9] . . . Miss Fanny lived a good deal 'in the clouds', a bit of a mystic and a dreamer. Mary used to tell me that if she asked her to bring home a *cake* or *fruit* or anything else, Fanny almost invariably brought back 'stamps'. She talked to me much of Ruskin: was a great reader and a lover of Gaelic songs—and could

sing these with great feeling, and play them too. . . . Miss Fanny was a loyal supporter of her Church: one of the finest women I have been privileged to know.

I cannot remember her taking a very active part in any of Oban affairs. She was constantly writing to people who like herself were interested in Highland folklore. She had a voluminous correspondence and so 'stamps' never seemed amiss![10]

Several years ago, also, an aged resident of Oban recalled the Misses Tolmie as 'gentle, retiring ladies' who took no part in the life of the community, so far as he could remember.[11] Miss Fanny did, however, take an active part in the Women's Guild. At the meetings, which were of a literary or musical nature, she sang or played and occasionally presided; once at least—with some trepidation, it is recorded—she gave a paper.

The minister, Dr Brown, observing that Miss Tolmie was a Gaelic enthusiast and had literary gifts in no small measure, suggested that she should write a Highland story for the parish magazine. This story, 'Oirig and Gormul: a fireside tale of the eighteenth century', appeared in six monthly parts, from January to June 1904:[12]

a sort of story I once wrote to please our Minister at Oban—when starting a Parish Magazine, and who wished it to be *Highland!* I then remembered a tale that I heard in Bracadale about a young woman who had been carried off by a passing vessel—and wove into it—my local lore—but no person or place being real—only the rhymes the young woman used to say aloud every night when she had perforce made her home in a far country beyond the Sea.

Gormul is an orphan of good family, adopted by her mother's foster-sister, Oirig. Their story is of life in a glen as seen through the eyes of a child, somewhat glamorized, though with some likeness to the author's own childhood in Minginish. A virtue of the story is the depiction of a way of life that persisted in essence in the Highlands up to Miss Tolmie's own day. The plot is direct but rather self-conscious in the telling. The happy ending is brought about, many years after the kidnapping of the girl, when a Bracadale sailor, shipwrecked on an island off the coast of South America, overhears a woman's voice chanting softly in Gaelic a jingle of place-names of his native glen. This of course is Gormul, the playmate of his childhood, now through a chain of circumstances the wife of the Spanish proprietor of the island.

In 1905 the Misses Tolmie, Mary and Fanny, accompanied by Mary Ross, removed from Oban to Edinburgh. They lived at first in a flat at no. 39 Merchiston Crescent, but the following year moved down to the 'main door' house at no. 37.

In the spring of 1906 the flat was the scene of a romantic family occasion, the marriage of John Mackenzie of Dunvegan, second son of John Tolmie Mackenzie (the Misses Tolmie's first cousin) to a niece of theirs, Margaret Tolmie from New Zealand—bride and bridegroom being second cousins of each other. John Tolmie Mackenzie was now an old man and his son John would succeed him in his various offices on his death in 1910.

The Carmichaels left Taynuilt and settled in Edinburgh about this time. Their daughter Ella was a gifted Celtic scholar and in a few years' time, along with Professor Mackinnon, was to launch and edit the *Celtic Review*. She became the second wife of William J. Watson, rector of Inverness Royal Academy, later—via the rectorship of the Royal High School, Edinburgh—to succeed Professor Mackinnon in the Celtic Chair. Neil MacLeod, son of the 'Skye Bard', and himself a bard, was a nearby friend; another friend was Archibald Menzies, the founder of the Reel and Strathspey Society in Edinburgh, who would drop in with his fiddle now and again, when there would be playing of old dance tunes and discussion of the words of *puirt a beul*.

A neighbour in a flat at no. 39, was David Davidson, a science master. His widow lived on there until not long ago, dying in 1958 a few weeks short of her hundredth birthday. She and her daughter recalled that Miss Fanny Tolmie often dropped in to visit them and had long chats with Mr Davidson, botany being one of their common interests. As the Davidson children grew old enough their father had provided them with tiny vascula and took them out on botanizing excursions. Miss Fanny was always interested to learn what they had brought home, and was characteristically pleased when on one occasion they brought back from Cauldstane Slap in the Pentlands a specimen of Grass of Parnassus, which she knew so well in Skye.

Throughout her life she was very fond of children. Today in many families, related or otherwise, a second and third generation have read well-worn illustrated books that were given by her to their elders, when they themselves were young. Children were perhaps a little in awe of her—her height and apparent great age had something to do with that—but they liked her. 'I am very old,' Mrs Davidson recalled her saying, 'but I never tell my age.' To young people at the turn of the century any woman in her sixties appeared timelessly old, none more so than Frances Tolmie, who habitually wore black, with mantle (or dolman) and bonnet rather than coat and hat. The darkness of her dress was relieved, however, by her fondness for lace and mauve bebe ribbons.

A pleasant social life centred upon no. 37 Merchiston Crescent. The Tolmie sisters had a large family connection and many friends, old and new. Frances Tolmie's nephew, John Tolmie at the Register House, eldest son of the minister brother,[13] and his wife and young daughter lived not far away. He and his cousins, Mary and Margaret Skene were closely associated with 'Aunt Fanny'; all three were musical.[14] Younger relatives, sent from the north to school in Edinburgh, were always welcome when they called, as were their elders who occasionally came to stay.

Fanny's friendship with the Constable and Cowan families endured, her closest ties probably being with Katie Constable, who had married William P. Bruce, paper manufacturer of Braeburn, Currie, and their daughters, Lucy and Mollie.

CHAPTER 11

EDINBURGH,
1908-11

THE FOLK-SONG SOCIETY

Let them, therefore, appear in their native simplicity and nakedness.
Patrick McDonald, quoted by Lucy Broadwood in the Introduction
to *Journal*.[1]

For a few years Fanny Tolmie, after sending Dr Henderson her MSS,
did not hear from him. He, however, was reminded of her and her
songs—if reminder was necessary—by an inquiry in the summer of
1907 from a young lady studying Gaelic with him in Sutherland.
Winifred Parker was of Highland descent, proud of her four Gaelic-
speaking great-grandmothers, 'a Rainy, a Rose and two Robertsons';
but she herself, educated in London, Paris and Dresden, had to acquire
her Gaelic. Still in her twenties, she was an enthusiastic worker on the
literary and educational side of *An Comunn Gàidhealach* and also a
member of the Folk-Song Society in London.

Her friend, Lucy Broadwood, honorary secretary of the Folk-Song
Society, was that summer and the previous one collecting Gaelic songs
in Arisaig. She wrote to Miss Parker, asking if she knew of anyone who
would underset the Gaelic words to the tunes and supply translations.

Dr Henderson at once suggested Fanny Tolmie. Not only that, but
learning of the work of the Society and of its *Journal* issued twice
annually, he felt that here at last might be the ideal repository for her
collection. Miss Parker agreed to take up the matter with Miss
Broadwood and carried away with her the four books of MS that Miss
Tolmie had sent him some years before. It was not, however, until
February 1908 that she called upon Miss Tolmie in Edinburgh.

Certain letters may here take up the story.[2]

Miss Parker to Miss Broadwood

18, Sloane Court,
S.W.

2.March. 08.

Dear Miss Broadwood,

I have been so frantically busy rushing about the country (to Edinburgh one week & Stirling another, and back here between) that I have had no time to write and thank [you] for your letter, or tell you of my visit to Miss Tolmie—you will be *charmed* with her, and should certainly make an effort to see her—she is the most fascinating old Highland lady—and sings and plays Highland music delightfully. I never heard a 'pibroch' sound well on the piano before—; she is very modest about her attainments—but it was the greatest contrast to hear her play her own simple 'pedal-bass' settings—with a wonderful feeling for the rhythm and value of the notes—and then a friend who had come in, and who played the usual excruciating arrangements in an unconvincing kind of way—Miss Tolmie was very anxious to impress upon me how different the Gaelic of educated people was from the dialects one hears—She has kept your m.s.s. and is *delighted* to give what help she can—I am sure you can absolutely trust her—she will do nothing, but what she knows about—but she says she must take her time about it.

Since writing the above I received the enclosed from Dr Henderson—(I forgot to tell you he asked me to thank you very much for the copy of the Folk Song Journal 'which was just what he had hoped for'—and he hopes he may have the pleasure of meeting you someday).

He had asked me to return the 2 m.s. (books of words) which he wanted for reference—so I now only have the 2 music books—I very hastily copied the word books—but *so* hastily that no one but myself, could possibly read them! Perhaps we can have a talk sometime soon about the best way to manage—I suppose you would want translations?—or not? I do not know whether Miss Tolmie would undertake these—

I am very anxious to have harp lessons—but I find my time so very fully occupied, it is quite impossible at present. Our deputa-

96

tion to the Secretary for Education was quite satisfactory on the whole—one cannot expect too much at first.

With kindest regards
Yours v. sincerely
WINIFRED M. PARKER

Dr Henderson to Miss Parker

14 Viewpark Drive,
Burnside, Glasgow
29.ii.08

Dear Miss Parker,

it is most kind of you to lend me that book on the Indian tribe— I can see it is very interesting. I received two Ms. in this parcel & Miss Tolmie wrote me ere you came to see her, she had my hurried note & I feel sure she would be heartily glad to see you. There is only one Miss Tolmie—she is unique & most delightful. She wrote me she felt it was the correct way of preserving her collection to bring it out in the Folk Song Socy publications. Accordingly under her own name I should wish it to appear. I will add a few words of introduction to let it be seen that it was done independently of any other view than a *bona fide* transcript from the folk. She committed it to my care to do with it as I thought fit but I refrained from giving it as a paper to any one for I held it a sacred trust from herself. Many folks would be glad to cull the cream of the collection & simply add a note of thanks to her at the foot. Miss Tolmie is a very retiring & modest nature & highly gifted & would readily give aid to any one interested but when so unique a collection as her's exists she ought to get the full credit for it & I hope Miss Broadwood & yourself will see that her collection gets a number of the Journal for itself. The work deserves it. I should like it proceed at once that Miss Tolmie may read the proofs & would like the Gaelic words given in full. She is no longer so young as she once was & it is desirable while her health remains to get this through the press in case of her not being free to go over it later on. One may delay too long & miss her superintendance of her work. This is just such a Collection as the F. Song Soc would treasure. I have been looking for five years for a suitable place for it & through you I am glad I have learned thereof.

Please set the matter a-going at once.

97

I hope I am not encroaching on your time. I would like you to convey our united greetings to Mrs Parker & we hope she is very well. Fall of snow here—& elsewhere.

faithfully yours,

GEORGE HENDERSON

In April (beginning thereof) I hope to have the Dragon Myth transcribed. I see the theme occurs in a version of Tristan & Isolde.

Miss Tolmie to Miss Broadwood

37, Merchiston Crescent,
Edinburgh.
March 5th. (1908)[3]

Dear Madam,

The notes which you committed to my care, and have given me much pleasure will be returned to you soon. At this moment, there are claims on my attention which in a few days will come to an end. I began with scanning the Songs you were taking down in Arisaig, and these, such as the 'Feasgar Luain'[4] of William Ross required a sort of waiting on them! Having mislaid Miss Parker's address, I send this note to you as a sign that though slow in returning the M.S. I am not forgetful.

Believe me to be, dear Madam, also with kind regards to Miss Parker—

Truly yours—

FRANCES TOLMIE

Miss Broadwood to Miss Parker

84, Carlisle Mansions,
Victoria Street, S.W.
Thursday
[5 March 1908]

Dear Miss Parker,

A great deal of Folk S. Society work after yesterday's Committee prevents me from writing more than a few hurried lines of *most* grateful thanks for your splendid help and delightful news. Before writing to either Miss Tolmie or Dr. Henderson can we meet & talk? I laid this generous offer before Committee & am authorised to give their best thanks & to get 'the Tolmie Collection' into print, as soon as *possible* & *convenient* to Miss Tolmie. If she prepares

98

and corrects proofs, & has a Journal to herself, it could perhaps immediately follow the next one (Mr Grainger's).

Could you possibly lunch here at *one* on Sunday (servants go out, hence this early time) or come to tea on Saturday any time after 4? Or could I come to you on Saturday morning at about 11 if that suited?

More when we meet. It is *delightful*—we were so proud at Committee to feel that our Society has inspired confidence from unknown Gaels!

Yours sincerely,
LUCY BROADWOOD

The minutes of the Society record that at that meeting on 4 March 1908—at Miss Broadwood's flat, no. 84 Carlisle Mansions, S.W.— there were present Sir Ernest Clarke (Chairman), Mrs Gibson (née Joachim), Mrs (afterwards Lady) Gomme, Dr Vaughan Williams and Messrs Frederick Keel, Fuller Maitland, Cecil Sharp and Gilbert Webb. Miss Broadwood brought to the committee the offer of Miss Tolmie and Dr Henderson 'to place Miss Tolmie's collection of Gaelic folk-songs (working songs, etc.) at the disposal of the Society, with a view to publication of them in a separate part of the *Journal* of the Society'.

Lucy Etheldred Broadwood (1858–1929) [Plate 12] was the great-granddaughter of the cabinet-maker, John Broadwood, who was born at Cockburnspath, Berwickshire, in the eighteenth century and went to London to make harpsichords for the Swiss, Burkat Tschudi. It is said that he walked to London. In any case, true to romantic tradition, he married his master's daughter and eventually owned the great pianoforte business, still 'John Broadwood & Sons'. On one side of the family Lucy Broadwood claimed Highland descent, through the Stewarts of Glenbuckie, of whom the late Sir Gilbert Murray was a distinguished descendant.

She spent her childhood at Lyne in Sussex and was essentially a countrywoman. The family had a town house also and there she met many European musical celebrities. She was a gifted and cultured woman with a particular talent for music, and her friends delighted in her singing of folk songs and songs of Purcell to her own accompaniment. As well as *English County Songs* (London, 1893) she brought out a

99

revised edition of her uncle's *Sussex Songs* (London, 1889), and later another volume, *English Traditional Songs and Carols* (London, 1908). Had circumstances compelled, she would in all probability have become a first-rate professional musician; but in that case she might not have become the mainspring for so many years of the Folk-Song Society, as secretary, editor and president.

Dear Miss Broadwood, [wrote Miss Tolmie on 13 March, 1908]

The other day I sent you on a card the reference which you wanted from your Portfolio, and did not thank you enough for the most interesting numbers, six in all, which you sent me of the Folk-Song Journal. I feel much honoured by your caring to have my somewhat imperfect Collection, as a contribution to the General Collection of British Folk-Songs, and to which I hope that Dr Henderson of Edrachillis will write a suitable Introduction, while I may add some notes of what I remember hearing on the subject of the Songs.

I hope soon to write to you about the Arisaig Tunes; and will not mention them on this occasion. I find that whatever I do is done in a zig-zag, meandering, intermittent manner, from little interruptions, and a weak eye—which has to be considered always; and is a check on all 'hurrying up'.—but still, not a hindrance by good day-light, only making one slow! May I offer a Postal Order for 10/6 . . . 1907 . . . as a sign of sympathy with the aims of the Folk-Song Society which I truly admire;[5] and should be as grieved if the English were to forget their Celtic-Teutonic lore—as if we were to lose our own completely,—as we are in danger of doing in this age of incessant and wonderful change.

I am, dear Miss Broadwood,
Yours with much respect—
FRANCES TOLMIE

There followed a flow of letters and MSS between Merchiston Crescent and Carlisle Mansions. Miss Tolmie's letters to Miss Broadwood, though none are available in the other direction, give a picture of the progress of the *Journal*. The early letters are mainly concerned with Miss Broadwood's Arisaig songs and, in particular, with a certain Cameron lament. The singer had given Miss Broadwood a tune that Miss Tolmie associated with other words. Two Cameron laments had been confused, one referring to Colonel John Cameron of Fassifern and the other to Donald Cameron, a noted sportsman.

Miss Tolmie discusses the two at length. In the course of a letter dated 24 March 1908 she writes:

> Not having lived in Lochaber I have little local knowledge of its songs and place-names. When-ever I get an opportunity I shall make enquiries as to *the original song going* with Tune No 4 . . . I shall be watching for that celebrated Cameron huntsman! The tune fixed upon, I see, has already been attached to a song of which I have never heard . . . My Grandmother would have known it & all of that generation. Printing was not so easy then; but the memory not over-taxed as it is now—and in the need of external aids for storing what it cannot use—such as Books—in which too much lies useless and forgotten like the curious remains found hidden away in a kitchen-midden among the Sand-hills of Bernera. It is a real pleasure to get some order into this confused web of memories half forgotten, and I do not feel it a trouble at all—my only regret being that I am not as quick about things as of old . . . Farewell today dear Miss Broadwood—and believe me to be sincerely yours—
>
> F. TOLMIE

In a P.S. she returns to 'the Cameron Huntsman—a gentleman of high degree of course—cadet of Lochiel . . . I shall not fail to ask about him if I meet anyone in Edinburgh—having a Lochaber association'.

The Cameron persisted in the correspondence until June; but on 22 June Miss Tolmie wrote that she was nearly ready with one section of her own songs. 'Could you kindly let me have the exact date on which they should be received by you?' In an earlier letter, dated 6 May 1908, she had written that she had had no expense in having the songs type-written,

> and instead made the acquaintance of a fine Hebridean from N. Uist, Mr Patrick Morrison, clerk with Messrs. Davidson. Squire Lawyer. 28. ~~George St~~ [sic] Charlotte Square, who refused to accept of ordinary payment for his trouble: 'I would do that much for the old Gaelic'—and is now going to be one of my Friends in town . . .

By October she had forwarded to Miss Broadwood copies not only of the tunes and texts in her own notebooks but additional songs noted from Mary Ross, and translations of them all. 'I have been helped in this matter', she wrote on 8 July 1908, 'by our old maid, Mary Ross—from Kilmaluag, Skye—who has done much for me in imparting her own recollections, and reviving mine.'

The committee, meeting on 23 July, decided that *Journal* no. 13, to appear in 1909, should consist of Miss Tolmie's collection of Gaelic songs and that 'such part should be somewhat larger than usual so as to include all the tunes and words that in the opinion of Miss Broadwood and Mr Fuller Maitland merited reproduction'.[6] Dr Henderson was to be co-opted to revise the Gaelic.

At the same time, as a matter of routine, the succeeding *Journal* was put in hand. A wise precaution it proved, for it was soon needed. The material appeared in 1909 as no. 13. 'Unforeseen difficulties', members of the committee were informed, had delayed the production of a double number that was to consist of 'a valuable, indeed unique collection of Gaelic songs, generously offered to the Society',[7] and it was therefore being reserved for a future occasion. Miss Broadwood, resigning from the general editorship, loyally promised to complete the editing of this *Journal* at whatever date it should be forthcoming. 1910 saw two further issues, nos. 14 and 15; and plans were made for no. 16, which however, eventually became the Tolmie *Journal*.

It is not surprising that this *Journal* turned out to be a larger and a longer undertaking than was at first anticipated. Not only was the number of songs much greater than had been contained in any previous issue—and in an unknown language at that—but there was the geographical complication of Miss Broadwood and Mr Fuller Maitland being in London, Miss Gilchrist in Southport, Miss Tolmie in Edinburgh and Dr Henderson in Glasgow—if not, from time to time, in Sutherland. Dr Henderson, brought in to revise the Gaelic, proved to be weighty and erudite. Miss Broadwood's niece, Miss Barbara Cra'ster, has written (January 1960):[8]

> unfortunately both he and Miss Tolmie had very definite & divergent views as to the correct spelling of the language, so the manuscript used to go backwards & forwards between them, for months, if I remember right, until at last my aunt had to insist on publishing the text as it then stood.

Miss Gilchrist, having studied the tunes, offered a theory as to their scales or modes. It was popularly held that there was a Highland pentatonic scale, but she claimed there were five, each with two six-note derivatives. She contributed an article on the subject to the Tolmie *Journal* and allocated the tunes to their place in her system; she also contributed copious annotations on tunes and subject matter—rather a larger share, in fact, than Miss Broadwood's. The latter, at the centre of operations, questioned Miss Tolmie as to the names and localities of singers and dates of notation and asked for all that she could tell regarding traditions and circumstances connected with the songs. Where Miss Broadwood was detached and objective in her documentation, Miss Tolmie—to whom each song was a landmark in her long life's experience—was reminiscent and diffuse.

Miss Gilchrist appears to have been indisposed and unable to do much during 1910—another cause for delay. By May 1911, however, things were really moving at last; and the story may again be taken up at this point by quotations from letters.

On 9 May Miss Broadwood writes to Miss Gilchrist:

How are you? I do hope keeping well, & still thriving on Sanatogen?

(1.) I enclose an item for the Tolmie Journal which you have not yet seen. (It was in the bundle you returned to me unopened.) Will you kindly comment thereon as to its place in your Scale-theory, etc. & return it to me—

(2.) Dr Henderson returned the MS. (such as I sent to you in vain last summer.) & I have lately been dealing with it, with my niece's kind help. We have classified and re-numbered the MS. largely according to your suggested list. We found still an *enormous* amount of titivating to be done, but have broken the neck of that. Dr Henderson has not altered much; nor *added* much as he considers the MS. bulky enough without further additions. After we have altered the numbering of songs in the *annotations etc.*: throughout, (the which has not yet been done,) & prepared the MS. as far as we can, will you like to have it to go thro' again before I begin to parley with the Scottish printer? Let me know your views, please. My niece & I go away the 2nd. week in June, abroad for 2 or more months, & I should like to arrive at some definite action as regards the Tolmie MS. before then, and if *possible*, get it into printers' hands. I have not stopped to trace melodies any further, but I understand from a letter of yours once that you have several new things to add in the way of annotation.

Dr. Henderson has mercifully cleared up some obscurities. But in several cases Miss Tolmie instead of correcting one false note in music has *re-written* the *whole*, giving once more *new* headings with *old* (*editorial*) mistakes which we had so carefully eliminated!! I think we must see the whole MS. thro' first proof before letting her have a sight of it again. Don't you?

Meantime Mr Keel is cheerfully preparing another Journal, which is to consist of an American's *very* interesting MS. of old England traditional songs—many of the stock ballad kind. . . .

A typical letter of Miss Tolmie's is that dated 22 May 1911:

Dear Miss Broadwood,

Let me now return the corrections, with the expression of my true regret that you should have so much of this kind of work to do. Please have no hesitation in sending on whatever you find to be not quite satisfactory. Your niece wrote about a verse in Ossian's warning to his Mother, and I am enclosing a copy of that free from the blemishes in the printed volume with the verses in the order desired—and the odd chorus in the middle which must have had a tune of its own, and cannot now be recalled. (My early notes of 1870 had become blurred & the names not distinct enough. The meaning becoming uncertain also)—
The last verses of 'Coisich a Rùin', if you think them too savage should be omitted, I think. I remember not being quite sure of 'Maibh's' patronymic which perhaps the Gaelic corrector may have observed, and supplied the right word. Some of the omissions astonish me where they occur.

Please convey my sympathy to Miss Gilchrist with the hope that she is now really strong again & equal to carrying on her invaluable assistance in the Folk Song Society. My sister Mary and Mary Ross send their kindest greeting.

With kind regards to your niece, believe me to be dear Miss Broadwood,

sincerely your—
F. TOLMIE

On 30 May 1911 Miss Broadwood wrote:

Dear Miss Gilchrist,

I have today despatched per registered parcel post to you the Tolmie MS. ① Everything is there excepting a very *short* introduction which I propose to make of Miss T. herself & the purpose of the collection. This will embrace certain stray notes of interest sprinkled amongst her letters.

My niece and I have laboured long over the MS . . .

③ Also *pray correct anything* which strikes you as needing it. I confess I have *not* again gone thro' all the *musical text*, leaving that to you. A good number of difficulties seem to have been cleared up by Dr Henderson-cum-Tolmie since last you saw the MS.

④ Pray add any important note on the songs ad libitum.

⑤ I believe that it will be unnecessary for me to have the MS. back from you, & I suggest that if you don't mind, that you sh.ld despatch the parcel to the printers as soon as you've done with it . . .

I am *that* tired with the rush of parties, late nights, 'musical events', editing, & coping with clothes-mongers that I am a perfect pulp.

I hope you are well & not too much overdone. . . .

On 31 May 1911 a letter follows from Miss Broadwood to say that she has that day written to make first arrangements with the printers, Messrs Robert Maclehose & Co., University Press, Anniesland, Glasgow. After making suggestions about getting MSS and proofs from hand to hand—from the printers to Dr Henderson, from him to Miss Gilchrist, then to Miss Tolmie and back to Miss Gilchrist, and finally back to the printers—she concludes, 'I am truly grieved to be giving you more work to do, & feel quite mean. But I *have* toiled over it. I couldn't have believed how much trouble vagueness can give—if it's vagueness in an unknown tongue!'

On 7 June 1911 Miss Broadwood writes to Miss Gilchrist:

The printers have my address to which to despatch the estimate (which I shall accept *whatever it is!!*). . . . I think that your plan of receiving proofs & MS. from the printer & despatching the MS. & duplicate proofs to Dr Henderson to send to Miss Tolmie & back to you is very good. I will not meddle with the matter, so will you kindly (in my name as well as your own) instruct printers, Dr. H. and Miss T. accordingly. Solemnly warning the latter to alter as little as possible, & telling her just what to do? I blush to give you so much trouble. . . .

Somewhere en route Miss Tolmie's address must have gone a-missing. On 25 July 1911 Dr Henderson writes on a postcard to Miss Gilchrist:

Yes; Miss F. Tolmie,
      37 Merchiston Crescent,
        Edinburgh.
I am happy to hear you are so advanced; & hope there may be no great delay now & that you have found the whole matter interesting.

'Dear Miss Gilchrist', writes Miss Tolmie on 2 August 1911, 'It is pleasant to be writing your name once more!' After giving some odds and ends of information asked for, she adds cryptically, 'All Dr Henderson's corrections I accept—they go beyond me in the name of Margaret Gillies and in the refrain of the little "port-a-beul".'

Miss Gilchrist may well have felt that they went beyond her also! A postcard to her from Dr Henderson, for instance, bearing the postmark 18 August 1911, reads

1. Batch 5 goes now to Miss T.
2. *Uaran mór* i.e., capital U. Diphthongization *ua* comes from older *o* regularly.
3. *Mo rogha ceòil* would be preferable; strike out—inn of rogha (which is accusative for nominative wrongly); ceòil is an old gen. case & liable to be influenced by nom. ceòl, since the more common gen. is ciùil which the assonance won't allow of here.
4. Thanks for bringing rest into Journal
                        from. faithfy yrs.
                            G.H.

Miss Tolmie at the same time had devoted four postcards and part of a letter to discussion of an accent which—like the cat, MacAvity— 'wasn't there'. *Snagach* ('spirited') in the Dunvegan fairy lullaby was to be found in some printed versions as *snàgach* ('snake-like'). The tune, which she believed not to have been recorded before, she noted carefully from the singing of the bard, Mr Neil MacLeod, a neighbour in Edinburgh at this time, whose many patient repetitions alone made it

2   Loch Coruisk

3   A Waulking in Skye

4   Frances Tolmie

5   Harriette Rigbye

6   Thwaite Cottage, Coniston

7 'Clennie' (Marion MacLellan)

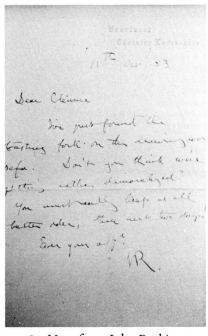

8 Note from John Ruskin

9 Mary Ross

10 The bardess, Mary MacPherson

11   The Black House, Kilmaluag, Skye

12   *Caristiona, Cumha Màthar*, 'A Mother's Lament'. Two sheets pinned together. Among the MSS in the National Library of Scotland

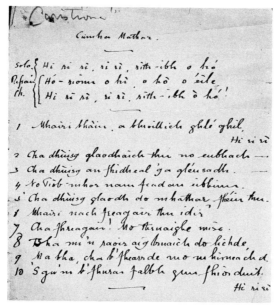

13   *Caristiona, Cumha Màthar*. Second sheet. (See Marjory Kennedy-Fraser, *A Life of Song*, pp.145f.)

14   Lucy Etheldred Broadwood

15   Participants at a folk music festival organized by
the Canadian Pacific Railway, Banff, Alberta, in 1929.
Left to right: Norman MacRitchie (Lewis), the author,
Alan Smith (Lewis), Marjory Kennedy-Fraser, Father
Donald Macintyre (South Uist)

16   Kilchoan Cottage, Dunvegan, with MacLeod's Tables in the background

17   Frances Tolmie in her old age

18   An invitation to tea, November 1925

19   Frances Tolmie with her grand-niece,
Margaret Hope Tolmie (afterwards Mrs
Prance), in 1921

possible to fix it correctly. As she herself was of the opinion that the first spelling was the correct one, and Mr MacLeod's singing of it confirmed her first impression, it might seem that there was no need to mention the intrusive accent at all. The final postcard (20 August 1911) ran:

If it be not too late, and if allowable, may I ask you kindly to put the initials of Mr. Neil MacLeod's name under the footnote relating to the word 'snagach' which has on several occasions been printed wrongly. A philologist could make a most interesting exposition of that word, & its English connexions.

F.T.

The note and initials are, accordingly, to be found on p. 174 of the Tolmie *Journal*.

On 21 August Miss Broadwood wrote from Glarus in Switzerland:

My dear Miss Gilchrist,

Alas! I am more sorry than I can say that you have had to spend such hours over the Tolmie MS. You have been an angel, & I feel a brute. . . .

You have my authority to delete any of Dr. Henderson's linguistic matter that seems really *too* beside the mark. In case where *interesting* meaning is thrown upon anything I sh.ld say *keep*. . . .

Again, my warm thanks & condolences. I foresee that *my* hour is coming now!

Yours in gratitude & most sincerely
LUCY BROADWOOD

During August the three-way postal traffic continued. Here are extracts from Miss Tolmie's letters to Miss Gilchrist:

22.8.11. Let me now return the MS., with the hope that I have duly attended to the points marked by you, and absurdly overlooked by me. It fills me with wonder how the eyes may be deceived in looking over such simple things, and I pray you to excuse my tendency to carelessness! I trust to do better over the next batch. . . .

Farewell now, dear Miss Gilchrist, and believe me to be over the Songs, yours with hearty good will,

FRANCES TOLMIE

Postcard, dated 1911 Edin. Aug. 24. (My love upon her who once lived at Lancaster.) The packet had just come in. I am engaged to go out of Town today, but shall endeavour to return the MS. this evening if possible—attending to all directions. Yours. F.T.

24.8.11. I am now posting the MS. and trust that I have in the main seen to the necessary marks: though not always neatly done. If I have failed in any thing, please return! To be received in penitence.

I was out in the country yesterday—a most glorious day. I was rowed on a lonely green pool on the lower slopes of the Pentlands by a laddie of 6 years of age—tame wild ducks skirting around the shore across an infinite variety of shadows—all sorts of green, with a deep blue in the middle. All grey today, and rain gathering. . . .

28.8.11. Let me now return the tunes with the necessary marks of R. V. and Fine. . . . You are wonderfully observing in all these little peculiarities of our native music. I regret to have given you the trouble of sending this again. . . .

Postcard, 29.8.11. Last evening a packet came, and another this morning which I shall return as quickly as possible, but perhaps not today by the afternoon post as usual—but tomorrow. . . .

31.8.11. Trusting that I have not overlooked any important point, I now return the 8th batch. The numbering of the verses, and the marking of the Refrains and Chorus, must have been irksome for you, and I think it wonderful how well you have made out the primitive, and half conscious arrangement in the original, of these separate parts. In No. 63—I seem to have gone against a previous correction of the MS. in correcting v. 2, 3, 4. These syllables found place in the tune according to the native ear, though the notation might have to be lengthened at times to suit the accent of a word—the same occasionally happening to a word also with regard to the tune. When I go and consult Mary Ross about a word, she thinks me very pernickety—'Who ever heard of such enquiries as are made now-a-days—the words chewed, and munched out of recognition'? As she does not write, though she reads well, she does not understand the necessity for exactness in the representation of spoken language on paper. But I am sorry about all the trouble you have had over these errors of every description. . . .

Returned from Switzerland and visiting at Vinehall, Robertsbridge in Sussex, Miss Broadwood wrote to Miss Gilchrist on 2 September:

My dear patient friend,

I can't thank you enough. Having sat like an owl in front of MS—letters—explanations & proofs I did, before yr last kind letter came just now, discover *much* to show me that I was wrong in my 1st supposition. And now I'm most grateful to know just what *has* been done. I'm allowed to brood over the work of editing here, but naturally can't get on so well as if I were working all day alone at home.

I go on *Thursday morning* early from here to 84 Carlisle Ms. SW, & leave that again (for a week) on Saturday the 9th.

    Idlerocks,

       Stone,

          Staffs

will be my address there.

OH! the relief it will be to all parties when this Journal is out! Sir E. Clarke recommends its being numbered No 16. & dated Dec. 1911. I also incline to this. It won't matter if we have only one Journal for the year, & this SHOULD be a gem in the end!

Much haste. I do hope you are not really very unwell. I can believe that you are $\frac{1}{2}$ killed by this work.

Yours vy sincerely,

L. BROADWOOD

The 'very definite & divergent views'[9] of Miss Tolmie and Dr Henderson were not confined to spelling. During September a difference of opinion arose over a song of which Miss Tolmie had noted the tune and some lines from Mary Ross in 1899. Dr Henderson weighed in with a longer version of the text he had taken down from a group of singers in South Uist in 1892, adding particulars they had given him as to the supposed authorship. Miss Tolmie asked Miss Broadwood to delete this version, considering that he had received it from an ill-informed source. In particular, she could not accept the statement that certain lines had been added by Flora MacDonald. She wrote at length and in some distress, outlining the life of her heroine, and declaring that these lines were quite foreign to her character and story. Compromise was reached by allowing Dr Henderson's version to stand but without the reference to Flora.[10] Humour broke through, however, in a marginal note to a letter to Lucy Broadwood bearing the postmark, 26 September 1911: 'What would you expect from S. Uist', says

Mary Ross with Skye disdain of the Outer Isles, 'but "Ròlaistean", rigmaroles, who eat Barley bread—not Oat,—have no sense of time, etc.'

During October Miss Tolmie visited her old Newnham friend, Mrs Bulley, at Hindhead, and the flow of proofs and letters continued. Her share, however, was nearly completed. Accepting Miss Broadwood's invitation to break her return journey in London, she wrote that she looked forward to spending a night at her residence and to laying her penitent head upon her pillow. Miss Broadwood was not to meet her: she would find her way from Vauxhall Station with some luggage in a cab.

Miss Barbara Cra'ster, Miss Broadwood's niece, recalled this visit, the only occasion on which she met Miss Tolmie. Her recollection was of 'a typical Scot—tall & upstanding—very intelligent & decided in her views'. She wrote that she did not remember that Miss Tolmie sang at all: 'I think I should not have forgotten it if she had.'[11]

Back in Edinburgh, Miss Tolmie posted to Miss Broadwood on 31 October the pages of 'Reminiscences'. They have supplied many clues to me in fitting her story together. In the accompanying letter she wrote:

> Amid these days of remembrance permit me to enclose some notes bearing on the songs, and how the light radiated from the abode of the revered Mr. T. Constable, and made clear what was before vague and confused. Without causing any re-printing of my own little introduction—perhaps you would mention this influence in becoming terms dear Miss Broadwood. I should be most grateful if you would just put in a few words with the sparkle of the dew on them.

And on 6 November 1911 Miss Tolmie wrote:

> Let me now return your Introduction which I think admirable, and shewing extraordinary understanding on your part of our native Music and language in which you have taken so deep and patriotic an interest. I thank you with all my heart. . . .

Writing on 10 November in reply to a query about the early history of the MacLeods in the Western Isles she adds, 'The Asiatic Studies are often in my hand, and were grand to dip into when in the train.

A fortnight has elapsed since you so kindly took me to the Railway Station.'

Their mutual interests were not confined to Gaelic song, tradition and custom. A. C. Lyall's *Asiatic Studies* may well have found shelf room beside Lafcadio Hearn's *Gleanings in Buddha-Fields* inscribed 'To Miss Frances Tolmie, in remembrance of our first meeting. Lucy E. Broadwood. September 1909.'

After her visit to Miss Broadwood's flat in Carlisle Mansions Miss Tolmie liked to refer to it as the *Grianan*, a Gaelic word meaning 'sunlit house' or 'place of happy associations'; and so, on 6 December, the following note accompanied a gift:

Once more, with the energy of youth I ascend to the hospitable 'Grianan' in London, to the lady who has so graciously given her aid in preserving in remembrance some of the domestic songs of joyous work of a bygone time, and in the name of the singers, kneeling before her, kissing her right hand and kissing her left, I pray that she will accept of this scarf of the tartan of Macleod with our earnest benedictions.

FRANCES TOLMIE (native of the Land of Macleod)
[*Marginal note*: with an Edinburgh Luckenbooth pin.]

One more letter may be quoted:

> Edinburgh.
> New Year's Eve, 1911.

Dear Miss Broadwood,

There is much on my heart to say, but I shall try and put it in as little room as possible, for Time presses for everyone; the great doors are closing from the force of a mighty wind, and however anxious I might be, I may never more cross my own threshold into the realm of imagination. But one need not though silent and still be dead, or indifferent, and we may always remember one another. I shall think of you always with delight, and wish you well for ever and peace and light to be in the Grianan, and music resounding there. I am filled with gladness when I look at the Journal of the Folk Song Soc. and am reminded of days gone by when I wished I knew a real Musician to whom I should commit the old songs which I grieve to see going into oblivion. And you came unsought by me, unknown to me, and took them under your care. You have pleased us all, my Sister Mary, Mary Ross, & myself. I am much gratified at the manner in which, in your able Introduction you have brought in the literary influence of Mr. Constable in widening my range of observation and throwing a reflex illumination on topics familiar to me from infancy, yet not seen in their relation to similar subjects elsewhere. We sent Mary Ross's Minister a copy the day after a handsome consignment of 30. numbers came from Messrs R. Maclehose & Co—and I posted one to Mr. Constable's daughter at Quinish in Mull, [*Marginal note*, Mrs Forsyth of Quinish] as she is not quite well just now, & it may amuse her to recognise some of the 'puirt' that I used to sing. A very noble person she is, as her Father and Mother were before her. Long may she and her dear sister live! all of the same quality. I merely mention [?this] as a sign of my appreciation of your nice delicate tact in blending each incident and giving it a vital bearing at the same time, on the origin and preservation of the songs and melodies.

You know dear Miss Broadwood that I am deeply grateful to you, that I am fond of you, and will so gladly do anything to help you in adding to the Collection which you began yourself. [Here follow details of inquiries she had been making on behalf of Miss Broadwood.]

This is all today, dear Miss Broadwood, ere some kind folk come in—I won't get my letter posted for New Year's Day. My warmest greetings to Miss Craster & yourself.

Ever affectionately yours. My Sister joining

F. TOLMIE

Points of emphasis in the letters of congratulation received by Miss Tolmie and Miss Broadwood were as varied as were their writers. At one extreme was non-musical Gaelic scholarship, as exemplified in Dr George Henderson and the Rev. Thomas Sinton; at the other, non-Gaelic musicianship of distinction, as practised by Sir Alexander Mackenzie and Dr Vaughan Williams. There were correspondents, associated with the Highlands and Islands, greatly interested but professing little knowledge of either music or Gaelic. The reaction of bilingual Gaels, familiar with the way of life that had nourished the songs, was mainly patriotic and nostalgic.

Of these last was Miss Kate MacRae (c/o Green, 51 Merchiston Crescent), who wrote, thanking Miss Tolmie for a copy of the Journal:

Dear Miss Fanny,

. . . I have been looking into it tonight, & many of the songs brought 'the tear to my ee', recalling the time & place where I heard them, & the dear singers. We had a faithful servant Rebeca Macpherson—she could neither read nor write, but her memory was stored with pathetic songs, which she used to sing sweetly to the children—(my nephews & nieces) I loved to hear her, & was moved by the pathos of the stories, that, about the woman who was left to drown by the cruel handmaid & the Lament for 'Gregor Cridhe' . . . I seem to know almost all Mary Ross's songs. . . .

The Rev. Thomas Sinton, for whose work Miss Tolmie had a great regard, wrote her from the manse at Dores, Inverness-shire, 'There never was such a collection made hitherto, and I would not have thought it possible for anyone now living to produce the like. It is difficult to express in words the peculiar wild, mystical way in which these fragments appeal to one.' Her 'own MacLeod', the chief, Norman Magnus, writing from Horsham, Sussex, was pleased to have the 'Lullaby of the Fairy Woman'; he had often been asked about it but had to confess that he did not know it. 'I will get my wife to play the air, your collection is of the greatest interest.'

Colonel Duncan Matheson of the Lews wrote from Kensington, thanking Miss Broadwood most warmly for the collection:

Nothing could appeal to me more, though unfortunately I do not know enough about music to understand the great interest of the melodies under that aspect. But they are just the plaintive airs one so continually hears on the West coast and especially among the fisher girls on the steamer returning to Lewis.

A London Gael, Mr John MacLennan, born near Garve in Ross-shire, and precentor at the quarterly Gaelic service at Crown Court Church of Scotland, Covent Garden, was impressed with Miss Broadwood's preface. 'It is perfectly plain to me', he wrote, 'that you write upon "Gaelic Song" to a far greater extent "from within" than I had thought possible, and I shall expect to be spoken to in Gaelic the next time I have the pleasure of seeing you!'

'My congratulations on your excellent preface', wrote Sir Alexander

Mackenzie, Principal of the Royal Academy of Music, describing the volume as 'a new departure into fresh ground. . . . It must have cost an enormous amount of labour.'

One of the first letters to reach Miss Broadwood was from Dr Vaughan Williams, dated December 28:

13 Cheyne Walk,
S.W.

Dear Miss Broadwood,

I have been carefully through the Gaelic volume & find some extremely beautiful tunes there notably. 9.10.13.17.25.32.35.36. 37.41.42.44.75.78.83.85.88.

What a strange country—so utterly different from our English Idiom—& what a study for a Celtic composer—for my self I feel lost and out of my element—though greatly admiring—among the mountains & mists & legends & chiefs—and long for my quiet Sussex downs and flat fields with large elm trees again.

Yours truly
R. VAUGHAN WILLIAMS

The *Journal of the Folk-Song Society* was at that time printed for members only; 1912, therefore, brought a large number of temporary members, many Scots among them, who paid a year's subscription in order to obtain the Tolmie collection.

At the annual general meeting in the Steinway Hall on the evening of Saturday, 16 March, Gaelic songs were included in the customary recital that followed the business. The singers were two London Gaels, John MacLennan, already mentioned, and Dr Farquhar MacRae. Lucy Broadwood had met them through Winifred Parker in 1908, about the same time as contact had been made with Miss Tolmie, and had phonographed and transcribed a number of songs from both. On this occasion, remaining seated as at a fireside, they gave songs of their native Ross-shire without accompaniment. Both in presentation and in language they provided a contrast to the English section of the programme, in which the names of Lucy Broadwood, Clive Carey, Cecil Sharp and Vaughan Williams figured as collectors, writers of accompaniments, or both. In spite of these contrasts, however, each section of the audience, English or Gaelic, may perhaps have found something familiar in listening to the older modal tunes of the other.

Frances Tolmie's collection of songs was published at last. Dr George Henderson, whose Gaelic scholarship had been so valuable, wrote thanking Miss Broadwood for his parcel of ten copies. He expressed his own great personal interest in the volume and assured her of his appreciation of the thought and care whereby she had made the whole enterprise a success.

'Many in future years', he added, 'will turn to these pages when more bulky and more pretentious volumes are forgotten.'

CHAPTER 12

EDINBURGH,

1907-15

I began to publish in 1907 and fortunately I met her in Edinburgh at that time.

Marjory Kennedy-Fraser[1]

The various delays between Fanny Tolmie's meeting with Dr Henderson at the Carmichael's in Taynuilt in 1900 and the eventual appearance of her collection in the *Journal of the Folk-Song Society* in 1911, had one curious result. In 1909, the year originally planned by Lucy Broadwood for its appearance, the collection was forestalled in the month of May by the first volume of the famous *Songs of the Hebrides* of Mrs Marjory Kennedy-Fraser (1857-1930).

Mrs Fraser, usually in company with her sister Margaret Kennedy, had been giving recitals of her songs from 1907. The first of these was on a February afternoon in that year when, as a subject in her customary winter lectures on *Lieder* (under the general title, 'Songs and Song-writers'), she spoke of 'A visit to the Outer Hebrides and Celtic Music'.[2] She illustrated her talk with adaptations of Gaelic song tunes that she had noted in the island of Eriskay in 1905; these she had arranged with pianoforte accompaniments and English words. Her Gaelic being limited to a few well-known songs and choruses,[3] she was dependent upon singers and others for translations; where such were not available she tells us that, *faute de mieux*, she wrote English words of her own.

The novelty and charm of the songs that emerged from this treatment, their polished performance by the two sisters (for both were highly-accomplished professional musicians), and Mrs Fraser's entertaining talk about the people, places and circumstances of her song gathering—all this ensured delighted acceptance by the non-Gaelic concert-goers to whom the songs were addressed. Gaelic-speaking Highlanders must have been very few in number in the early audiences.

Following the impression made by her first recital, Mrs Fraser 'straightway published one or two of the songs, with my piano settings and translations' and 'decided to resume the work of collecting seriously, as soon as possible'.[4]

That summer, in company with her daughter Patuffa, she made a second collecting expedition to Eriskay, and the first of many to Barra. Recitals at two Pan-Celtic gatherings, one in Edinburgh in the autumn of 1907, the other in London in 'early 1908', led to an undertaking by the music publishers, Boosey and Company, London (now Boosey & Hawkes) to bring out a volume of the songs.[5]

Not until the late spring of 1908 did she meet Kenneth Macleod,[6] who became her Gaelic collaborator. Meanwhile she had made the acquaintance of Frances Tolmie, who was living in 37 Merchiston Crescent, Edinburgh, while she herself lived at 95a George Street, in the centre of town. The following letter[7] indicates the kind of help she was receiving:

37. Merchiston Crescent.
Feb. 4th [1908]

Dear Mrs.Kennedy-Fraser,

The remaining songs are enclosed, all correction being welcome. Any information regarding the subject of any song will be promptly forwarded when required.

Sincerely yours,
F. Tolmie

Twenty-six letters from Miss Tolmie were preserved by Mrs Fraser, after whose death they were returned to relatives of Miss Tolmie; because of their particular interest they were passed to the Rev. Dr Archibald MacDonald, who was Miss Tolmie's nephew by marriage and co-editor of *The MacDonald Collection of Gaelic Poetry* (Inverness, 1911). Letters, or parts of them, referring to particular songs that Miss Tolmie gave are quoted in chapter 14; those that follow here are of a more social nature.

37. Merchiston Crescent,
Nov. 30th [1909]

Dear Mrs. Kennedy-Fraser,

Let me express in a few lines how much I was impressed at both your Recitals of our native melodies arranged according to the principles of Art.

I listened with much pleasure, as I recognised each familiar strain, but at the same time with bewilderment, and a sense of my own profound ignorance of the region into which you were leading the audience, and a strong desire to hear everything *over*, and *over* and *over* again, and learn in truth. Could one leap at a bound into all this inner meaning and exposition of our Hebridean life to which you have devoted your genius, without preliminary experience, however true one's power of Intuition might be?

Aspiring, waiting, and thanking Miss Kennedy and you with all my heart for a great Lesson, and with kindest regards to you, and to Mr. Kenneth Macleod who has done his part so admirably, believe me to be, dear Mrs. Kennedy-Fraser.

Sincerely yours,
FRANCES TOLMIE

March 31st (1910)

It was delightful to sit in peace listening to your earnest and enlightening Lecture last evening . . . reminding us of the real and necessary basis of musical patriotism: an acquaintance with the principles of Music in general, and with those scales on which our native melodies are founded, in particular. A course of lectures from you on this subject would be of immeasurable benefit to us all, Highland & Lowland . . . and give correct precision to our judgment and taste. . . .

Sincerely yours,
FRANCES TOLMIE

My niece, Mrs. MacDonald of Kiltarlity Manse, who sat beside me, greatly admired the accompaniments, as well as the songs.

There are no letters for 1911. From May onward, as has already been told, Miss Tolmie was fully occupied with her work on the *Journal*; glimpses of her are to be found, however, in the minutes of the Celtic Union, Edinburgh.

This society, dating from 1894—a dozen years after the establishment of the Celtic chair in the university, and two after *An Comunn Gàidhealach* ('The Gaelic Association')—met in the rooms of the Philosophical Institution at no. 4 Queen Street and was a haunt of the Gaelic intellectual élite of that day. 'The Misses Tolmie' appear regularly among the names of members attending. An evening of real Gaelic gaiety must have been that of 14 March 1911, when the Rev. Neil Ross delivered a lecture entitled *Cuairt do n' Ghaidhealtachd* [sic], 'A Trip to the Highlands' in Gaelic blank verse, which 'in Mr Ross's hands . . . added an indescribable charm to the narrative'. The minutes report that Fanny Tolmie's old friend, Alexander Carmichael, was in the chair and was 'thanked in Gaelic, for his discharge of the duties of the chair'. His daughter, Mrs Ella Watson, had also used Gaelic in her contribution to the discussion, and Neil MacLeod, the bard, rounded off the evening with a 'humorous speech' of thanks, also in Gaelic.

Out of the eight or so meetings each winter season three were musical evenings. Margaret Kennedy, Archibald Menzies and the young composer William B. Moonie are named among those who arranged the programmes. By way of contrast to conventional Highland songs—mostly in English—traditional Gaelic singing by Miss Tolmie received special mention in the minutes of 1912.

> February 7. A musical evening arranged by William B. Moonie, John Bartholomew, advocate, presiding. 'Miss Tolmie's "Waulking Song" [unspecified] roused the enthusiasm of the meeting to a high pitch'.
>
> March 27. A musical entertainment arranged by Archibald Menzies, Harvey Shand in the chair. 'Miss Tolmie's rendering of the "Lament of the Water Kelpie" (in Gaelic) reminded the audience, of the "Good old Times" by its pathos and sweetness'.[8]

On 5 January 1910 Mrs Kennedy-Fraser had given at the Celtic Union a recital drawn from her first volume of the *Songs of the Hebrides*. She may possibly have included her English version of the 'Water-Kelpie', which is found there.[9]

Miss J. F. Mackinnon, a long-time member of the Society, remembers as a girl one occasion when Miss Tolmie sang. She was not on the pre-arranged programme but sang at the request of her friend, Archibald Menzies.

That summer Mrs Kennedy-Fraser persuaded Kenneth MacLeod to go with her to his native island of Eigg, which he had not revisited for twenty years.[10] There, staying at Laig House, she had a letter from Miss Tolmie in Edinburgh, dated 30 July 1912.

How very, very kind of you to write to me from Eigg, and share your happiness in that sacred island with me and also I thank you for letting me know that you had been kindly welcomed to Skye! I can follow you about, and listen once more to the local tales. Have you been to 'Slochd-a-Ghliongain'[11]—and have you heard of the horse that fell into that awful 'Slochd', and emerged all alive, from the depths under the sea—over in Sleat?

I should be glad if Mr. Kenneth were to be the minister of Eigg. It is a cause for regret that the parish should be vacant so long—a charge that used to be filled with great dignity in our remembrance. It is not an isolated charge—nor are the people rude or rustic—far from it. I wish you much satisfaction in your 'turus'[12] dear Mrs. Kennedy-Fraser going round by Arisaig, till you return to Edinburgh. I send 'beannachdan'[13] to all the kind folk, and my special regards to 'Mr Coinneach'—we used not to say the surname of our Ministers. I hope that Miss Patuffa is enjoying her stay in [Iona] . . . and with Mary joining, am

Affectionately yours
FRANCES TOLMIE

The next two letters concern Mrs Kennedy-Fraser's arrangement of the 'Lay of Fraoch', which appears in the album *Sea Tangle* (London, 1913) as 'The Daughter of Maeve'.

August 8th [*1912*]
Your note is delightful and I admire much, and with all my heart all that Mr. MacLeod and you have done in the short time, and am so glad that you had a calm sea, coming away. You shall certainly have Leabhar-na-Feinne, which I pray you to keep as long as you require to have it; unless I learn anything to the contrary, it shall be posted to St Abb's Haven by tomorrow evening—you may be staying on there, or you may be returning home, when I could hand it in quite easily myself. You know how welcome you are to have

it, but I'll make a copy of the original for you. That's what should be!

> Yours in haste.
> Dear Mrs. Kennedy-Fraser,
> F. TOLMIE

August 9th [*1912*]

If on looking over the 'Leabhar' which I now send, you would like the contribution from dear Dr. Carmichael written out, please send it back and I would gladly do it.

Please do not associate my name in any way with the translation, which on my part was only a tentative effort, to be corrected and passed [?] by the Master, Mr Kenneth himself: I do not wish to step out among the scholars—I am ready enough to appear among those who remember.

> Ever yours,
> F. TOLMIE

September 5th 1912   (Re-directed to St. Abb's Haven,
                                                Berwickshire)

Believing that Miss Kennedy and you are now back in Edinburgh from your grand round, and Miss Patuffa I hope, safe home from Iona, let me express my warm thanks to you for your delightful letter from Eigg, and the cards that followed from various points of your long journey, shewing that you had been warmly welcomed everywhere, & that your work of both *revival* and *evolution* was understood, and valued by those who listened to the Celtic strains from the Hebrides. I wonder if you have seen Ultonian-Ballads gathered in the Hebrides, and translated into English by Hector Maclean, 1892, among which I have found a version of Fraoch, both in Gaelic & English. You have only to send a card,—it goes to you. I am writing to Mr. Kenneth thanking him for a generous present of grouse, & mentioning it to him in case he might like to have the Collection by him. Should a card come from you, I would send the book on, on Monday, as our abode will be closed on Saturday. With our kindest greetings,

> Affectionately yours,
> F. TOLMIE

In a different vein are the following:

Oct. 21st. 1912

Thanking you for the announcement regarding the Beltane Conference, I hope to attend it on Thursday 24th. With kind regards to Miss Kennedy & Miss Patuffa, believe me to be,

Sincerely yours,

F. TOLMIE

The meeting was held in Glasgow. Miss Tolmie was present, but it so happened that Mrs Kennedy-Fraser missed her train. That evening Miss Tolmie wrote:

I cannot let the day draw to a close without sending you a few lines to express the general regret at the Art Rooms in Renfrew St. Glasgow, when your Telegram was read, & we learned that you had lost your train. We were sorry for you, as well as for ourselves . . .

She goes on to name the speakers who filled the gap, and concludes: 'I came away before the party had dispersed as my train was leaving at 6, and I had promised to be home early. They did their best to fill up the void caused by your absence.'

Writing on 25 October, Miss Tolmie acknowledged tickets sent for a Scottish concert on the 26 October, at the same time promising to attend a meeting the following week regarding the formation of a certain 'Beltane Society' with whose objects she declared her sympathy, even though she might not be available to help in any way. Nothing more, however, seems to have been heard of this Beltane Society. After the Scottish concert Miss Tolmie wrote:

Oct. 26th [1912]

I cannot let the day go by without sending a note to express how truly we enjoyed the Concert of native song last evening, and our hope that Miss Kennedy and you were not over-tired after your generous exertion to entertain and delight us all—within a wide compass from gay to grave, of which a striking example might, I believe, be found in your rendering of the 'Deil amang the Tailors', when, on the left hand one learns with awe, the 'Fear Mòr'[14] himself arriving with measured, inevitable strides among the merry tailors! 'Fraoch' was most impressive. But I need not enter into details. It was all so charming and homelike, producing the illusion of innocent cottage firesides, as well as of elegant Drawingrooms, while there was a cool breathing of fresh air around us which kept us all alert amid our dreams and visions of by-gone times. Accept, I pray of my grateful thanks for all this pleasure: & for the comfortable seats given us.

With kindest greetings to Miss Kennedy and Miss Patuffa, believe me to be, dear Mrs. Kennedy-Fraser,

Affectionately yours,

FRANCES TOLMIE

The album of nine songs entitled *Sea Tangle, Some More Songs of the Hebrides* was published for Mrs Kennedy-Fraser by Boosey (London) on 8 January 1913. This is doubtless the 'new copy of the songs' mentioned in the following letter.

January 12th [1913]

On awakening this morning [Sunday] from a sound and beneficent sleep, my first recollection was a most pleasant one of the hours spent in your 'Grianan'[15] yesterday amid showers of sleet and rain. Let me first of all apologise for any droll incompetence on my part with regard to the Express so kindly sent on by you, and to which I sent no reply till I arrived in person. There was a *flaw about that incident* which I cannot explain,—about which you are no doubt perfectly indifferent. It was delightful to be in your charming family group with Mr. Kenneth. And you accepted my attempt at translation most generously—but I am not stopping there without an effort to do better! And the new copy of the songs you gave me with my name inscribed with much grace! Mary Skene was equally pleased with the volume made over to herself—. It is not lost upon her! She has very nice perceptions, and has a piano of her own down at Fettes College[16] where she can play over the accompaniments, and encourage others to sing, should she not raise her own voice. She certainly has not fluent Gaelic, as Portree for many years has got perked up on Lowland, & even English lines!. There is no use talking about this side of of our Hebridean existence—it is too much complicated—like the separation of the Sister Kingdoms of Scotland & Ireland since the times of Queen Elizabeth; and the over-throw before then, of the Macdonald dynasty, with a streak of religious fanaticism among the politics of the three Kingdoms interacting on one another.

It pleased me much to listen to Miss Patuffa's music; and to know Marley who is a health-causing inmate for mind & body, and a most precious possession! And then Miss Kennedy—you shod me so kindly and set me on my way. I remembered all this on awaking, and must thank you all again for a delightful afternoon.

Yours most sincerely,
FRANCES TOLMIE

On Tuesday, 21 January, Mrs Kennedy-Fraser introduced her new album at a recital in the Music Hall, George Street. She was assisted by her two sisters, Mrs Matthay, the reciter, and Miss Margaret Kennedy, the singer, with Mrs Begbie, harp and Miss Winifred Smith, violin. Referring to this concert, Miss Tolmie wrote:

January 22nd [*1913*]

Last evening, my sister being better, and a friend staying with her, I had the great pleasure of feeling quite free to repair to the Music Hall, and listen once more to the ancient melodies of our country adapted to the conditions of the present day. In peace I sat hearing each varied theme needing so much care and experience in arrangement and performance, & which seemed so fitted to the personality of each player and singer, & reciter; and have only one remark to make that I never enjoyed a concert more.

The bearers of your own special tickets, came away full of enthusiasm and delight. Farewell now, dear Mrs. Kennedy-Fraser—wishing a blessing on each head, and heart, and hand, believe me to be,

Affectionately yours
FRANCES TOLMIE

Mary Tolmie died in December 1913. Fanny remained in Merchiston Crescent until the spring of 1915. Her advancing years, the coming of war and the deaths of older friends—among them Alexander Carmichael and Neil MacLeod—inclined her towards returning to Skye to end her days there and to be buried, when her time came, beside her father. This last, her younger relatives looked upon as a rather romantic notion; she had been so young when he died that she could surely have very little recollection of him. They, perhaps, knew nothing of the early episode she had confided to Lucy Broadwood of her 'first prayer' as he lay dying in the bed with its bird-patterned curtains.

Miss Margaret Skene has told of how Aunt Fanny in her later years in Edinburgh was harassed at times by visitors who would come 'bouncing in' with some inquiry to which, at the moment, she could find no reply. The eager visitor gone, she would go through to the kitchen, and she and Mary Ross would be heard conversing in Gaelic and humming snatches of tune. Aunt Fanny was slow and deliberate in mind and movement, aimed always at meticulous accuracy, and could not be hurried. To get something right, to be true to oneself or another person one must at times draw aside and concentrate: 'I know [she writes] that a certain degree of reserve is necessary to pursue order where many interests & sympathies crowd in—one cannot respond to the best of people sometimes, when there [are] many claims on the attention.'[17] A fortnight might pass before she had solved the problem whatever it was.

In April or May 1915 the move was made. Accompanied by Mary Ross, she left Edinburgh to spend a night en route in the manse at Kiltarlity. That must have been the occasion when a young Free Church missionary student caught sight of two tall women in Beauly,[18]— possibly on the railway station—but no one could tell him who they were. Both were dressed in black, the more striking of the two—'with long face and piercing eyes—wearing a veil of the type worn in the early days of cars . . . might have been taken for a member of some Anglican sisterhood'.[19] Not until eight or nine years later did the Rev. Donald Mackinnon, by that time Free Church Minister in Portree, recognize in Dunvegan the mysterious lady he had seen at Beauly.

Miss Tolmie was to occupy a cottage near the harbour, but at first stayed for a time with her cousin John Mackenzie and his wife Margaret Tolmie (her niece) from New Zealand, who had been married at 37 Merchiston Crescent nine years before. John had meanwhile succeeded his father, John Tolmie Mackenzie, as factor to MacLeod of MacLeod, as harbour master and in other public capacities.

The following letter from Dunvegan, Isle of Skye, addressed to Mrs Kennedy-Fraser is dated 28 May [1915]:

In reply to your question, I regret that I have no more Gaelic words to that tune, to which you refer. It was usually sung in an impromptu manner, according to circumstances. If I remember

125

exactly the song to which you allude, (for the collection has not yet been unpacked) it begins with a refrain representing the Cock as announcing before Dawn to the initiated in his language, the events, especially the courtships & weddings of the coming time; thus giving opportunity to the singer who led the refrain, for droll associations of names, as well as serious forecasts of genuine feeling among the parties mentioned—she could add what she liked and vary it to suit the taste of the 'waulking-board', as well as that of the interested audience.

> Refrain.
> The Cock 'will be crowing'—
> (a form of present tense)
> an hour before day.
> V.I. He announced,
>   who is coming.
> a short refrain—
> V.II. another line.

I cannot remember the words I wrote—but you are free in English or Gaelic to do, as these waulking women did. Any other question I shall always gladly answer.

Mary Ross has come, but we cannot get into the house yet, as a dilatory man has left his things lying there, & mine are ready to enter. My peats are being cut in the moor. Very few ships are coming in, and we are to have no coal this year.

With kindest remembrances to Miss Kennedy, and Miss Eilidh,[20] and hoping that Professor Kennedy Fraser is well, believe me to [be] ever affectionately yours,

FRANCES TOLMIE

Now in her mid-seventies, she felt, in spite of wartime stringencies, a satisfaction in returning to the place to which she belonged. Through all the upset of moving house she was as intellectually alert and as helpful as ever.

CHAPTER 13

'SONGS OF THE HEBRIDES'

I do not wish to step out among the scholars—I am ready enough to appear among those who remember.

Frances Tolmie

I had certainly brought home with me a good haul of tunes—others could collect and write down the Gaelic words.

Marjory Kennedy-Fraser[1]

The *Journal of the Folk-Song Society*, no. 16, 1911, remains the definitive edition of Frances Tolmie's collection of traditional Gaelic songs. Keith Norman MacDonald's *Gesto Collection* (appendix, pp. 1–68) and his *Puirt-a-Beul* form a valuable complement, supplying Gaelic words for ten songs in the *Journal* that have English translation only, except for the line of Gaelic underlying the tune. The very lack of editing in MacDonald's works ensures the preservation of the songs as Miss Tolmie heard and noted them, without 'improvement' or alteration.

In different guise are the derivatives from some of her songs as presented by Marjory Kennedy-Fraser in *Songs of the Hebrides*.[2] The various volumes contain 212 songs with pianoforte accompaniment and some 120 unaccompanied tunes (with or without words) in the introductions. Twenty-one of the former (to 22 tunes) and four of the latter are identifiable as having originated with Miss Tolmie. In the early days of their acquaintance it is likely, from internal and other evidence, that Miss Tolmie lent to Mrs Kennedy-Fraser her own copies of *The Gesto Collection* and *Puirt-a-Beul*, in which certain of her songs were to be found [Plates 12 and 13]. In assessing the debt of Mrs Kennedy-Fraser to Miss Tolmie it is all along important to bear in mind the dates of their acquaintance and the timing of their respective published collections of songs. Miss Tolmie's and Mrs Kennedy-Fraser's titles and ascriptions are listed side by side in appendix B of this book.

When the two ladies met in 1907 Mrs Kennedy-Fraser was an established music teacher and lecturer; she also worked for some years as music critic on the *Edinburgh Evening News*. She was a daughter of David Kennedy (1825–86), the noted Scottish singer who from 1866 carried out his project of singing Lowland Scots songs to emigrated Scots throughout the British Empire and in the United States.

Kennedy had left his native Perth and the trade of house-painter to follow a musical profession in Edinburgh as precentor in Nicolson Street United Presbyterian Church, concert singer and teacher. Twice married, he trained his five sons and six daughters as singers; as they grew up they accompanied him in threes and fours on his extensive tours and often adventurous journeys.[3] Between times they enjoyed periods of vocal study with noted continental teachers, chiefly in Milan. The tragedy at Nice in 1881, when two daughters and a son perished in a fire at the Théâtre des Italiens, where they had gone to hear Donizetti's opera *Lucia di Lammermoor*, aroused much public sympathy and was long remembered.

Marjory, the fifth of the family and second child of the second marriage, was her father's accompanist off and on from the age of twelve. She had her share of continental study, including spells in Milan with Lamperti and in Paris with Mathilde Marchesi. In 1887 she married her mother's young cousin, Alec Yule Fraser, who at the age of thirty-two became headmaster of Allan Glen's Technical School in Glasgow. He died in 1890, leaving her with a son, David, and a daughter, Helen Patuffa.

Returning with her two children to Edinburgh, she took up music teaching. She was presently joined by her sister, Margaret, who had studied at the Royal Academy of Music in London and was to have a long and successful career as singer and teacher of singing. Jessie, the youngest, also went to the Academy; in 1893 she married her pianoforte professor, Tobias Matthay.

Matthay (1858–1945), in his teaching at the Royal Academy, in his own Pianoforte School and in *The Act of Touch* (London, 1903), and other books, exerted a wide and refreshing influence upon the pianoforte teaching of his day, preaching a persuasive rather than an aggressive approach to the keyboard. His sister-in-law became his enthusiastic disciple; the accompaniments she wrote later relied for their most effective performance upon Matthay's principles, particularly in the matter of *tempo rubato*.

In 1900 Mrs Kennedy-Fraser became a founder-member of the Edinburgh Musical Education Society, an offshoot from the Incorporated Society of Musicians, which had been established some years earlier. I myself, a member from 1912, look back with pleasure on those fortnightly meetings in the university music classroom (now the Reid Concert Hall), presided over by Professor Frederic Niecks[4] and later by Professor Donald Francis Tovey. Lectures on new composers, new music, new books on music and allied topics were delivered to appreciative young music teachers, who were mainly pianists. Mrs Kennedy-Fraser's lectures on *Lieder*, which she entitled 'Songs and Song-writers', were in turn an offshoot from the EMES, and lasted through the winter seasons from 1903 to 1907.[5]

My contemporaries and I were immensely stimulated by her and her teaching. She had clearly been well trained as an accompanist by her father, and as a singer by celebrated continental teachers; she had seen the world; above all she had a flair for putting over whatever she had absorbed herself. She began her collecting in the early 1900s at the beginning of the Edwardian age, with which she may be closely identified. The Victorian age was gone; a new era of liberation had come, expressing itself in a variety of social forms—dress, dance, mode of thought and manner of speech, women's suffrage and the Labour movement. Permeating all this there was amongst the intelligentsia a fascination with what one might term the nebulous, as evidenced in Debussy's *Pelléas et Mélisande*, Maeterlinck's *Blue Bird*, Barrie's *Peter Pan*.[6] Marjory Kennedy-Fraser was abreast of her time, and so when she found that her first Hebridean lecture-recital in Edinburgh in 1907 aroused great interest, then, as she herself says, she felt justified in confining herself in the future to Hebridean research and song [Plate 15].

The seed of the *Songs of the Hebrides* is to be found earlier, when Mrs Kennedy-Fraser became acquainted with L. A. Bourgault-Ducoudray's volume of Breton folk songs, with their apt accompaniments and singable French translations.[7] 'I felt that there might still be a like work to do among the Scots Gaels, and that I could do it, if only I knew where to begin.'[8]

The Ducoudray Breton songs had come to her notice in 1895. They were borrowed for her by her sister, Mrs Matthay, from the Welsh singer, Mary Davies. At that time Mrs Kennedy-Fraser was gathering material for some lecture-recitals on Celtic music (Scottish and Irish Gaelic, Manx, Welsh, Cornish and Breton) that she was to give at the 'Summer Meeting' conducted by Patrick Geddes and J. Arthur Thomson,[9] at the Outlook Tower on the Castle Hill. Geddes (1854–1932), Professor of Botany at Dundee, a man of boundless energy, capable of excelling in each of many fields in which he was interested, is remembered chiefly as a pioneer of town-planning.[10] At the Outlook Tower he attracted summer and winter what was sometimes described as a 'colony' of writers, artists and intellectuals. He attributed the idea of organizing the 'Summer Meetings', held between 1887 and 1899 and said to be the first real summer school in Europe, to the well-known vacation courses conducted from 1874 at Chatauqua, New York.

In 1895 Geddes and his author friend, William Sharp, (1855–1905) embarked upon a publishing enterprise. Under the imprint, 'Patrick Geddes and Colleagues', they published an imaginative but short-lived 'northern quarterly', the Evergreen (1895–7), and the first two books of 'Celtic-flavoured' stories by 'Fiona MacLeod'. Geddes and his wife guarded the secret of the writer's identity, and only later was it revealed that the mysterious 'Fiona MacLeod' was Sharp's alter ego.[11]

At the Outlook Tower Mrs Kennedy-Fraser met the artist John Duncan (1866–1945), who chose Celtic mythological subjects for many of his pictures. In 1904 he was painting on the island of Eriskay and wrote to tell her that this was the very place for the research into Celtic song that she had in mind, and that she should come out there as soon as possible. She had other plans that year, however. The following year he wrote her more urgently that there were two American lady collectors, one already on the spot and the other due shortly,[12] and advised her to come without delay.

In the early August of 1905 Mrs Kennedy-Fraser set out. John Duncan put her in touch with several singers—the youngest a child of six—who sang songs to her of which she noted the airs.[13] Later she was to write that she had brought home a good haul of tunes—others could collect and write down the Gaelic words. Father Allan MacDonald, the much-loved priest, folklorist and poet of Eriskay, promised to send words to her, but he died in the influenza epidemic that broke out shortly after her return.

In 1907 she gave her first recital. That summer, with her daughter, Patuffa, she revisited Eriskay and made the first of many visits to

Barra. Meanwhile she had published one or two of her songs with English words and accompaniments, and it must have been about then that she met Miss Tolmie.

The latter's note of 'Feb. 4th' [1908] was apparently received by Mrs Kennedy-Fraser after her return to Edinburgh from London with the Boosey contract for *Songs of the Hebrides*, and before she 'had to cross the Minch earlier than usual in order to go on the hunt for the words of the airs I had collected there the previous summer'.[14] The next two letters, both revealing, fall into place before Mrs Kennedy-Fraser's journey north.

37 Merchiston Crescent
March 7th [1908]

Dear Mrs. Kennedy-Fraser,

Let me express my regret to be so dilatory in sending these Airs and the song of Ailein Duinn which you fancied the other day, and I hoped to send immediately. A variety of accidents hindered me, and I must now wait till next week.

But I am not forgetting. Asking you to forgive this somewhat abrupt note, which must on no account give you the trouble of writing in return—with kind regards to Miss Kennedy, Mr. Fraser, believe me to be

Sincerely yours
FRANCES TOLMIE

March 10th [1908]

Let me enclose the songs in which you are interested, in the hope of doing better another time. No reference is needed but the 'Gesto Coll.' But Ailean Donn, the Maclean is not in the same list, and may go among your Hebridean gatherings, (without our name), *and open to enlargement of the words*—the first verses of which we have not.

We are of the Hebrides [?when we turn] as well as the folk of Barra and Eriskay.[15] Please remember us most kindly to Mr. and Mrs. Watson[16] when you meet them at Inverness. Wishing you a prosperous journey—believe me to be

Sincerely yours,
F. TOLMIE.

I may have forgotten some air or song, which I trust you will ask for when you return.

It was not until the 'late spring of 1908' that Mrs Kennedy-Fraser met Kenneth MacLeod, who became her Gaelic collaborator.[17] Frances Tolmie, who had still had no further word from Dr George Henderson, to whom she had entrusted her MSS five years earlier, responded generously when asked for help. The first volume of *Songs of the Hebrides* was now in preparation. Of some forty-five songs with accompaniment that it was to contain, five were to come from Miss Tolmie, three of them already in print (see appendix B, nos 4, 5 and 6). Another song, *Clò nan Gillean* appeared unaccompanied as an illustrative tune in the introduction.[18]

The song of *Ailein Duinn*, referred to as 'fancied the other day' in the first of the two letters just quoted—that of 7 March [1908]—was in *The Gesto Collection*, appendix, (p. 61), headed *Ailean Donn*.[19] This song, *Ailein Duinn shiùbhlainn leat*, 'Brown-haired Alan, I would go with you', is still current in oral tradition. As Mrs Kennedy-Fraser's 'Harris Love Lament' its tune both in pitch and time is near enough to Miss Tolmie's version, the alteration of key and time signatures being immaterial in performance. The Gaelic words for singing were drawn from the few lines given in *The Gesto Collection*. Kenneth MacLeod preceded the song in *Songs of the Hebrides* with further traditional couplets, along with an English translation, not intended to be sung. Example 23 shows the tune as given, transcribed from the MS, in my article, 'The Tolmie Manuscripts', which appeared in the *Journal of the English Folk Dance and Song Society*, vol. vi, no. 3, of December 1951.

Cumha an eich-uisge, 'Lamentation of the water-horse' (*Journal*, 7, and Example 9 in this book), was in *The Gesto Collection* as 'The water Kelpie's song, when his wife left him'. Miss Tolmie was taken at her word (see her letter of 10 March 1908), and no other 'reference' was given. Songs 1, 2, 4 and 5 in appendix B of this book were early notings or recollections of Miss Tolmie's.

Ailean Donn, 'The MacLean', (no. 3 in appendix B), had on the other hand been noted by Frances Tolmie from Mary Ross in Oban in 1899, a few years after the former's return from England, while she was renewing her Gaelic studies. It provides a good example of what Mrs Kennedy-Fraser and Kenneth MacLeod between them did to a song they got from Miss Tolmie.

Example 23

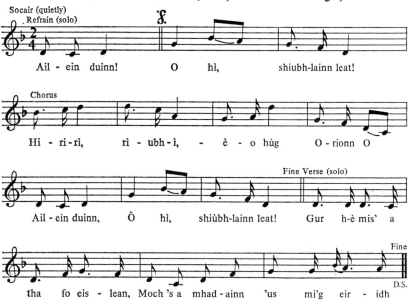

Ailein Duinn, o-hi, shiubhlainn leat! (Waulking song)
(Brown-haired Allan, o-hi, with thee would I go!)

TRANSLATION

(S.R. and Ch.) Brown-haired Allan, O-hi, with thee would I go.
(V.) Under grief am I, Rising early in the morning.

This lament for Brown-haired Allan is associated with a drowning off the Isle of Harris and is known with many variants throughout the Hebrides and the Western mainland. It may be compared with 'Shiùblainn, Shiùblainn', (*Journal*, 67), which bears an interesting note.

First the text: Mary Ross's song, *Ailean Donn* is a lament sung by a woman for her father, three brothers, her child, and—greatest grief of all—her husband, 'the MacLean', all lost by shipwreck. Text and tune went into the notebooks Miss Tolmie sent to Dr George Henderson after they had met in 1900. There are two more transcriptions of the Gaelic text among the MSS, differing slightly from each other. I have chosen one of them, giving first the solo and chorus refrains, then Miss Tolmie's translation of the Gaelic text:

133

Ailein Duinn.

Waulking Song
(not in Gesto
Coll.)

Solo   Ho rionn éile, o-ho, ì o-ho!
Chorus O-hì ibh o, ho-ro, hù-o,
        Ho rionn éile, o-ho, ì o-ho.
Solo   Cha b'è sid a rinn mo chradh-lot!
        Ho rionn eile, o-ho-ì oho!
Chorus O-hì ibh o, ho-ro, hù-o,
        Ho rionn eile, o-ho, ì o-ho.

After referring to various forms of misfortune, the Mourner continues:

'That was not what caused my anguish,
But the wave that over-turned the Boat.
My Father was there and my Brethren three,
And the Darling whom I bore, and reared.
5 But this was not the cause of my poignant grief,
But He who had taken me by the hand;
MacLean of the fair white bosom!
Allan the Brown-haired; mouth of winning speech,
Mouth of mirth and joyfulness.
10 Ruler of Mankind. How great was my love towards thee.
I used to recognise the movement of the boat
And thou love one in the chief place.

'Little Gull! O white Gull!
Come hither and tell thy news!
15 When didst thou leave the fair men?'
'I left them on the island of the sea,
Back to back, without breath,
Mouth downwards—shedding blood.'

O! how am I sorely distressed,
20 That thy bed should be among the Sea-wrack,
That the Seals should be thy Guard;
Thy white Candles, the lofty Stars,
And thy violin music, the murmur of the Sea.

Frances Tolmie must have experienced great pleasure in noting such a song from Mary Ross, who recalled it from the singing of the waulking women in Kilmaluag in her childhood in the 1850s. It is a fine poem and would have called for alertness and a good memory on the part of the leader of the singing, who had to supply a line or 'verse' within each round of solo and chorus refrains.

Miss Tolmie, as seen from the letters quoted above (p. 131), gave this song (presumably Gaelic text, translation and tune) to Mrs Kennedy-Fraser who derived from it 'The Seagull of the Land-under-Waves'. In some of the songs she used, Mrs Kennedy-Fraser adhered to the folk versions given to her by Miss Tolmie, but in the case of *Ailean Donn*, 'the MacLean', she gave rather free rein to her fantasy. For the English text Mrs Kennedy-Fraser paraphrased Miss Tolmie's translation of the few stock lines of apostrophe to a seagull and its reply; the complete tune is employed to carry but one stanza of meaningful words. Mrs Kennedy-Fraser balances this stanza with a repetition of the tune on the pattern of the original Gaelic, consisting of meaningless vocables, except for a concluding meaningful eight-syllable line of 'verse'. Two such double rounds of the tune make up 'The Seagull of the Land-under-Waves'.

In the *Journal* Miss Tolmie entitles her version of the song, *Hó rionn eile*. She gives only part of the text (quoted above from the MS) omitting the opening lines (1–7 above) and putting the following lines in a different order. Miss Tolmie's and Mrs Kennedy-Fraser's versions are shown in Examples 24 and 25.

Example 24   *Journal, 48*

Hó Rionn Eile

Sung by Mary Ross,
from Killmaluag, Skye, at Oban, 1899

'Hó rionn éil-e, O - hì - a - hó!   O - hì, ibh   o,   Hó - ró hù - ò.

Hó rionn éil - e, O - hì   a - hò!   1. Ail-ein duinn   beul   a'mhànr-ain.

135

2. *Beul an t-sùgraidh, 'sa chiùl
ghàire.
3. Rìgh nam fear! bu mhór mo
ghràdh dhuit.
4. Gu'n aithnichinn siubhal do bhàta
5. 'S tu fhéin a ghaoil air ràmh
bràghad.
6. O gur mis'tha air mo sgaradh
7. Gu bheil do leabaidh anns an
fheamainn;
8. Gur h-iad na ròin do luchd-faire

9. Do choinnlean àrd na reultan
geala;
10. 'S do cheòl-fidhle gaoir na mara.
11. Fhaoileag bheaga, fhaoileag bhàn
thu!
12. Thig a nall, is inn's do
naigheachd.
13. C'àit an d'fhàg thu na fìr gheala?'
14. 'Dh'fhàg mi iad 's an eilean mhara.
15. Cùl ri cùl, is iad gun anail.'

TRANSLATION

(*Refrain*: Hó ríonn, etc., *Chorus*: Ohì, etc.) 1. 'O Alan of the brown hair, mouth of tender tones, (R. followed by Ch.) 2. of mirth, and of melodious laughter! 3. Noblest among men, great was my devotion to thee. 4. I could recognise the movement of thy boat, 5. and thou, beloved, at the stroke-oar. 6. How it grieves me 7. that thy bed is the sea-ware; 8. that those who wake thee are the seals; 9. thy tall candles the shining stars; 10. and thy violin music the murmur of the sea. 11. O little gull, O white gull! 12. Come hither, and give me thy tidings. 13. Where hast thou left the dead [*lit.* white] men?' 14. 'I left them on an island of the sea, 15. back to back, and without breath.'

* The refrains for solo and chorus come before every line and after the last one.

NOTE The small notes are as Miss Tolmie sang the song to Mrs Kennedy-Fraser on the latter's phonograph. A tape-copy of the phonograph recording exists at the School of Scottish Studies. (Francis Collinson).

Comparison of the two versions shows that Marjory Kennedy-Fraser, by slowing down the value of the notes, while retaining the intervals, has lost the original vital rhythm of the tune. The song, with its fine pentatonic-scale intervals, has become a vehicle for vocal display.

Nor is this all. Kenneth MacLeod has added to the 'Seagull' twenty-seven lines in Gaelic and English, but not intended to be sung. They fall into four stanzas, the first having one line less than the others. Each stanza begins with the line, *Fhaoileig bhig is fhaoileig mhara*, 'Little seagull, ocean seagull', the first continuing with five lines of the original, modified. Eight lines from another song, *Coisich a rùin*, 'Hasten thy pace, beloved' (*Journal*, 53) are the basis of stanzas 3 and 4. The second stanza, after the opening line, is new, and there is a reference to 'Ruairi Og' (young Roderick MacLeod of Dunvegan), although the subject of the original is a MacLean (*Leathanach*)! To summarize: five lines from the original, eight from *Coisich a rùin*, ten new lines and four apostrophes to the Seagull, add up to the twenty-seven from Kenneth MacLeod. Mary Ross's old song, *Ailean Donn*, has been utterly transformed.

Example 25

Songs of the Hebrides
vol. 1, p. 85

The Seagull of the Land-under-Waves

Old Skye Air from Frances Tolmie
Words from Kenneth Macleod

English adaptation and pianoforte
accompaniment by
Marjory Kennedy-Fraser

Everything that Mrs Kennedy-Fraser got from Miss Tolmie in the way of songs was given to her either in MS or in print. Mrs Kennedy-Fraser defined her method in the following terms:[20]

In setting the airs we have in no case altered the melodies. We have tried merely to set them in a harmonic and rhythmic framework of pianoforte wrought-metal, so to speak, as one would set a beautiful stone, a cairngorm or the like, and have tried by such setting to show the tune the more clearly—have tried to bring out its peculiar character.

Mrs Kennedy-Fraser declared that she was 'not a mere folk-song enthusiast'.[21] In the course of an address to the Celtic Congress in 1924 she included the above paragraph. This was clearly her avowed method.

The next song of Mrs Fraser's which I shall discuss is 'Sea Sounds', a song she associated with the 'The Seagull' as amongst her best. 'Sea-Sounds' was drawn from *Iùraibh o-hì, iùraibh o-hù*, a favourite song of Frances Tolmie's. It had old associations, carrying Miss Tolmie back to 1863 when she learned and noted it from Oighrig Pheutan (Effie Beaton) who was over eighty then and recalled her mother's recollection of Dr Johnson's visit to Ullinish in 1773.

'Sea-Sounds', like the 'Seagull', is made up of only a small portion of the text of the original—lines 1, 9, 14, 13, 15, 11, 17, 19, in that order, forming four stanzas, each separated by a few bars from the next. The Gaelic refrain vocables do not quite coincide, *o-hó* for *o-hù*, *hó rionn éile* for *o ho eile* but verse and refrain are matched to the note-succession as in the original with, however, a difference in timing.

The original song, *Iùraibh o-hì, iùraibh o-hù*, is a lament, not for a sea-going man but for a huntsman or gamekeeper. A grief-stricken woman, imagining herself revisiting the place where she lived a year earlier, is on a hillock, where she can hear the sounds of nature but not a single human voice. The resulting song, 'Sea-Sounds', opens with a couple of lines of nostalgia for 'the Isles' and 'dear lov'd island sounds', and concludes with a vague desire to see a boat 'or curach from the isles rowing'. The Gaelic, incorporated in Mrs Kennedy-Fraser's version, begins with the first line of the original (as shown in Example 8, p. 34).

Kenneth MacLeod, in his introduction to this song, took 'Sea-Sounds' as his cue and enlarged upon the nostalgia of Gaels living outwith the Highlands or Islands. He ascribes a comment about the fishermen's slow sad singing indicating a heavy catch, not to Oighrig

Pheutan, aged over eighty in 1862, but to a fictitious 'young maiden of the moonlight' whom he identifies in a footnote as 'a venerable gentlewoman beloved of all who love goodness and music; and she still sings *Iuraibh o hì, iuraibh o hó*—as this book knows'.[22] In fact, Oighrig Pheutan's song was a solemn recollection of an earlier day; but thanks to Mrs Kennedy-Fraser and Kenneth MacLeod, out of the original deeply-felt lament has emerged a sentimental nostalgic drawing-room song.

Mrs Kennedy-Fraser was fascinated by the theme of the jealous woman. Her composition, 'Sea-Tangle, or The Sisters', comprises four airs, of which two are derived from *A' Bhean Eudach*, 'The Jealous Woman', the well-known fulling song and lullaby current in differing versions throughout the islands and north-west mainland of Scotland. She equated the song with the widespread Child ballad, 'The Two Sisters',[23] with which it has the common theme of one woman drowning another out of jealousy, though in form and content they differ.

In *A' Bhean Eudach* the protagonists are mistress and serving-maid, the former the wife of a man of substance[24] and the mother of three, whereas the 'Two Sisters' are unmarried girls. A well-known Scottish version of the latter is 'The Twa Sisters O' Binnorie' which opens as follows:

> There were twa sisters sat in a bower
> There cam' a knight to be their wooer
> He coorted the eldest wi' glove an' ring
> But he lo'ed the youngest abune a' thing
> The eldest she was vexed sair
> And sair envied her sister dear.

This ballad is in third-person narrative form; *A' Bhean Eudach* is, however, in the first person, the musings of the victim as the tide comes in and she drowns. The scene of 'The Two Sisters' in most versions is a river; the elder pushes the younger into the water, and the body floats downstream until discovered—at a miller's dam, for instance. In some versions the song ends here; in others a supernatural element is introduced, such as the passing minstrel who strings his harp with locks of the victim's hair and plays in 'her father's ha', the harp strings singing of themselves, naming and denouncing the criminal.

The song, *A' Bhean Eudach* basically has nothing weird about it; its strength lies in its down-to-earth credibility. Kenneth MacLeod, however, in his preamble to 'Sea-Tangle' adds a detail found in neither of the originals, the suggestion by the elder 'half-sister' to re-enact a childhood game, whereby she would weave the gold-brown hair of the younger into the gold-brown seaweed or tangle clinging to the rocks.

This addition became the opening of the song, 'Sea-Tangle', in the form of an incantation by the 'jealous one' as she goes about her deadly weaving. In the key of G, with forty-four bars in 3/4 time, it carries a reference to the song 'S fhada bhuam a chì mi 'n ceò, 'Far away I see the mist'.[25] It is introduced by twelve bars, in which the first four notes of Example 30 (see appendix C), associated with the exclamation uvil, uvil, are heard twice. These four notes, elongated at each repetition to four bars, are used as a *leitmotiv* in this song (180 bars in all), which is cast somewhat in the form of a miniature solo cantata or a *cante-fable*. The opening incantation is followed by a modulatory section to suggest the incoming of the tide, culminating in the outcry of the drowning woman, uvil, uvil. The words of the next part of 'Sea-Tangle' are again only a shadow of the original. They are set to the air of Example 29 (see appendix C), beginning with the second half; its form might thus be expressed as 'B A B'. A short section of ten bars returns to the 3/4 time, a chant on two notes, the drowning mother expressing blessings upon her children. Her last thoughts in the final section are of her youngest, a babe at the breast. The song ends with the outcry, uvil, uvil, twice in A flat, followed dramatically by the third of C major.

When one examines the song 'Sea-Tangle' it is easy to say that Mrs Kennedy-Fraser has inflated her material. 'Sea-Tangle', like all her works, was written for performance. Those of us who, around the beginning of the First World War, heard her sing and speak this story were carried away by her intensity, her artistry and by the novelty of the subject. 'She held you in the hollow of her hand', commented one of my friends recently as we spoke of her magnetic personality and the quality of her performance.

'Sea-Tangle', as performed by Mrs Kennedy-Fraser—and only its creator could do it justice—was very impressive, a strange, even grim story. She would enlarge upon her theory of the origin of such a legend—a rock seen above the water at high tide, light-brown seaweed falling away from either side of it, suggesting the head and hair of a woman drowned. When she first presented this song at one of her 'Saturday evenings' it made such a deep impression upon a rising young artist, Stanley Cursiter, later to be Queen's Limner, that he painted a few days after a small water-colour of just such a rock, and presented her with it. I long admired this little picture on the wall of Mrs Kennedy-Fraser's music-room at 6 Castle Street, when I went there for lessons.

One day I had a lesson from her on 'Land of Heart's Desire' (Example 27, over page).

This song, she told me, was founded upon a tune of only four bars which she got from Frances Tolmie, and is headed 'Air collected by Frances Tolmie in N. Uist'. After a short introduction of harp-like chords the little tune makes its first appearance, having already been stretched to six bars. Mrs Fraser uses no new musical material, the tiny tune being spread over a background of arpeggios to the length of fifty-five bars. The words, in English only, are by the adapter. The effect is that of a very simple improvisation. Perhaps its very simplicity accounts for its popularity.

And what of the original (Example 26)?

Example 26   *An Gàidheal*, vol. ii (1873), p. 165

Tuireadh bean mhic-ant-shaoir

Key F or E

:S | s:–:s | m:–:m | D:–:–|s : m :S| s:–:s | m:–:s₁ | D:–:–|m:r:m| r:–:d | d:– ‖
A nìgh'n ud thall,   Hùg ó, An cois na tràghad,   Hao - rì,   hó - ró.

It is not to be found in Miss Tolmie's MSS. for the simple reason that it was not of her collecting. There is, however, a letter to Mrs Kennedy-Fraser, dated 26 August 1910, from Miss Tolmie, in which she writes,

> I enclose a recollection of a tune from North Uist, which appeared in the 'Deò-Gréine' when it first came out.[26] It was in Sol-fa and I cannot remember by whom it was contributed—and another of those various airs to which the 'Bean Eudach' was sung . . . Mr. Kenneth may remember it. . . .

Adapted into 'Land of Heart's Desire', this was to prove a favourite

Example 27

Songs of the Hebrides,
vol. 2, p. 34

Land of Heart's Desire

Set to English words by
M. Kennedy-Fraser

Air collected by Frances Tolmie in N. Uist
Arranged by Marjory Kennedy-Fraser

Land o' Hearts De-sire,* Isle of Youth, Dear Western Isle, Gleaming in sun - light!

Land o' Heart's De - sire, Isle of Youth!......................

Far the cloudless etc.

* The Celtic Paradise

song at Mrs Kennedy-Fraser's recitals. It would be sung with ecstasy by Margaret Kennedy in her rich mezzo-soprano voice, her sister Marjory accompanying her with nicely calculated *tempo rubato* and gradation of tone. The theme, 'thou and I' in a green isle wandering free on sheen-white sands under a far-stretching cloudless blue sky, or dreaming in star-light, thrilled its listeners. The very vagueness of the words appealed to the imagination. It was easy both to sing and to listen to. Unlike the original, it was about rather than of the Hebrides. Its fanciful pictures, as is the case in other songs of Mrs Kennedy-Fraser's, lack the realism of true Gaelic poetry, that realism which Frances Tolmie always loved and respected.

No doubt the versions of Marjory Kennedy-Fraser and Kenneth MacLeod were very charming, even exciting, but it is a period charm. The two collaborators had translated their material, whether from Frances Tolmie or from other sources, into drawing-room songs that made too facile, too voguish an appeal to last.

CHAPTER 14

DUNVEGAN,
1915–26

We knocked at the door of a cottage close to the sea and it was opened by a very tall straight old woman.[1]

Miss Tolmie gave the name 'Kilchoan' to the semi-detached cottage which she was to occupy for the rest of her life [Plate 16]. Kilchoan is near Strontian, where Fanny lived from the age of twelve to fourteen in her brother's manse. The house is to be seen on the shore side of the road that skirts Loch Dunvegan and links the village with the castle. From the back, looking left, she could see 'MacLeod's Tables' (the hills, Healaval More and Healaval Beg); looking right, and from the side window of her dining-room, she enjoyed a view of Uiginish House where she was born. John and Margaret Mackenzie, her cousin german and niece who had been married in her house in Merchiston Crescent in 1906, were in Dunvegan House, separated from 'Kilchoan' by only a couple of fields and the road leading to the harbour.

John had now succeeded his father, John Tolmie Mackenzie, as factor to MacLeod of MacLeod and in various other offices, including those of postmaster, harbour master, parish councillor and Justice of the Peace. He was the second son of a large family of whom two brothers, Murdoch, the elder, and Hector, the one next to him in age, were respectively medical officer and factor over in North Uist. All three were keen historians and genealogists and their cousin Frances shared these tastes.

Their grandmother, daughter of Seoc Tolm, was the aunt Annabella, Mrs Hector Mackenzie, from whom Frances Tolmie had noted songs in the early 1860s. That was when Miss Tolmie had been living with her mother and sister at Bracadale manse and later at Ebost farm, a six-mile walk from Dunvegan. In 1915, at seventy-five, she was still a good walker and delighted in reviving these memories.

Staying with her for a time at first was her niece, Margaret Skene, to whom in Oban some years earlier Mary Ross had demonstrated in Gaelic the anatomy of a fowl. Born in Portree in 1872, she had trained as a nurse in the 1890s. She made history when, on being offered the post of Queen's nurse at Acharacle, Argyll, she accepted on condition that she would not be required to wear the customary long wide cloak. The committee were taken aback; a nurse, they thought, should look like a nurse. She knew, however, the hazards of wind and weather she would have to face, and the likelihood that some of her visits would have to be made by boat. She had been in and out of boats from child-hood and knew well the story of the drowning of her grandfather, Dr Donald MacAskill, when a sudden squall and restless cattle capsized the boat as he neared his own island of Eigg, and he became entangled in his heavy cloak. She got her way; discarded along with the cloak were the equally unpractical white starched bonnet strings.

I had the privilege of knowing Miss Skene in her last years—she died in 1961—and she told me much about her aunt. A generation younger than Miss Tolmie, Miss Skene was always very close to 'Aunt Fanny'. She stayed with her often, for long or short periods, in Dun-vegan. A great delight of Aunt Fanny's was to entertain for the evening some of her *cailleach*, 'elderly women' friends. Mrs Mary Nicolson, who had succeeded Mary Ross as maid, would prepare a 'sumptuous tea' (Miss Skene's phrase) and in cap and apron pour out for the guests. Tea things cleared away and washed up, Mrs Nicolson would re-appear, cap and apron removed, to take part in the *ceilidh*.

The room in which they sat had much to remind their hostess of the past. There were pictures, both oils and water-colours, painted or owned by Miss Rigbye; two or three, depicting Skye-scenes, were the work of S. Marshall Bulley, the husband of Miss Tolmie's old Newn-ham friend, Annie Armitage. Her piano was—naturally, one might say—a Broadwood; keeping it company was a *prie-dieu* chair that had belonged to Miss Rigbye. Over the sofa hung a water-colour of Thwaite Cottage, Coniston, painted by Arthur Severn, which was described to me by Meg Mackenzie as showing the long two-storeyed house 'with a pussy on the lawn lapping milk out of a saucer'.[2] At Christmas 1915 Miss Tolmie received from 'Joanie' Severn a copy of *The Devil's Motor*, which consisted of numerous illustrations by Arthur, her husband, to a shortish text by Marie Corelli.[3]

The war years went by. Tolmie nephews and great-nephews from Australia and New Zealand came on leave to Dunvegan and—as in so many large families—there was the heartbreak felt for those killed in action.

Norman Magnus was MacLeod chief at this time. He and his wife, as well as his brothers Sir Reginald and Canon Roderick, visited Dunvegan annually. There they and their families were always sure of a warm welcome from Miss Tolmie.

Other old friends sought her out, and new admirers also. After the war three young women on holiday came to her door. One of them, Mrs de Glehn (then Miss Marion Cassels) wrote some years later:[4]

In the summer of 1919 I was with a small party of friends at Dunvegan in Skye and being all much interested in Gaelic songs and folk-lore we determined to try to make the acquaintance of Miss Frances Tolmie. She had come to end her days where they began at Dunvegan, which is a most beautiful little place on the shores of a sea loch and close to the ancient castle of Macleod, the oldest inhabited castle in Scotland.

We knocked at the door of a cottage close to the sea and it was opened by a very tall straight old woman. She was severely dressed in black, but in her hand she carried a black satin fan, and she said with the most delightful friendliness and grace 'You are welcome, ladies.' Then she asked why she was being honoured with our visit and we replied that her fame as a collector of songs had brought us to her door and that we hoped she would talk to us a little about the old island life which she had known so well. She felt I think that our interest was real and she allowed us to spend the most entrancing time in her society. She talked of her childhood 75 years ago when the whole island was thickly populated and every farm house was full of large and happy families. . . . We asked if she would sing us one of her ancient songs and to our joy she consented, and that was a most unforgettable experience. Her pleasant speaking voice suddenly turned into the rough voice of one of the old peasant women. She sang in the traditional manner and her singing seemed to open up the past and give us a feeling of the remote savage life of the Hebrides and of its 'blood stained and dreadful history.' She

146

sang for some time explaining first what the songs were about . . .
She had the old ways, and they have disappeared.

The following year Lucy and Mollie Bruce of Braeburn, Currie,
Midlothian, granddaughters of Mr and Mrs Thomas Constable, to
whom Frances Tolmie owed so much, spent a week at 'Kilchoan' with
their mother's former governess. I myself was to have the privilege of
meeting Miss Lucy Bruce and Mrs Hector Burn-Murdoch. They had
heard of Fanny Tolmie, of her songs and her stories, from their childhood. About the time Miss Tolmie removed from Oban to Edinburgh
in 1905 she had lent Lucy Bruce, then eighteen years of age, a translation by Samuel Laing of the *Heimskringla or Chronicle of the Kings of
Norway*. 'I read all the volumes of it with great interest', Lucy Bruce
wrote me in a letter, dated 17 August 1952:

> she took us a drive to Sligachan, & had an interesting story of folk
> lore or fairy lore to tell us of all the places we passed on the route.
> What a wealth of folk lore & folk music was hers—& she looked
> like one of the ancient norns of the Norse myths, or of the race of
> the Valkyrie, so tall & gracious & stately & fair to look upon.

The road from Dunvegan to Sligachan took them through Ebost and
Bracadale, places that Fanny Tolmie associated with Oighrig Ross and
Little Margaret and the songs they had taught her sixty years before.

The Rev. Dr Donald Mackinnon, of the Free Church, Kennoway,
Fife, told me of how in Portree in the early 1920s he had corresponded
with Miss Tolmie on genealogical matters and she had invited him to
visit her. It was not until one day in 1923 or 1924 that, happening to
be in Dunvegan on business and using a hired car, he asked the driver
before leaving to take him to 'Kilchoan'. Miss Tolmie, however, was
out and they turned back. Just then he caught sight of a figure approaching them on the road—the striking-looking lady he had seen some years
before at Beauly [Plate 17].[5] He stopped the car and got out to speak to
her; she greeted him warmly, and invited him to accompany her back
to her house, but he could not spare the time. However, he walked
with her as far as her gate, and then she returned with him to the car.
They repeated this walk in 'Scotch convoy', traversing the same ground
several times, before finally taking leave of each other, talking the whole
time. He was delighted to hear from her all manner of detail about the
Beaton family of Skye, the famous doctors, on whose genealogy he was

doing research at the time. He never met her again; when she died at the end of 1926 he was in Canada.

In 1924 Frances Tolmie was elected an honorary member of the Royal Celtic Society, founded in 1822 at the instance of Sir Walter Scott at the time of George the Fourth's visit to Edinburgh. It was an all-male society, of which its outward and visible sign was the wearing of Highland dress. At the centenary it was decided to elect some lady honorary members. Frances Tolmie was among the third group of two or three, elected in 1924; Mrs Marjory Kennedy-Fraser preceded her by a year.

Frances Tolmie's scholarship was by now respected among Highland historians, folklorists and genealogists, with many of whom she was in close touch. One of her correspondents was the Rev. Canon Roderick MacLeod of MacLeod, the clan historian. The following letter to him from Miss Tolmie was kindly lent to me by his daughter, Mrs Brenda Osbaldeston-Mitford:

Dunvegan—Isle of Skye
May 6th 1925

Dear Mr Rory,

Your kindness in sending me two Numbers of the Scottish Historical Review I feel very deeply, from a patriotic as well as personal point of view. Amid the changes of recent times it is good to learn how our Fore-bears lived in other days under very different conditions, which though hard in some respects—are yet venerated, as the Good Old Times, by us all! We may rejoice over the comforts and conveniences of the Modern Age—while the Heart goes back reverently to the memories of the brave and devoted Chief and his own folk through War and Peace. And there were always saints in the Church down through the ages; them all transmitting to us our inborn blessings, in these later days of comparative quiet and Recollection of what our Fathers aimed to be—true to those from whom *they* sprang. I am no Politician nor a Theologian—but a Spectator on the Field of Life, especially in our Island Principality. I am very glad to have this Reading of our story from your pen, dear Mr. Rory. The first Number was read aloud to me by Meg Mackenzie, who enjoys doing so. I am spending the winter with my kind cousins at Greenhill, and can hardly believe that I stayed about 6 months with them:—so wonderful was the melting away of each month and so many were our interests—they so full of their duty at the Hall, and the Club, and the Nursery [?School]. It has been a wild winter and spring—as if one storm were raging all the time with breaks of a calm and heavenly evening now and then!

We were very glad that Sir Reginald was here with his party just when we had about 10 days of sunshine and cold, dry wind in April. After his departure, the storm set in again, and heavy showers of hail and rain. Our gardens are in a very backward state.—But we hope for better days soon. The Cuckoo was heard over at Uignish on May 1st.

The Countess is much engaged over improvements at her Beehive and seldom is seen on this side of the Loch. Our kind neighbour Mr Budge of the Hotel is seriously ill of some dropsical disorder: The place is full of stir by the coming and going of Officials of the Estate—of the Roads; of the Agricultural Board—Travellers from City firms—and Inspectors of Health and Schools. But we have no minister, so some of us go to the U.F. Church. There are great improvements going on at the Castle, in the garden as well as the placing of Electric apparatus within. If 'our own Macleod' comes in summer (my title for our chief in my childhood) I hope that the Roads may be better; as they could not be worse!—because of the heavy carting of timber still going on! O! I pray to be most kindly remembered to Mrs Macleod. I [was] calling at the Shoemaker's lately and was conversing with Mary Macaskill who was really very [?middling]. Donald Maclean himself has been very ill, but is now almost well; he was suffering from some chill. I offer my kindest Remembrances to Mrs. Mackenzie, and to Mrs. Mitford —to Mrs.—(suddenly gone from me)—and believe me to be, dear Mr. Rory—Yours most gratefully—and respectfully—

F. TOLMIE

She continued to enjoy playing the piano and on one occasion—either in 1923 or 1924—played Highland airs at a concert in the village hall. John Mackenzie presided and, as was the custom, ceremoniously escorted her on his arm to the piano on the platform. Later she was persuaded to sing, but this time remained below the platform, seated on a chair, erect and stately as ever, 'like a queen' as Meg Mackenzie said. Her songs were 'cheered to the echo': *puirt a beul*, a seal song learned from Kenneth MacLeod, *Dubhach, ho Leathag*, and then—

149

memory reaching back over eighty years to her mother's singing in the
nursery at Uiginish—*Uamh 'n Òir*, 'The Cave of Gold'.

Mu'n till mise,
Mu'n ruig mise,
Mu'n till mise
   A Uamh 'n Òir.
Bidh 'chlann uchda
'N am fir fheachda,
'S cha till mise
   Ri mo bheò!
'Ere I return, ere I attain, ere I return
from Uamh 'n Òir,
babes, borne in the bosom [will be] men, bearing arms.
But never more shall I return.[6]

I myself had the privilege of meeting Miss Tolmie in 1925. After
four years of teaching singing in the Nicolson Institute, Stornoway, I
had been appointed to Portree Secondary School and other smaller
schools in Skye. Although a few of us from the mainland had formed a
class to study Gaelic,[7] in Stornoway my contact with the language had
been slight. In Skye I came to realize how much I needed it, especially
when facing the Gaelic-speaking baby classes in some of the little
schools I visited. At home in Edinburgh I had had piano lessons from
Mrs Kennedy-Fraser and a few lessons on her songs, and was familiar
with the name of Frances Tolmie from the pages of *Songs of the Hebrides*.
It was in Skye, however, that I first saw *Journal* no. 16 of the Folk-Song
Society. A well-worn copy was lent to me by Miss J. C. MacDonald
('Miss Toonie'). I was greatly attracted by this small volume, and felt
how interesting it would be to hear what the real old Gaelic songs
sounded like, as sung by their collector, Miss Tolmie. Now I learned
that she was living in Dunvegan. I had to visit the school there once
every three weeks—it was twenty-five miles away—so I wrote and asked
if I might call upon her. A charming little note invited me to tea with
her on a November afternoon [Plate 18].

She received me in the dining-room of her cottage, a tall, stately
figure, eighty-five years of age. I found her to be a delightful talker and
the possessor of a happy sense of humour. She told me of how her real
collecting began, of her knitting rounds when she was twenty, of how
her mother insisted that she have an escort on her long walks over the

Bracadale moors, and of how, in preference to a girl of her own age, she had chosen to be accompanied by one or other of two elderly women, Oighrig Ross and 'Little Margaret' Gillies. Then she described how her songs came to be published by the Folk-Song Society. Looking back on that conversation, I am struck by the way circumstances provided not only the work to be done and the person to do it, but also a fitting repository for it.

She spoke feelingly of her singer-friend, Mary Ross. 'Alas, poor woman, she is now lying on her deathbed at Kilmaluag.' After singing two or three songs to me, Miss Tolmie brought out Dr Keith Norman MacDonald's *Gesto Collection*.[8] Turning up the song of the *Gruagach*, she invited me to follow music and text as she sang. At that time I was perhaps more interested in the story than the actual song. She next produced the *Journal* and sang one or two more songs. Her singing was natural and pleasing to listen to. Although I cannot remember what the songs were, I recall clearly the impression the printed music gave me of being but a skeleton of what she actually sang. It is only today in an awareness of how traditional Gaelic singers ornament their tunes that I realize how much I missed of the nature of Miss Tolmie's singing. There was undoubtedly a certain flexibility of pitch; she herself remarked, with a glance at the little Broadwood in the corner, that these songs did not go well with the piano.

From the beginning she had been encouraged by Alexander Carmichael and others to write down all she heard and learned. 'Fortunately,' she said, 'I was able to write down the tunes in sol-fa.'[9] Later, visiting North Uist, she had noted further songs. She went on to tell me how she had kept her notes for many years, 'a rolled-up bundle of manuscript'. One day in 1900, when visiting the Carmichaels at Taynuilt, she met Dr George Henderson, the famous Gaelic scholar and author, at that time Lecturer in Celtic subjects at Glasgow University. It was not until a couple of years later that she actually sent the notebooks of her songs to him. Five years in fact were to elapse after that before they were brought to the notice of Lucy Broadwood and the Folk-Song Society through Miss Winifred Parker, who heard of them from Dr Henderson.

I met her again a couple of times, but only briefly. One occasion I recall was near Dunvegan School, as the pupils were dismissing for lunch. She recognized me and we talked for a few moments. Again I recall her tallness and the neatly tied black bow beneath her chin.

Standing by was a little girl, Betty Steel (Mrs Campbell), who some years later was a colleague of mine in Lochmaddy, North Uist. I have often reproached myself since that I did not make opportunities to return to Miss Tolmie often to learn some of her songs as she sang them.

In the first days of 1927, returning from vacation in Edinburgh, I was storm-stayed in Kyle of Lochalsh for the night. The train was late, the weather very rough, and the last ferry had gone. On the boat in the morning there was talk of the funeral the previous day of the great old lady of Skye who had died on New Year's Eve. Many people had been there in Duirinish churchyard in spite of the weather. About a fortnight earlier on a wet and stormy night she had heard the wail of a cat on the roof, and opened the skylight of her bedroom to let the creature in. In so doing she fell and broke her femur. Complications followed and she did not recover.

CHAPTER 15

CONCLUSION

All my songs have been learned just within the innocent circle of
my home duties and are a true remnant of an early time.

Frances Tolmie

The value of the Tolmie collection lies not only in the songs themselves,
their words, their stories and their tunes, but in the circumstances in
which Frances Tolmie learned them; each one had a personal association
for her. Indeed the chronological table (appendix A) is a biography in
itself. In fact it is through marshalling these dates and piecing them
together with details of her life from other sources that it has been
possible to tell her story.

Her gathering of these songs was different from that of the professional collector of today, a collector who is generally a stranger to the
singers and often a non-musician, a person interested and at home more
in the text than in the tune. Frances Tolmie had the best of it here, for
she had enough musical knowledge and experience to note the tunes,
while the language was native to her. She was bilingual in Gaelic and
English from her earliest days.

She had another important asset in that she was not separated from
her singers by any kind of recording machine. Collecting has come to
have a different meaning from what it had to her. Today songs may be
recorded by someone who has no knowledge of music or of the language
that is sung, and the record may go to two others as well, one to transcribe the test, the other the tune. The process may involve three
people, and suggests the assembly line in a factory.

In Frances Tolmie's day only a pencil came between the singer and
the writer of text and tune. She herself had the unusual skill—self-

acquired—of being able to write down the tunes. She took pains: the tunes and words in the notebooks are carefully written, both her hand-writing and music manuscript being most pleasing to look at, individual in style, graceful and legible. It may be emphasized that the songs she learned from Effie Ross and 'little Margaret' Gillies between 1860 and 1862 were taught to her most carefully by these two women and, of course, in one of her two native languages.

In the preparation of her MSS for Dr George Henderson after their meeting at the Carmichaels' she added the following on the last page of the two notebooks:

> When I lived in Bracadale with my Mother at the Manse—and at Ebost—I used to walk long distances visiting various hamlets when I used to superintend knitting work supplied to the women by our much revered Miss Emily MacLeod of MacLeod who was away in England then. I always had as my escort either Oighrig Ross or Mairearad bheag nigh'n Domhnuill 'ic Ruaraidh—both elderly and most interesting and willing to sing all the way to their young associate—and tell old-world tales. The younger women, even then, were becoming *dull* inwardly, and outwardly imitative of the new smart ways—and mixing English words with their ordinary speech, following the fashion prevailing among those who had been 'sous' [i.e. 'south']. and more than 'sous'—i.e. into England. Effie [Oighrig] Ross was somewhat crazed, but very suitable as my companion on all occasions. These dear women are all dead. I might have learned more had I been older and wiser.[1]

The singers of all her songs were dear to her and that is what makes the collection so personal. Her scholarly care was a tribute to the singers, their songs and the whole culture they manifest: whether the singer or story-teller was rich or poor, sound in mind or crazed, never made any difference to her. Not that she did not also keep abreast of published Gaelic material of her day. In correspondence both with Miss Gilchrist as well as with Miss Broadwood in 1909 she referred to the various well-known collections of Gaelic songs that were then appearing —the *Celtic Lyre*, Sinclair's *Òranaiche* and others, remarking at one point, that songs she cared about were only now coming into books, adding characteristically that many of the other songs contained in such books were not as congenial to her 'as the simple strains of my old waulking women always were'.[2]

In Skye she had real friendship for her elderly escorts, Effie Ross and 'little Margaret', whose parents' recollections went as far back as the mid-eighteenth century. At the same time she loved to be with her little nieces and nephews at her brother John's manse: in fact many a nursery song found its way into her collection.[3] In Edinburgh through the friendship of the Constables she was brought into direct contact with many literary personalities of the day. Fanny Tolmie was travelled, well-read, equally at home in various cultures, mixing with the most distinguished and the humblest.

Hers was a position to be envied: 'without seeking, without asking' on her part, so much seemed to come her way. Matilda Wrench was the first of a series of cultured women of means who gave her financial security, without which she would have had neither leisure, advanced study nor foreign travel. Nor was that all. Harriette Rigbye, Josephine and Isabel Cowan,[4] and eventually Lucy Broadwood and Anne Gilchrist of the Folk-Song Society, all furthered her and her work in their own way. Frances Tolmie's experience with Keith Norman MacDonald, *The Gesto Collection* and *Puirt-a-Beul* has been described. In The Folk-Song Society she found the scholarship she had long needed. She found, in fact, two musicians, for Anne Gilchrist's share of the actual editing of the *Journal*, including her suggested scale system, nicely balanced that of Lucy Broadwood. They brought different, but complementary, qualities, musical, literary—and both very human—to the work. Their liberal annotations, chiefly regarding the tunes, side by side with Miss Tolmie's own, largely concerned with the stories and circumstances of the song subjects, add up to a volume that today still retains its freshness.

Frances Tolmie's personality impressed all those whose *ménages* she shared, even when hers was nominally a subordinate capacity. As governess to Katie and Mamie Constable and as companion for over twenty years to Miss Harriette Rigbye, she was anything but the pale down-trodden female of popular fiction. Her niece Menie MacLellan ('Clennie') was no different; as governess to the Severn children, she not only endeared herself to their mother, 'Joanie', but also consoled the ageing and often rather sad Ruskin.

The Highland girl, Frances Tolmie stood out from her class and generation in that her studiousness was given full scope. She was amongst the earliest women students at Cambridge, higher education for women being then in its infancy. Although she was only at Newnham for two terms she undoubtedly left her mark. There she was known by her fellow-students as 'the Great One'.[5] She was always gracious and dignified, with her red-gold hair, her blue eyes and the Tolmie build. Fanny was, however, one of the *Tolmaich Mhóra* in more ways than physical build: her mind was wide-ranging, her outlook broad, though within Victorian limits. 'Aunt Fanny would never have told a vulgar story', said one of her nieces; 'I doubt if she would have understood one.' That perhaps is an over-statement. Who, in any case, could have read Aunt Fanny's mind? Only once was there a question of the possible bowdlerizing of material sent to Miss Broadwood:[6]

> [I] pray you not to be uneasy that I have changed any words in Song 53, for the sake of conventional propriety. I had it from two sources, giving the preference to the singer of best ability and general knowledge, resulting in correct intuitions. . . . That was the reason I changed the words, led by comparison between the two from whom I heard the song.

She was modest about her work; it was the songs and singers that mattered to her. Confident of the honesty of her own collecting, she was equally aware of the achievements—or otherwise—of others. With the utmost generosity she would share her songs with anyone who cared to ask.[7]

It is a little difficult to assess her musicianship. Singing and piano-playing were an essential part of her way of life, and in both she was an amateur in the true sense of the word. Her singing has been described to me as 'light' and 'soft',[8] which was my own impression when I heard her in Dunvegan in 1925. Musicianship in her day, however, as far as young women were concerned, meant piano-playing. Other relatives of hers, now gone, have been unanimous that her sisters, Jane (Mrs Skene) and Mary were better pianists, as were some of her nieces, for instance Mary and Margaret Skene, and some of her grand-nieces. Her niece, Menie MacLellan appears to have been the best pianist of them all. In her later days in Edinburgh and Dunvegan Miss Tolmie is spoken of as playing the piano a lot. Her playing on one occasion served as a welcome to Winifred Parker, who had been invited to tea with her in Edinburgh: 'When I arrived her sister opened the door, and Miss Tolmie sat at the piano playing the "Robertson Rant" in my honour. (My forbears on two sides were Robertsons.)'[9]

Frances Tolmie's accompaniments, or rather basses, to the songs she diffidently sent Dr Keith MacDonald for *The Gesto Collection* are very simple, often no more than a sustained octave in the bass. Harmony was not considered to be part of a young lady's musical education and she had been taught it neither by Mary Yaniewicz nor Frau Weisse. On the other hand there were in her versions none of the crudities to be found unfortunately in only too many published arrangements of Gaelic or Lowland Scots songs. She had a moderate knowledge of tonic sol-fa, the system of sight-singing developed by the Rev. John Curwen (1816–80), which from the 1840s onward swept the country.[10] She made only one or two slips in her transcriptions.[11]

Songs were but one facet of Miss Tolmie's world of folklore; tales, superstitions, legends, sayings, bird calls, children's games with their spoken rhymes, genealogy and place-names were all within her purlieu.[12] Something of her manifold interests is to be found in her notebooks, small in quantity compared with present-day standards, but each item characteristically revealing.

Frances Tolmie's work and her life were all of a piece: whatever she did, her character shone through. So many people, relatives and friends have been pleased to talk about her. Her impressive personality can be seen in the following anecdote—one of many—told me by her grand-niece, Mrs Margaret Prance [Plate 19].[13]

Aunt Fanny was travelling to London. . . . She noticed that the only other occupant of the carriage looked very miserable—a middle-aged, gaunt, plain-looking creature.

Aunt Fanny began to talk to her, whereupon she poured out her tale. She had been Housekeeper to an old Widower . . . and had married the old man, expecting to inherit his money.

He was old, cantankerous and ailing, & she had now discovered that his money had been his first wife's and would go to his family on his death. So she had left him, in the house where they lived. Aunt F. told us that she had remonstrated with her, 'And do you mean to say that you have left that poor frail old gentleman all alone in that house?' No doubt she said more too! When they reached London the woman asked Aunt F. where she was staying, & Aunt F. gave her the name of her Hotel. Then they parted. Aunt F. was dining later in her Hotel when the woman appeared & said: 'I have been thinking over what you said, and I am going back by the night train.'

Aunt F. treated her to dinner & saw her off. Then she wrote to my Father & asked if he knew the couple, since we lived in the same street. We only knew them by sight, but were able, in due course, to tell Aunt F. that the couple were to be seen walking slowly along the street, arm in arm as of yore!

Her instinctive sympathy with others found its expression equally in her work. Songs were to her above all human documents. She was not a collector in the objective sense of the word. It is not correct to state—as I have heard—that she 'went about collecting'. There is no record of her having noted songs from the women she visited in the course of her knitting rounds. About the only instance of her collecting 'from the outside', is when, living in Oban, she was asked to go to Dervaig in Mull to note a song that someone wanted.[14]

She was singer more than pianist, yet she played Highland music both for her own pleasure and that of others. My own recollection of her singing is that it was like listening to an unknown musical language. Following the music in the *Journal* that she handed to me—I greatly regret that I do not recall what the songs were—I could see that the printed notes gave the skeleton of the tune, but I was ignorant of the style in which she was singing. I felt as one does in a foreign country of which one has learned the language up to a point, and would like to stay there long enough to feel at home in it.

But I remember her height, her graciousness and dignity and am reminded of Miss Lucy Bruce's remark that she was 'like a character out of a ballad' and of the girls at Newnham naming her 'The Great One'.

And yet—if one could turn time backwards—at Struan in Bracadale in the Isle of Skye, on a warm summer afternoon, it is not too difficult to conjure up two persons from more than a century ago—one, a young girl with red-gold hair, her imagination feeding on the Gaelic songs and stories of the other, her companion, old Oighrig Ross, as they walked over the moors together.

NOTES

BIBLIOGRAPHICAL NOTE

Rather than compile a formal bibliography I have simply named in the notes the various books and magazines I have used, as they occur in the text. All authors and my many informants are also named in the index.

GAELIC NOTE

Gaelic orthography still suffers from a licence that English has lacked for a long time, and I have not attempted to change any spellings in what I quote from printed or MSS sources. On the other hand I have not felt constrained to echo idiosyncratic spellings when myself referring to persons, places and things in Gaelic, but have aimed rather at a self-consistent and non-controversial usage. [Thus, *Fear Bhàlaidh* = The Laird of Vallay, or the song entitled 'The Laird of Valley'. *Fear Bhàlai* = Miss Tolmie's song, *Journal*, 92.]

INTRODUCTION AND ACKNOWLEDGMENTS

1 Tacksman: 'One who holds a tack or lease of land . . . in the Highlands, a middleman who leases directly from the proprietor of the estate large pieces of land which he sublets in small farms' (*Shorter Oxford English Dictionary*).

2 Compiler of *Carmina Gadelica*, in two volumes, Edinburgh, 1900.

3 The Folk-Song Society was incorporated in 1932 with the English Folk Dance Society (founded by Cecil Sharp in 1911) to form the present English Folk Dance and Song Society. The *Journal of the Folk-Song Society* no. 16, being the third part of vol. iv, which came out in December 1911, and which contains the Tolmie collection, is referred to hereinafter simply as the *Journal* or occasionally as the Tolmie *Journal*. Songs from the *Journal* are referred to by their number. The quotations here are from Lucy Broadwood's introduction, p. v.

4 In 'The Gaelic Oral Tradition', *Proceedings of the Scottish Anthropological and Folklore Society* vol. v, no. 1, 1954, p. 14.

5 The songs collected by Frances Tolmie are to be found in two appendices (numbered pp. 1–33 and pp. 34–68), to *The Gesto Collection of Highland Music*, edited by Keith Norman MacDonald, published in Leipzig in 1895 (henceforth called *The Gesto Collection*). The appendices, printed separately, followed within six years after publication and are to be found in later editions of the work. Songs quoted from this collection are referred to as *Gesto*, followed by the appendix page number.

6 *Songs of the Hebrides*, vols 1–3, London, 1909, 1917 and 1921.

7 Initiated by Zoltán Kodály, followed by letters in the press, including one in *Scotsman* of 30 March 1950, written by Douglas Kennedy, the then Director of the English Folk Dance and Song Society.

8 Daughter of the Rev. Dr Archibald MacDonald, Kiltarlity, joint editor of the *MacDonald Collection of Gaelic Poetry*, Inverness, 1911; his wife was a niece of Miss Tolmie's.

9 R. Ethel Bassin: 'The Tolmie Manuscripts', *Journal of the English Folk Dance and Song Society*, vol. vi, no. 3, 1951, pp. 61–8.

CHAPTER 1: UIGINISH, SKYE, 1840–4

1 A well-known Gaelic saying.

2 The abduction of Rachel, wife of James Erskine, Lord Grange, an Edinburgh judge, a story of domestic strife and political intrigue, has been re-told by I. F. Grant in *The Macleods*, London, 1915 (pp. 401–4), who names various sources. The incident above is from Hector Hugh Mackenzie, *The Mackenzies of Ballone*, Inverness, 1941, pp. 88f, who refers to Robert Chamber's *Traditions of Edinburgh*, Edinburgh, 1912, p. 216.

3 Usually referred to as 'the General' to distinguish him from other chiefs who bore the name Norman.

4 'The Red Man'; from the predominant colour of his checked suit and plaid in the painting by Allan Ramsay in Dunvegan Castle.

5 Most of the songs I shall be quoting are to be found in *Journal*. I refer to them as *Journal* followed by the song-number only. I have compared these with the MSS. In one case I have quoted a MS version. In quoting texts from the *Journal* songs I have kept Frances Tolmie's spelling, but have sometimes taken the liberty of writing out Miss Tolmie's prose versions as lines of verse. I have not changed any of the words. I have, however, omitted Anne Gilchrist's modal annotations. I have also used Keith Norman MacDonald's *The Gesto Collection of Highland Music* (see note 5 of the introduction) and his *Puirt-a-Beul*, Glasgow, 1901, reprinted 1931, henceforth called *Puirt-a-Beul*. The Gaelic text of Example 1 is from the latter, p. 48.

6 In MS on ten sheets of exercise-book paper among Lucy Broadwood's papers in Cecil Sharp House, London. Henceforth called 'Reminiscences'. It is given here as appendix D. I shall not give page numbers since the work is so short. The Broadwood papers contain much valuable Tolmie material. Unless otherwise stated, all letters to and from Miss Broadwood are in the Broadwood papers.

7 James Wilson, *A Voyage round The Coasts of Scotland and the Isles*, Edinburgh, 1842, pp. 430f, quoted by Hector Hugh Mackenzie, op. cit., p. 101.

8 See chapter 3, p. 20.

9 On his first taking up duty in Kilmallie it was apparent that the preaching of the Gospel required to be preceded by a more muscular Christianity, the separating of combatants in the churchyard. His strong arm inspired respect, and before long he put a stop to such an unseemly method of settling differences. See Rev. Donald Mackinnon, 'The Mackaskills of Rudha 'n Dùnain', *Clan Macleod Magazine*, Edinburgh, 1951, vol. ii, no. 17, p. 25. The whole article, found on pp. 22–7, is informative.

10 Mackenzie, op. cit., p. 100.

11 John Mackenzie, letter to Miss Broadwood, 2 February 1927. The Rev. Donald Mackinnon writes, 'one of her best poems was a lament which she composed to her brother, the young heir of Coll, who was drowned when on a visit to her at Eigg', Mackinnon, op. cit., p. 25.

12 John Mackenzie, letter to Miss Broadwood, 2 February 1927.

13 He was always known afterwards as *Tàillear a' Mhairt*, 'The Tailor of the Cow', and his family as *Clann Tàillear a' Mhairt*. See *Journal*, p. xii.

14 Mackinnon, op. cit., p. 27.

CHAPTER 2: RUDHA AN DÙNAIN, STRONTIAN, BRACADALE, 1845–57

1 The journey to Talisker and arrival there was related to me in 1952 by Mrs Brenda Osbaldeston-Mitford, as described to her by Miss Tolmie.

2 Personal communication from Neil Morrison, now resident in Edinburgh.

3 The spelling of Rudha an Dùnain varies from one writer to another: in my quotations I have reproduced the different versions given to me.

4 Loch Coruisk is the subject of one of Turner's sixty-five vignettes, illustrating the first edition of Scott's *Collected Poetical Works*. To Ruskin it was a simile for his sorrow over the death of Rose La Touche, 'a dark lake in the fields of my life as I look back—Coruisk with Sarcophagus Mountains round'. Quoted by Peter Quennell, *John Ruskin: The Portrait of a Prophet*, London, 1949, p. 282.

5 John Mackenzie, letter to Miss Broadwood, 2 February 1927.

6 *Journal*, p. 156. There follows a reference to *Journal*, 50 (i).

7 As described in Frances Tolmie's story, 'Oirig and Gormul'. See appendix E.

8 'Farm manager' (Scots).

9 An undated note among the Broadwood papers.

10 About twenty-five years ago I was struck by a remark made by a minister's wife, bilingual and well-educated, as she sat with her first child on her knee: 'It would seem strange to speak anything but Gaelic to a *baby*.'

11 This may have been the Rev. Donald Fraser (1822–69) who in 1857 became parish minister of Fearn, Ross-shire. See *Fasti Ecclesiae Scoticanae*, Edinburgh, 1928, vol. vii, p. 57.

12 An undated note among the Broadwood papers.

13 Ibid. *Cuagach* means 'clumsy'.

14 See Francis Collinson, *The Traditional and National Music of Scotland*, London, 1966, pp. 93–101.

15 *Journal*, p. 146.

16 'The word "tweed" for homespun or "kelt" was unknown in those days' *Journal*, p. 148.

17 This description of a waulking is drawn from the *Journal*, pp. 147–9, amplified by my own observation and participation in one held in the Island of Lewis in 1922. Mrs Donald Mackay, Valtos Farm, Balallan, had had a short web, possibly a suit-length, dyed, spun and woven from the fleece of her own sheep and she kindly arranged for my benefit this waulking, or shrinking preparatory to tailoring. The occasion was not ceremonial but purely functional. There were four of us taking part, two on each side of a table in a small outhouse. The waulking women still displayed in their singing all the vigour of an established tradition. See also J. L. Campbell, ed., *Hebridean Folksongs. A Collection of Waulking Songs. Made by Donald MacCormick*, with tunes transcribed by Francis Collinson, Oxford, 1969, pp. 3–16, 'The Waulking Described'.

18 *Journal*, p. 149.

19 Collinson, op. cit., p. 68.

20 This overlapping of couplets is characteristic of songs in many other languages, including French-Canadian, Russian, Ukrainian and Greek. Alan Bruford of The School of Scottish Studies, University of Edinburgh, mentions also Breton and Faroese in this connection.

21 In the *Journal*, 50, it is given its alternative title, *Bean Mhic a' Mhaoir*, 'Wife of the son of the Maor [or Bailiff]' but appears as *A' Bhean Eudach* in Keith Norman MacDonald's *Puirt-a-Beul*, Glasgow, 1901, pp. 44f. The Gaelic song which is known in many versions, was to be used by Mrs Marjory Kennedy-Fraser. It will be discussed in more detail in chapter 13, pp. 139–40. See also appendix C.

22 This outline is from a MS in my possession. *Journal*, 50, (ii), and *Puirt-a-Beul*, p. 45 are also more or less similar.

23 The Rev. Donald Mackinnon, *The Clerical Sons of Skye*, Dingwall, 1930, p. 26.

24 'Reminiscences.'

25 Between the descendants in Scotland of the three brothers who emigrated 120 to 130 years ago and their cousins—in ever-widening degree—close ties have endured. Visits have taken place in both directions right up to the

present, including those of sons and grandsons in the Anzacs during the First World War.

26 This volume came into the possession of Margaret Frances Tolmie Skene (1872–1961), a niece of Frances Tolmie. Miss Skene passed it on to a relative, Douglas Henderson, Regius Keeper of the Royal Botanic Garden, Edinburgh, who kindly lent it to me.

27 As told to me by Margaret Skene.

28 *Journal*, p. 270.

29 'Reminiscences'. Square brackets indicate my own annotations.

30 Ibid.

31 Ibid.

32 See Murdo MacLeod: 'Gaelic in Highland Education', *Transactions of the Gaelic Society of Inverness*, vol. xliii, 1960, pp. 305–34. I am grateful to William Gillies of the Department of Celtic, Edinburgh University, for his help in the latter part of this chapter. (Editor.)

CHAPTER 3: EDINBURGH, 1857–8

1 Mrs J. T. S. Watson, *Pathmakers in the Isles, 1850–1949*, Edinburgh, 1949. I have also drawn on early Minutes and Reports of the Ladies' Highland Association, in the Church of Scotland Offices, Edinburgh.

2 Malcolm Gray, *The Highland Economy, 1750–1850*, Edinburgh, 1957, pp. 124–41.

3 Watson, op. cit., p. 15.

4 Matilda Wrench, ed., *Visits to Female Prisoners at Home and Abroad*, London 1852.

5 J. A. W. Neander, *Life and Times of St Bernard*, London, 1843.

6 Matilda Wrench, *The Highland Glen; or, Plenty and Famine*, 4th ed., London, 1848.

7 Ibid., pp. 67f.

8 Ibid., pp. 12f.

9 From a private letter to Effie MacNeill, dated simply 'Sept. 26th, Kilchoan'. It was shown to me by the recipient in the early 1950s. I do not know its whereabouts now.

10 'Reminiscences.'

11 'Reminiscences.'

12 See Percy A. Scholes, ed., *Oxford Companion to Music*, 4th ed., London, 1942, pp. 452; 586.

13 I myself heard a divertimento of his on 7 December 1958 in Edinburgh at one of Eric Robert's Connoisseur Concerts. During the Edinburgh Festival of 1965 the Polish violinist, Henryk Szeryng, unveiled a plaque to the memory of Yaniewicz on the wall of no. 84 Great King Street, Edinburgh, where he

once lived. It was to this house that Fanny Tolmie went for music lessons from his daughter Mary, in the year 1857–8. The grave of Yaniewicz in Warriston Cemetery was discovered after a sixteen-year search by a fellow Pole (see *Scotsman*, 30 August 1965).

14 'Reminiscences.'

CHAPTER 4: BRACADALE, 1858–62

1 *Journal*, p. 144.

2 Ibid., pp. 156; 144.

3 *The New Statistical Account*, Edinburgh, 1845, pp. 295–9, describes the Bracadale glebe as comprising thirty-six acres.

4 *Journal*, p. 144. The old manse is now called Balgown House, and in 1953 when I stayed there, the proprietress was Mrs C. MacDonald.

5 MS in my possession.

6 The local explanation given for the title of the Spoilt Dyke is that a dyke was knocked down on top of the MacDonald corpses in order to form a mass grave. This battle of Millegàraidh is said to be the second and (to date) last occasion of the waving of the Fairy Flag of Dunvegan. See I. F. Grant, *The MacLeods*, London, 1959, p. 86.

7 The Gaelic text of this lament of thirty-four lines will be found in Keith Norman MacDonald, *Puirt-a-Beul*, Glasgow, 1901, p. 47; the *Journal* gives an English translation of the whole and Gaelic of the first line only. A condensed version of this translation is in Francis Collinson, *The Traditional and National Music of Scotland*, London, 1966, pp. 8of.

8 This song appears as *Oran an t-Each Uisge—Nuair Theich a Bhean Bhuaidh*, 'The water Kelpie's song when his wife left him', in *Gesto*, p. 20.

9 *Journal*, p. 146.

10 See also *Puirt-a-Beul*, pp. 45f.

11 *Journal*, pp. 219f. The last comment is by Anne Gilchrist. In fact, as William Gillies points out, 'the hornless animal' or 'the grey one' are simply *kennings*, i.e. periphrastic avoidance of the name, for the seal. Such practice is a matter of taboo.

12 See appendix C for different versions.

CHAPTER 5: EDINBURGH, 1862–6

1 A. Cowan & Sons is now incorporated in the Reed Paper Group.

2 See *Alexander Cowan, of Moray House and Valleyfield. His Kinsfolk and Connections*, compiled by his grandson, Charles Brodie Boog Watson, privately printed at Perth, 1915, passim.

3 1814–1900; fifth son of Alexander Cowan; created a baronet in 1894. Extracts from the private diaries were kindly given in 1955 by his grand-daughter, Mrs Ella Errington of Beeslack. Beeslack is described in John Small, *Castles and Mansions of the Lothians*, Edinburgh, 1883 (pages unnumbered), as 'castellated Gothic' and stands to the north of Penicuik.

4 Elizabeth, Janie and Joan.

5 A widowed sister who kept house for Sir John Cowan, he himself being twice a widower.

6 Eldest son of Sir Walter Scott (also Walter), classmate of Charles, the eldest of the Cowan sons, at the Royal High School.

7 James Cowan (1814–95) continued his father's tradition of an annual family gathering round the Christmas tree.

8 Robert Michael Ballantyne (1825–94), author of *Coral Island*.

9 The Rev. Thomas Chalmers, D.D., leader of the new Free Church in 1843, was a second cousin of John Cowan.

10 Moray House had been dwelling-house and paper warehouse for Alexander Cowan's father and elder brother. It was sold to the North British Railway in connection with the building of the Waverley Station and the laying down of a line from Berwick to Edinburgh. The site was re-sold to the Free Church and on it was built the Normal School, involving the destruction of a 'peerless garden'. On this site the Moray House College of Education now stands.

11 Told me by Marie L. Barker; she was reporting a recollection by Hans Eggeling, formerly of the Department of German, Edinburgh University.

12 See The Ladies' Highland Association Annual Report for 1865. There were eventually 160 'Ladies' Schools', which gradually closed, as schools under the 1872 Education (Scotland) Act were set up.

13 These three songs are to be found as follows: 'Lament for McLeod, younger of Raasay', *Gesto*, p. 17; 'A Song about the Gruagach', *Journal*, 42, *Gesto*, p. 19; 'Ailein, Ailein', 'Alan, Alan, long is thy slumber', *Journal*, 64, *Gesto*, p. 16.

14 Ladies' Highland Association Annual Report for 1869.

15 The Wrench family tree was lent to me by the late Miss Winifred Wrench, sister of Sir Evelyn; family detail was kindly supplied by F. A. Wrench, Sheffield.

CHAPTER 6: PORTREE, NAIRN, NORTH UIST, CONTIN, 1866–73

1 Of the Skene family of seven, the two daughters, Mary (1863–1933) and Margaret (1872–1961) were later to be closely associated with 'Aunt Fanny'. See chapter 10 onwards.

2 Margaret Skene told me of one such crossing when she was a child in the late 1870s.

3 Their mother, Barbara Tolmie, wife of Captain John MacDonald, tacksman of Scolpaig, had been—like Miss Tolmie's father and Mrs Hector Mackenzie —one of the large family of Seoc Tolm.

4 For comments upon the qualities of John MacDonald (1824–88), a man described as 'possessing the implicit confidence of proprietors and tenants alike' (Alexander Carmichael in appendix A of the Report of the Napier Commission of 1883, p. 455), see H. H. Mackenzie, *The Mackenzies of Ballone*, Inverness, 1941, pp. 97ff.

5 This note comes in the MS, after twenty-five couplets in Gaelic.

6 On an undated note among a list of singers in Miss Tolmie's handwriting, among the Broadwood papers in Cecil Sharp House.

7 See *Journal*, p. 271, note.

8 Miss Emily knew Gaelic and was musical. As a girl she on one occasion sang Gaelic songs to Mendelssohn and Moscheles who had come to dinner at the house of her father (twenty-fourth Chief) in London. The two composers then sat down at the piano and improvised duets upon the airs. This was about 1833, for such improvisations were a feature of their London recitals at the time. (Told me by Mrs Brenda Osbaldeston-Mitford in Edinburgh, August 1955.)

9 *Journal*, p. 146.

10 Afterwards re-named 'Esdaile', Kilgraston Road, Edinburgh, closed as a school in 1967. Margaret Tolmie married the Rev. Archibald MacDonald, D.D., minister of Kiltarlity, Inverness-shire, joint author with the Rev. Angus MacDonald of Killearnan of the well-known *The Clan Donald*, vols 1–3, Inverness, 1896–1904, and *The MacDonald Collection of Gaelic Poetry*, Inverness, 1911.

11 See Anne Gilchrist, 'The Song of Marvels (or Lies)', *Journal of the English Folk Dance and Song Society*, vol. iv, no. 3, December 1942, pp. 113–21. See also the annotation in *Journal*, pp. 190f.

12 Told at Dunvegan in June 1954 by Mrs Mary Frances MacDiarmid, youngest of the family of Mr and Mrs Donald Allan Tolmie, while on a visit from New Zealand.

CHAPTER 7: CAMBRIDGE, 1873–4

1 For the early history of higher education for women see Vera Brittain, *Lady into Woman, A History of Women from Victoria to Elizabeth II*, London, 1953; see also B. W. Welsh, *After the Dawn. A Record of Pioneer Work in Edinburgh for the Higher Education of Women*, Edinburgh 1939.

2 I treasure a copy of *Ladies in Debate*, Edinburgh 1936, by Lettice Milne

Rae, given me some years ago by Mrs Elizabeth Siddons Budgen, who was a niece of Dame S. E. S. Mair.

3 Masson Hall was in the south-west corner of George Square, until demolished to make room for the University's new library. It is now a student hall of residence in Lauder Road.

4 Mary Agnes Hamilton, *Newnham. An Informal Biography*, London, 1936, p. 106.

5 Katherine Bradley (up in 1874), who, together with her friend, Edith Cowper, published poetry under the joint pseudonym of 'Michael Field'.

6 Hamilton, op. cit., p. 107.

7 *Newnham College Roll Letter*, Cambridge, January 1928, privately printed, p. 40.

8 Relatives say she was not quite six feet, probably a couple of inches less.

9 *Newnham College Roll Letter*, pp. 40f. Miss B. A. Clough signed the whole obituary. In addition to quotations given here it included contributions by Mrs Marion de Glehn and Mrs Kennedy-Fraser, and information drawn from the *Journal*.

10 Mrs Rachel Marshall, Cambridge.

11 *Newnham College Roll Letter*, p. 41.

12 From a copy of the will in the Scottish Record Office, General Register House, Edinburgh.

13 Details kindly supplied in a letter, dated 4 September 1968, from Mrs A. B. White, Registrar of the *Newnham College Roll* at that time.

14 Told me by Margaret Skene, Frances Tolmie's niece. 'Wrennie', 'Miss Wrennie' or 'Miss Rennie' are different versions of what must have been her aunt's pet name for her benefactor and friend, Mathilda Wrench.

CHAPTER 8: CONISTON, 1874–95

1 In MS notes headed 'Preliminary answer to questions (put by L. E. Broadwood)', dated 1908. Among the Broadwood papers. (Henceforth called 'Preliminary answer'.)

2 *Journal*, p. 146.

3 Mrs Severn devoted herself to Ruskin from 1873, when he acquired Brantwood, Coniston, until his death in 1900. She and her husband and family lived in the old Ruskin house at Herne Hill in London, but spent much of the year at Brantwood.

4 *The Diaries of John Ruskin*, selected and edited by Joan Evans and John Howard Whitehouse, vols 1–3, Oxford, 1956–9, vol. 2, p. 760. (Henceforth called *Diaries*.)

5 The full title conveys a sense of the milieu in which it was compiled. It is: *Hortus Inclusus Messages from the Wood to the Garden Seat in Happy Days to the*

Sister Ladies of the Thwaite, Coniston by their thankful Friend John Ruskin, LL.D., Orpington, Kent, 1887. The wood was Brantwood, Ruskin's house; the garden was that of the Thwaite.

6 E. T. Cook and A. Wedderburn, ed., *The Works of Ruskin*, Library Edition, London, 1909, vol. 37, Letters II, 1870–89, p. 324.

7 Ibid., p. 343.

8 Helen Gill Viljoin tells me that among the Ruskin diaries and letters bequeathed to her by Frederick G. Sharp, there are two letters from Miss Rigbye to Ruskin, one from Lausanne, 3 November 1886, and the other from Capri, 12 January 1887. There are references to 'Miss Tolmie' or 'Frances', but merely casual, for instance, 'Miss Tolmie sends grateful thanks for your kind remembrance of her.'

9 The box from Mudie's, received monthly or otherwise, was eagerly awaited by a great many people living in the country. Mudie's circulating library in Oxford Street, London, was founded in 1843 and closed in 1937. It thus marks an era initiated by development of cheap mail and rail-traffic and closed by the spread of county libraries. I recall the pleasure that a group of us subscribers to Mudie's felt in the 1920s in the Island of Lewis whenever our Mudie box arrived.

10 I was kindly shown in 1952 the MS diaries of George Holt by his nephew, W. M. Rawdon Smith.

11 See chapter 6, p. 59.

12 *Diaries*, vol. 3, p. 1135.

13 *Diaries*, vol. 3, p. 1135.

14 *Diaries*, vol. 3, p. 1137.

15 Told me by Margaret Skene.

CHAPTER 9: OBAN, 1895–1900

1 Letter to Anne Gilchrist, 8 June 1909.

2 Anna M. Stoddart, *John Stuart Blackie*, Edinburgh, 1895, pp. 4f.

3 Ibid., p. 112.

4 Rev. Thomas Murchison, D.D., 'The Beginnings of An Comunn', *Souvenir Programme*, Jubilee National Mòd at Oban, 12–16 October 1953, p. 13.

5 Ibid.

6 Ibid.

7 Letter from Francis Tolmie to Anne Gilchrist, 8 June 1909.

8 *Journal*, 49; the song is dated 1896.

9 'Reminiscences.'

10 See the letter from Frances Tolmie's cousin, and nephew by marriage, John Mackenzie, Dunvegan, to Lucy Broadwood, 2 February 1927. 'She was

always so pleased to lend her manuscripts to friends who showed an interest, and I much fear that many of them have accordingly disappeared. . . .'

11 Head of the Gesto family in his day, the eldest cadet branch of the MacLeods of Dunvegan, he made a fortune as a tea-planter in India. Returning to Skye, he bought the estates of Greshornish and Orbost and built and endowed the Gesto Hospital. He died unmarried in 1869. See Donald Mackinnon and Alick Morrison, *The MacLeods. The Genealogy of a Clan*, Edinburgh, 1971, *passim*.

12 Letter from Frances Tolmie to Lucy Broadwood, 24 November [1908]. Square brackets denote that the year has been deduced from contents and other information. Round brackets show that an envelope bearing the postmark has been preserved. Not until late in life did Miss Tolmie put in the year in dating her letters.

13 R. W. Chapman, ed., *Johnson's Journey to the Western Islands of Scotland and Boswell's Journal of a Tour to the Hebrides with Samuel Johnson, LL.D.*, London, 1934, p. 53.

14 Letter from Frances Tolmie to Lucy Broadwood, 24 November [1908].

15 Ibid.

16 'Preliminary answer' (see note 1 to chapter 8). In the last section Miss Tolmie writes 'I am 68 years old this very day—and cannot sometimes hasten like a young person'. That day was 13 October 1908.

17 In the *Souvenir Programme*, p. 18, an amusing glimpse of the bardess is given:

From 'The Oban Times' Report, 1892

The Skye poetess (Mrs Mary Macpherson) introduced this competition (female voices). She shook hands with all the gentlemen on the platform, and then invaded the judges' portion of the platform, shaking hands very heartily with the Rev. Dr Stewart, who conducted her to the singer's desk amid applause. Mrs Macpherson sang 'Breacan Màiri Uisdein'. She was not in good voice, but her song was listened to with the greatest respect and attention. It should be mentioned that before she sang she eulogised Lord Archibald Campbell for his defence of the tartan. Lord Archibald Campbell, at the conclusion of her song, conducted the Skye poetess off the platform in the most chivalrous and thoughtful fashion, amid loud applause.

18 See chapter 6, p. 56.

CHAPTER 10: OBAN, EDINBURGH, 1900–7

1 This was how she described it to me when I visited her in 192

2 *Journal*, p. 146.

3 As title page of one of the MS notebooks in the National Library of Scotland.

4 The song is *Journal*, 63. The note is amongst the MSS in the National Library of Scotland.

5 This section is drawn from *Journal*, pp. 147f., and MS notes in the National Library of Scotland.

6 *Journal*, p. 148.

7 'Preliminary answer' (see note 1 to chapter 8).

8 Letter to me from Mrs Rachel Marshall, 24 August [1952].

9 Member of the 'Wee Free Kirk', a nickname given to the minority of the Free Church of Scotland which stood apart when the main body amalgamated with the United Presbyterian Church to form the United Free Church in 1900.

10 Letter to me, undated, but enclosed with another, dated 14 September 1952.

11 In answer to an enquiry made by Angus MacLeod, formerly Rector of Oban High School.

12 Letter to Lucy Broadwood, 8 July [1908]. 'Oirig and Gormul' is reprinted in full as appendix E.

13 The Rev. John William Tolmie, in whose manse his sisters Fanny and Mary with their mother had spent over a decade, had died in 1886. His granddaughter Margaret, the daughter of John Tolmie at the Register House, married as her second husband Basil Prance of the Indian Civil Service.

14 Margaret Skene told me that on New Year's Day John Tolmie would go to hear *Messiah* at noon in the Music Hall (the Assembly Rooms, George Street, Edinburgh), his score under his arm, then at night he would dress up and sing comic songs at Carrubber's Close Mission in the Canongate, while she played his accompaniments.

CHAPTER 11: EDINBURGH, 1908-11.
THE FOLK-SONG SOCIETY

1 Patrick McDonald, *A Collection of Highland Vocal Airs, . . .* [etc.], Edinburgh, 1784, preface.

2 All the letters in this chapter, including the letters of appreciation of the Tolmie *Journal*, are, unless otherwise stated, to be found in the Broadwood papers. I have reproduced any oddities of spelling, etc.

3 See chapter 9, note 12.

4 'Monday evening.'

5 10s. 6d. was at that time the annual subscription to the Society.

6 Minutes of the Committee of the Folk-Song Society for 23 July 1908.

7 Ibid.

8 These remarks were made in some notes made in January, 1960, that Miss Cra'ster sent to Captain Evelyn Broadwood who passed them on to me.

9 Ibid.

10 See the *Journal*, pp. 207–10. The song is no. 51, *Cumha Sheathain*, 'Lament for Shehan [Sethan]'.

11 See note 8 above.

CHAPTER 12: EDINBURGH, 1907–15

1 *Newnham College Roll Letter* (see note 7 to chapter 7), p. 43.

2 Marjory Kennedy-Fraser, *A Life of Song*, London, 1929, pp. 103; 120.

3 Ibid., pp. 78; 113; 114.

4 Ibid., p. 121.

5 Ibid., pp. 140f.

6 Ibid., p. 144.

7 The twenty-six letters from Miss Tolmie to Mrs Kennedy-Fraser upon which I draw in this and the following chapter, are in the National Library of Scotland.

8 The Rev. John Macintyre (now in Strathpeffer) kindly provided me with these entries in the Celtic Union Minute Book for the Sessions from 1909 to 1938. His successor as honorary secretary, Donald MacPhail, gave me further access to the minutes. Direct quotations are between inverted commas.

9 Marjory Kennedy-Fraser, *Songs of the Hebrides*, vol. i, London, 1909, pp. 94–7.

10 M. Kennedy-Fraser, *A Life of Song*, p. 174.

11 'Hole of the Clanking.'

12 'Tour.'

13 'Blessings.'

14 'Great Man', i.e. the Devil.

15 'Sunny spot.'

16 Mary Skene (Margaret's older sister) was matron of one of the houses of Fettes College, Edinburgh, from about 1912 to 1920. Her 'fireside' hospitality and her extraordinary kindness are recalled by W. C. Sellar, G. P. S. Macpherson and R. S. Hardie in *Fifty Years of Fettes. Memories of Old Fettesians 1870–1920*, Edinburgh, 1931, edited by H. R. Pyatt, pp. 227; 245; 254.

17 MS note in Frances Tolmie's hand. Amongst the Broadwood papers.

18 Kiltarlity, Inverness-shire, is about five miles from Beauly.

19 Told me by the Rev. Dr Donald Mackinnon.

20 Gaelic for Helen, Patuffa's first name.

CHAPTER 13: 'SONGS OF THE HEBRIDES'

1 Letter from Miss Tolmie to Mrs Kennedy-Fraser, 9 August 1912, quoted

in chapter 12, p. 121. Marjory Kennedy-Fraser, *A Life of Song*, Oxford, 1929, p. 119.

2 *Songs of the Hebrides*, published in London, appeared as follows: vol. 1, 1909; vol. 2, 1917; vol. 3, 1921. Other publications of Mrs Kennedy-Fraser are: *Sea Tangle*, London, 1913; *From the Hebrides*, Glasgow and London, 1925; *More Songs of the Hebrides*, London, 1929.

3 Described by Marjory Kennedy in *David Kennedy, The Scottish Singer*, Paisley, 1887, and in condensed form in *A Life of Song* by Marjory Kennedy-Fraser, London, 1929. After her marriage to Alec Fraser in 1887 Marjory Kennedy assumed the name of Kennedy-Fraser.

4 Reid Professor of Music from 1891 to 1914; biographer of Chopin.

5 She was assisted, for the most part, by her brothers, Charles and John and her sister, Margaret. Charles became a doctor but never ceased to be a singer. John gave up law in Edinburgh for music in London, but he died in early middle life. For details of the lectures see *A Life of Song*, p. 103: 'These lecture-recitals occupied the winters of 1903–7. In the latter year one of the afternoons was devoted to "A visit to Bayreuth and Wagner's *Parsifal*", another to "A visit to the Outer Hebrides and Celtic Music" '.—A revealing conjunction.

6 See *A Life of Song*, p. 117, where Mrs Kennedy-Fraser during a visit to Eriskay, on looking into 'the oily depths' of a sea-inlet, 'murmured "Pelleas and Melisande" '.

7 *Trente Mélodies populaires de Basse-Bretagne, receuillies et harmonisées par L. A. BOURGAULT-DUCOUDRAY. Avec une traduction française en vers adaptée à la musique par FRANÇOIS COPPÉE*, Paris, 1885. Collected in Brittany in 1881 at the instance of the Ministry of Public Instruction and Fine Arts of the French Government.

8 *A Life of Song*, p. 101.

9 1861–1933. Professor of Natural History in the University of Aberdeen.

10 Patrick Geddes acquired the Outlook Tower in 1892, enlarged it and laid it out as a kind of sociological museum. It is capped with a 'camera obscura'. His many improvements to Edinburgh include the renovation of forty closes in the 'Royal Mile' and the extension of the commodious flats in Ramsay Garden, beside the Castle Esplanade. See Philip Boardman, *Patrick Geddes, Maker of the Future*, North Carolina, 1944, *passim*.

11 Rutland Boughton (1878–1960) used as libretto for his successful opera, *The Immortal Hour*, 'Fiona's MacLeod's' play of that name and some of the latter's poems.

12 They were Miss Evelyn Benedict and Miss Amy Murray. The latter published an article in the *Celtic Review* for April 1906, containing seven songs of her collecting in Eriskay; her *Father Allan's Island*, Edinburgh, 1936, contains several songs noted in Eriskay. See J. L. Campbell's centenary article,

'*Songs of the Hebrides*, a re-appraisal of Marjory Kennedy-Fraser', *Scots Magazine*, Dundee, January 1958, pp. 307–14.

13 On my own first visit to Eriskay in the summer of 1939 John Duncan was still referred to affectionately as *Iain a' Chladaich*, 'John of the Shore'. I had the privilege of visiting him in Edinburgh in the summer of 1940, when he told me of Mrs Kennedy-Fraser's first visit to Eriskay, and of the first tune she noted—which became the well-known 'Eriskay Love Lilt'.

14 *A Life of Song*, p. 141.

15 Miss Tolmie's gentle protest seems to hint that she had been hearing more than she relished of the singers and songs of these two islands.

16 William J. Watson, rector of Inverness Royal Academy, and his wife, Ella, née Carmichael. In 1908 he became rector of the Royal High School, Edinburgh; subsequently he succeeded Donald Mackinnon in the Celtic Chair of the University in 1914.

17 *A Life of Song*, p. 144.

18 Introduction to *Songs of the Hebrides*, vol. 1, p. xxiv. Mrs Kennedy-Fraser gives various titles to the introductory matter in the successive volumes; for convenience I refer to all as the 'introduction'.

19 Samuel MacLean, in 'Realism in Gaelic Poetry', *Transactions of the Gaelic Society of Inverness*, vol. xxxvii, 1946, pp. 80–114 (see especially p. 91f), quotes a poem with some lines similar to Miss Tolmie's, including the reference to the *Leathanach*, 'MacLean'. Its opening line is *Ailein duinn, a nì 's a nàire*. This and the following lines may be Miss Tolmie's missing verses (see letter of 10 March [1908], quoted on p. 113).

20 *Songs of the Hebrides*, vol. 2, p. xix.

21 Address by Marjory Kennedy-Fraser to the Celtic Congress held in the Isle of Man in July 1924, published in *A Celtic Song-Book Chosen by A. P. Graves*, London, 1928, p. 81.

22 *Songs of the Hebrides*, vol. 1, p. 124.

23 'The Twa Sisters', no. 10 in Francis James Child, *English and Scottish Popular Ballads* (1882–98) (New York, 1956, vol. I, p. 118). Twenty-one versions from Scandinavia and the British Isles are given in this volume. See also Paul Brewster, 'The Two Sisters', *Folklore Fellows Communication*, no. 147, Helsinki, 1953.

24 In the *Journal*, 50, Miss Tolmie uses the alternative title for this song, *Bean Mhic a' Mhaoir*, 'The Wife of the Son of the Maor [or Bailiff]'.

25 See J. L. Campbell, ed., *Hebridean Folksongs. A Collection of Waulking Songs. Made by Donald McCormick*, with tunes transcribed by Francis Collinson, Oxford, 1969, pp. 193; 338.

26 As can be seen, the tune is actually not in *An Dèo-Gréine* but in *An Gàidheal*, vol. ii, (1873), p. 165. The well-known pseudonym 'Abrach' is attached to it. As printed it consists of five bars. Miss Tolmie was quoting

from memory in her letter. She confuses *An Gàidheal* with *An Dèo-Gréine*, the one-time organ of *An Comunn Gàidhealach*, which afterwards became *An Gàidheal*.

CHAPTER 14: DUNVEGAN, 1915–26

1   *Newnham College Roll Letter* (see note 7 to chapter 7), p. 44.

2   Margaret and Henzell Mackenzie, known as Meg and Zella, were the daughters of Miss Tolmie's first cousin, John Tolmie Mackenzie, and sisters of John Mackenzie the factor. They used to live at 'Greenhill', Dunvegan.

3   Marie Corelli, *The Devil's Motor. A fantasy.* Illustrated by Arthur Severn, London, 1910.

4   *Newnham College Roll Letter*, pp. 43f.

5   See chapter 12, p. 125.

6   See chapter 1, p. 4 for the music. The song was identified by Mrs Barbara Fraser (neé Beaton) in a letter to me from Rhodesia.

7   We enjoyed the teaching of Norman MacLeod, Classics Master, afterwards rector of Madras College, St Andrews.

8   This was the presentation copy given to Miss Tolmie by Keith Norman MacDonald, inscribed 'To my dear friend and coadjutor Miss Fanny Tolmie, June 30th, 1902'.

9   Miss Tolmie mentions also in connection with 'Herrot's' songs in North Uist about 1870 that she marked the tune in sol-fa, in case she should forget. It was well-known among her relations that she used tonic sol-fa.

CHAPTER 15: CONCLUSION

1   Tolmie MS in the National Library of Scotland. The epigraph of this chapter appears as a marginal note written down the left-hand side of this passage.

2   Letter to Anne Gilchrist, 8 June 1909. In the Gilchrist papers in Cecil Sharp House.

3   There are families, related and otherwise, who still treasure well-worn children's books given by Frances Tolmie to their parents when they were young.

4   Half-sisters of Sir John Cowan. They took her on an early visit to Switzerland.

5   Letter to me from Mrs Rachel Marshall, 29 August [1952].

6   Letter to Miss Broadwood, 26 September 1911.

7   Sometimes, however, Frances Tolmie was disappointed with the treatment meted out by editors to Gaelic songs. Two of Mary MacLeod's songs, *Fuaim an Taibh*, 'The sound of the ocean' (*Journal*, 98) and *An Crònan*, 'The croon'

(*Journal*, 99) with a few others of her repertory went into Donald Campbell's *Treatise on the Language, Poetry, and Music of the Highland Clans . . .*, Edinburgh, (first published in 1862). She writes that she had sent some songs to Campbell at Alexander Carmichael's request, that Campbell, however, though 'full of zeal had not correct enough knowledge' and that his book therefore 'teems with extraordinary mistakes'. Letter to Miss Broadwood, 20 June [1909].

8   Letter to me from Mrs Rachel Marshall, 29 August [1952]. Contrast the impression given by Mrs de Glehn (p. 147).

9   It was through Winifred Parker that Lucy Broadwood came into touch with George Henderson of the Folk-Song Society. Letter to me from Winifred Parker, 23 June 1953.

10   At such concerts as the one in the Crystal Palace, which Miss Tolmie attended with Sir John Cowan and party, it is common knowledge that the '4000 children singing' had been trained by tonic sol-fa.

There is a tradition that the idea of tonic sol-fa occurred to a young woman, unnamed, while on a visit to Skye, on hearing the system of notation by vocables used by pipers, called *canntaireachd*, said to have been devised by the MacCrimmons, pipers to the MacLeods of Dunvegan. (Francis Collinson, personal communication.)

See also his *Traditional and National Music of Scotland*, London, 1966.

11   *Crodh Chailein*, 'The cattle of Colin', (*Journal*, 84), ascribed to Isabel Cameron of Mull, is re-written correctly in the list of *corrigenda* in the *Journal*, vol. xvii, 1912. This tune is known in many forms. The corrected version in vol. xvii of the *Journal* is a charming example in the mixolydian mode.

12   In John Francis Campbell's *Leabhar na Féinne*, vol. 1, London, 1872, are her versions of a couple of ballads, as already noted (p. 58). Verses of her collecting are to be found in Rev. Angus MacDonald and Rev. Archibald MacDonald, eds, *MacDonald Collection of Gaelic Poetry*, Inverness, 1911, and information from her in George Henderson, *Survivals of Belief among the Celts*, Glasgow, 1911.

13   In a letter to me, 30 April 1968.

14   *Òran ionndrainn*, 'A song of longing remembrance', *Journal*, 96 (i).

APPENDIX A

Chronological table of the
songs in the *Journal of the Folk-Song Society*,[1]
vol. iv, no. 16, London, December, 1911

Date	Song no.	Title in Gaelic and English	Ascription
1843–4	1 and 4	†*Uamh 'n Òir (i) and (iv) (The Cave of Gold)	An early nursery memory, Skye.—F.T.
	80	*Na Caoraich's na Gobhair* (The Sheep and the Goats)	From Eigg. Learnt in early youth in Skye.—F.T.
	22	*Buain na Rainich* (Cutting the Bracken)	An early memory from Uiginish, Skye.—F.T.
1845	3	*Uamh 'n Òir* (iii) (The Cave of Gold)	A nursery recollection, Skye.—F.T.
1846	2	*Uamh 'n Òir* (ii) (The Cave of Gold)	Learnt in early childhood, Skye.—F.T.
1848	62	*Thog am Bàta na Siùil (The Boat hoisted the Sails)	Remembered from childhood in Minginish, Skye.—F.T.
1850	65	*Clò nan Gillean* (The Young Men's Kelt, *or* Cloth)	As sung by the waulking women at Rudh'-an-Dùnain, Skye.—F.T.
1852	63	*Chaidh na fir a Sgathabhaig (The Men have gone to Scavaig)	Remembered from childhood in Minginish, Skye.—F.T.
1853	105	*Oran an t-Saighdeir* (The Soldier's Song)	Sung by Patrick Macleod (young shepherd), at Rudh an Dùnain, Skye.

[1] The titles and ascriptions are printed exactly as given in the *Journal*, except that capitals have been supplied in converting to lower-case [Editor].

* Also in *The Gesto Collection*.

† Also in *Puirt-a-Beul*.

Date	Song no.	Title in Gaelic and English	Ascription
1854	50	†*Bean mhic a' Mhaoir* (i) (The Wife of the Son of the Maor [or Bailiff])	Remembered from early youth in Minginish, Skye.—F.T.
1860	103	*Fàill ill o-ho-ro*	A memory from Eigg, revived at Bracadale Manse, Skye.
	9	*Na creid iad* (Believe them not)	Learnt in infancy, at Uiginish, Skye, and heard at Bracadale Manse.—F.T.
1861	10	*Am faca tu'n gobha?* (Hast thou seen the smith?)	Fragment heard at Bracadale Manse, Skye.—F.T.
	16	*Slàn gu'n tig Aonachan* (Be it well with Aonachan)	Sung by Oighrig Ross, Bracadale, Skye.
	26	*'Fac thu na féidh?* (Hast thou seen the deer?)	Sung in the nursery at Bracadale Manse, Skye.
	28	*Till an crodh, Dhonnachaidh!* (Turn the cattle, Duncan)	Sung in the nursery at Bracadale Manse, Skye.
	29	*Dh'fhalbh an triùir Mhaighdinnean* (i) (The three maidens have gone away)	Sung in the nursery at Bracadale Manse, Skye.
	30	*Maolruainidh Ghlinneachain* (Maolruaini Ghlinneachain)	ditto.
	38	*Dhomhnuill, a Dhomhnuill!* (Donald, o Donald)	ditto.
	39	*Brochan lom, tana lom* (Gruel thin and meagre)	ditto.
	40	*Poca sìl an t-sealgair* (The huntsman's bag of grain)	ditto.
	42	**Oran mu'n Ghruagaich* (A song about the *gruagach*)	Sung by Oighrig [Effie] Ross (cottar), Bracadale, Skye.
	44	*Chall ò ro hì*	ditto.

Date	Song no.	Title in Gaelic and English	Ascription
1861	45	*Là Millegàraidh* (The day of Millegàraidh)	ditto.
	52	*Chaidh mis' dh'an tràigh (i) (I went to the shore)	Sung by Margaret Gillies (cottar), Bracadale, Skye.
	52	*Chaidh mis' dh'an tràigh (ii) (I went to the shore)	Sung by Oighrig Ross (cottar) Bracadale, Skye.
	79	*Tha'n crodh air na lòin* (The cattle are on the marshy lands)	Sung in the nursery of Bracadale Manse, Skye.
	81	*Tha 'n crodh-laoigh 's an fhraoch* (The calving-cows are on the heather)	An early memory from Eigg, revived.
	82	*Cò ni bhùirich?* (Who will bellow?)	Sung in the nursery at Bracadale Manse, Skye.
	83	*'S tràth chuir a ghrian* (Early has the sun)	Sung by Janet Anderson (nurse at Bracadale Manse, Skye), who learned it in Eigg.
	97	*Oran do Mhac-Griogair o Ruadh-Shruth* (A song to MacGregor of Ruaro)	Sung by Janet Anderson (nurse), Bracadale Manse, Skye.
	98	*Fuaim an taibh* (The sound of the ocean)	Sung by Margaret Gillies (cottar) Bracadale, Skye.
	100	*Shibeag, Shibeag!* (Little Sibella)	An Eigg memory, revived at Bracadale Manse, Skye.
1862	7	*Cumha an eich-uisge* (Lamentation of the water-horse)	Sung by Kate MacDiarmid (cottar), Minginish, Skye.
	11	*Tha sìor chóineadh am Beinn-Dórain* (There is constant wailing in Ben Doran)	Sung by Mrs H. McKenzie, Dunvegan, Skye.

Date	Song no.	Title in Gaelic and English	Ascription
1862	43	*Cumha Mhic-Leòid (Lament for Macleod)	Sung by Roderick Macleod (cottar) Bracadale, Skye.
	50	†Bean mhic a' mhaoir (ii) (The Wife of the Son of the Maor [or Bailiff])	Sung by Mrs Hector Mackenzie, Dunvegan, Skye.
	61	†Oran mu'n Ghruagaich-mhara (A song about the mermaid)	ditto.
	64	*Ailein, Ailein, 's fhad an cadal (Alan, Alan, long is thy slumber)	Sung by Oighrig Ross (cottar) Bracadale, Skye.
	91	*Hó ró, hùg o, hùg o	Sung by Margaret Gillies (cottar) Bracadale, Skye.
	99	An crònan (The croon)	ditto.
1863	74	*Oran Arabhaig (A song of strife)	Sung by Margaret Gillies (cottar), Ebost, Bracadale, Skye.
	75	Iùraibh o-hì, iùraibh o-hù	Sung by Oighrig Beaton (cottar) Bracadale, Skye.
1864	57	Hé, mannd' thu (Ay, bashful thou)	Sung by Mrs Hector Mackenzie, Dunvegan, Skye.[2]
1870	12	An cubhrachan (The sweet little one)	Sung by Janet Anderson (nurse), Contin Manse, Ross-shire.
	17	'Mhnàthan a' ghlinne so! (Ye women of the glen)	As sung in the nursery at Contin Manse, Ross-shire.
	32	Colann gun cheann (The headless body)	Sung by Mrs MacPherson (Mary MacDonald), poetess, at Contin Manse, Ross-shire, 1870.

[2] I have kept to Miss Tolmie's dating here, even though Mrs Mackenzie died in 1862 [Editor].

Date	Song no.	Title in Gaelic and English	Ascription
1870	37	*Tha chu' ag is 'gug-gùg' aice* (The cuckoo calls)	Sung by Jessie MacDougall, servant at Nairn, from Moidart, Inverness-shire.
	46	*Cumha bhràithrean* (Lament for brothers)	Sung by Janet Anderson (nurse), Manse of Contin, Ross-shire.
	53	*Coisich a rùin!* (Hasten thy pace, beloved)	Sung by Margaret M'Leod (cottar), Portree, Skye.
	78	*Oran do Dhomhnull Gorm* (A Song to Donald Gorm)	Sung by Harriet M'Vicar (spinner), North Uist.
	85	*Laoidh Dhiarmad* (The Lay of Diarmid)	Sung by Margaret MacLeod (cottar), Portree, Skye.
	86	*Laoidh Fhraoich* (The Lay of Fraoch)	ditto.
	87	*Laoidh Oscair* (The Lay of Oscar)	ditto.
	90	*Am bròn binn—aisling Righ Bhreatainn* (The Melodious Sorrow— The Dream of the King of Britain)	ditto.
	92	*Fear Bhàlai* (MacDonald of Valey)	Sung by Harriet M'Vicar (spinner), North Uist.
	93	*Oran do Mhac-Iain-'ic- Sheumais* (A Song to the Son of John-Son-of-James)	ditto.
1871	88	*Cumha Dhiarmad* (Lament for Diarmid)	ditto.

Date	Song no.	Title in Gaelic and English	Ascription
1871	89	*Comhairl' Oisein dha 'mhàthair (Ossian's Warning to his mother)	Sung by Margaret MacLeod (cottar), Portree, Skye, and Mrs M'Vicar, North Uist.
	104	'N uair theid thu dh'àirigh-bhuachain (When thou wilt go to Buachain Sheiling)	Sung by Mrs M'Neill, Newton, North Uist.
1896	49	Caoidh Màthar (A Mother's Mourning)	Sung by Mary Ross, from Killmaluag, Skye, at Oban.
1897	5	Oran tàlaidh an eich-uisge (The lullaby of the water-horse)	Sung by Mary Ross, from Killmaluag, Skye.
	6	Caoidh an eich-uisge (Lament of the Water-Horse)	ditto.
	84	Crodh Chailein (The Cattle of Colin)	From Miss Isabel Cameron, from Mull.
	95	Oran do Ghilleasbuig òg, a Heisgeir (Song to young Gilleasbuig of Heiskir)	Sung by Mary Ross, from Killmaluag, Skye.
1898	8	Ba-bà, mo leanabh (Sleep, sleep, my Child)	From Mrs Boog Watson of Edinburgh.
	33	†*'Nuair thig mo bhodach-sa dhachaidh (When my old Man comes home)	Sung by Mary Ross, from Killmaluag, Skye, at Oban.
	47	Ill iù, hill ó, illean is ó	ditto.
	76	Eile na hùraibh o-ho	Sung by Mary Ross from Killmaluag, Skye.
	77	†O hi ibh ò (Greeting across the sea)	ditto.
1899	19	†An cù bàn (The white dog)	ditto.

Date	Song no.	Title in Gaelic and English	Ascription
1899	48	*Hó rionn eile*	Sung by Mary Ross, from Killmaluag, Skye, at Oban.
	51	*Cumha Sheathain* (Lament for Shehan [Sethan])	Sung by Mary Ross from Killmaluag, Skye.
	59	*Hó leib-a chall ó*	ditto.
	102	*Cha dean mise car a chaoidh* (My strength is gone for evermore)	ditto.
1900	13	*Dean cadalan* (Sleep thou awhile)	Sung by Mary Ross, from Killmaluag, Isle of Skye, at Oban.
	15	*'S milis Mórag* (Sweet is Morag)	Sung by Mary Ross, from Killmaluag, Skye, at Oban.
	18	*Siùd a leinibh* (Rock thee, o child!)	Sung by Mary Ross, from Killmaluag, Skye.
	23	*Hó! Mhórag bheag!* (Ho! little Morag!)	ditto.
	27	*Togaibh è, togaibh è* (Rear ye him, rear ye him)	Sung by Mary Ross, from Killmaluag, Skye. Edinburgh.
	29	*Dh'fhalbh an triùir mhaighdinnean* (ii) (The three maidens have gone away)	Sung by Mary Ross, from Killmaluag, Skye.
	54	*Hó ró, lail ó*	Sung by Mary Ross, from Killmaluag, Skye.
	55	*Cumha bantraich* (A widow's lament)	ditto.
	56	*Hug ó rionn ó*	ditto.
	58	*Air fàir an là* (At dawn of day)	ditto.

Date	Song no.	Title in Gaelic and English	Ascription
1900	67	*Shiùbhlainn, shiùbhlainn* (I'd follow thee, follow thee)	ditto.
	70	*An long Éireannach* (The Irish ship)	ditto.
1901	66	*Hill-ean is ó hug ù* (The cattle are lowing in the pasture)	ditto.
	96	*Oran ionndrainn* (i) (A song of longing remembrance)	Sung by Mr MacLachan, Dervaig, Island of Mull, 1901. Heard also at Quinish, Island of Mull.
	96	*Oran ionndrainn* (ii) (A song of longing remembrance)	Sung by Mary Ross, from Killmaluag, Skye.
1902	36	*Eóghann Bàn* (Eoghan the Fair-haired)	Sung by Mrs Arch. MacDonald, Cleadale, Eigg.
	73	*Hó ró, thùgaibh i* (Hó, ró, give it ye!)	Sung by Mrs MacLean (crofter's wife), Castlebay, Barra.
	94	*Alasdair 'mhic, o-hó* (Alexander, son of Colkitto)	ditto.
1906	31	*Na trì eòin* (The three birds)	Sung by Mary Ross, from Killmaluag, Skye.
1907	35	*Gaol nam ban* (Most loved of women)	ditto.
	60	*'Illean ò, rò mhaith hò!* (O youths most excellent)	Sung by Mary Ross, from Killmaluag, Skye. Edinburgh.
1908	14	*Tha na féidh, o-ho* (The deer are there, o-ho!)	Sung by Mary Ross, from Killmaluag, Skye.
	20	*Oran tàlaidh na mnà-sìdhe* (The Lullaby of the Fairy-Woman)	Sung by Mr Neil MacLeod, Gaelic Bard.

Date	Song no.	Title in Gaelic and English	Ascription
1908	24	'S aighearach mi (Joyful am I)	Sung by Mary Ross, from Killmaluag, Skye.
	25	An téid thu bhuain mhaoraich? (Wilt thou go and gather shell-fish?)	Sung by Mary Ross, from Killmaluag, Skye. Edinburgh.
	41	*Griogal Cridhe (Beloved Gregor)	A memory from earliest days in Durinish and Minginish, Skye.—F.T.
	68	Oran teannachaidh (A song for tightening the cloth)	Sung by Mary Ross, from Killmaluag, Skye.
	71	'Chraobh an iubhair (O Yew Tree)	ditto.
	72	Goiridh an coileachan uair roimh là (The Cock will crow an hour before Day)	Sung by Mary Ross, from Killmaluag, Skye.
	69	Iù ri ribh ò!	ditto.
	101	Caoidh leannain (Mourning for one loved)	Sung by Mary Ross, from Killmaluag, Skye, at Edinburgh.
Undated	21	'Phiuthrag nam piuthar (Little sister of sisters)	From the notation of the late Rev. John MacDonald of Harris.
	34	Ciod è 'ghaoil? (What is it, love?)	Sung by Miss Isabel Cameron, from the Island of Mull, who learned it from her nurse, a native of the Island of Eigg.

APPENDIX B

Songs which Frances Tolmie gave to Marjory Kennedy-Fraser.

KEY

Tolmie:	T.J.	Tolmie *Journal* i.e. *Journal of the Folk-Song Society*, vol. no. 16, London, 1911. The song no. is given.
	G.App.	Appendix to *The Gesto Collection of Highland Music*, compiled and arranged by Keith Norman Mac-Donald, Leipzig, 1895. The page no. is given.
	P.B.	*Puirt-a-Beul*, collected, arranged, and annotated by Keith Norman MacDonald, Glasgow, 1901. The page no. is given.
Kennedy-Fraser:	SH	*Songs of the Hebrides*, collected and arranged by Marjory Kennedy-Fraser and Kenneth MacLeod, vol. I, London, 1909; vol. II, London, 1917; vol. III, 1921. The volume no. is given in Roman capitals, the introduction page no. in small Roman figures, and the text page no. in Arabic figures.
	ST	*Sea Tangle. Some more Songs of the Hebrides*, collected and arranged by Marjory Kennedy-Fraser and Kenneth MacLeod, London, 1913. The page no. is given.
	FTH	*From the Hebrides. Further Gleanings of Tale and Song* by M. Kennedy-Fraser and Kenneth MacLeod, Glasgow and London, 1925. The page no. is given.
	MSH	*More Songs of the Hebrides*, collected and arranged by Marjory Kennedy-Fraser, London (no date, but after 1927). The page no. is given.

No.	T.J.	Tolmie		Reference and Title			Ascriptions	
		G.App.	P.B.		Ref.	Kennedy-Fraser	Tolmie	Kennedy-Fraser
1	65	—		Clò nan Gillean (The young men's kelt, or cloth)	SH,I,xxiv	Clo nan Gillean	As sung by the Waulking Women at Rudh'-an-Dùnain, Skye, 1850.	Noted from Miss Frances Tolmie in the spring of 1908. . . .
2	34	—		Ciod è 'ghaoil? (What is it, love?)	SH,I,74	A Soothing Croon from Eigg	Sung by Miss Isabel Cameron, from the island of Mull, who learned it from her nurse, a native of the island of Eigg.	'A good example of such a coaxing sympathising croon from the Island of Eigg, as noted from the singing of Miss Frances Tolmie of Skye, is here given.'
3	48	—		Hò rionn eile (Ailein duinn, beul a' mhànrain) Example 24	SH,I,84	The Seagull of the Land-under-waves	Sung by Mary Ross, from Killmaluag, Skye, at Oban, 1899.	Old Skye air from Frances Tolmie. Words from Kenneth Macleod.
4	7	20		Cumba an eich-uisge (Lamentation of the water-horse) Example 9	SH,I,94	Skye Water-Kelpie's Lullaby	Sung by Kate Macdiarmid (cottar), Minginish, Skye, 1862.	Old Gaelic words and tune from The Gesto Collection.

No.	T.J.	G.App.	Tolmie P.B.	Reference and Title			Ascriptions	
					Ref.	Kennedy-Fraser	Tolmie	Kennedy-Fraser
5	75	—	47	*Ibraibh o-bì* / *Ibraibh o-bù* / *Example 8*	SH,I,124	Sea Sounds (*Gair na Mara*)	Sung by Oighrig Beaton (cottar), Bracadale, Skye, 1863.	Air and words noted from the singing of Frances Tolmie.
6	—	61	—	*Ailean Donn* (Brown Allan) c.f. *Example 23*	SH,I,130	Harris Love Lament (*Ailean Donn*)	Note on MS: Oighrig Ross, 1861.	Melody noted from the traditional singing of Frances Tolmie.
7	86	—	—	*Laoidh Fhraoich* (The Lay of Fraoch) *Example 14*	ST,24	The Daughter of Maeve (A version of the Dragon Myth)	Sung by Margaret MacLeod (cottar), Portree, Skye, 1870.	Words collected from various sources by Kenneth MacLeod. Air noted from the singing of Miss Frances Tolmie.
8	—	—	44 2nd tune	*A' bhean eudach* (The jealous woman) *Example 28*	ST,1 SH,II,55	The Sea-Tangle (or The Sisters)	Skye tune	Collected and arranged by Kenneth MacLeod and Marjory Kennedy-Fraser.
9	50 (1)	—	44 1st tune	*A' bhean eudach* (The jealous woman) *Example 29*	ST,1 SH,II,55	The Sea-Tangle (or The Sisters)	T. J. Remembered from early youth in Minginish, Skye 1854. P.B. Eigg Tune.	Collected and arranged by Kenneth MacLeod and Marjory Kennedy-Fraser.

		Tolmie		Reference and Title			Ascriptions	
No.	T.J.	G.App.	P.B.		Ref.	Kennedy-Fraser	Tolmie	Kennedy-Fraser
10	49	—	—	*Caoidh Màthar* (A mother's mourning) *Plate*	ST,19 SH,II,182	Caristiona	Sung by Mary Ross, from Killmaluag, Skye, at Oban, 1896.	Clanranald air collected by Frances Tolmie.
11	43	52	—	*Cumha Mhic-Lèoid* (Lament for MacLeod) *Example 7*	SH,II,xx		Roderick MacLeod (cottar), Bracadale, Skye, 1862.	No title; referred to as a 'passionate 17th century lament, by the famous poetess, Mary MacLeod'. No words.
12	76	—	—	*Eile na bùraibh o-bo* *Example 21*	SH,II,xxii		Sung by Mary Ross, from Killmaluag, Skye, 1898.	Rowing Song, From Skye. From the singing of Frances Tolmie.
13	100	—	—	*Shibeag, Shibeag!* (Little Sibella)	SH,II,15	Coll Nurse's Lilt ('Shibeag, Shibeag')	An Eigg memory, revived at Bracadale Manse, Skye, in 1861.	Collected by Miss Frances Tolmie.
14	—	—	—	*A' bhean eudach* (The jealous woman) *Example 29*	SH,II,34	Land of heart's desire	[See chapter 13, p. 143, letter dated 26 August 1910.]	Set to English words by M. Kennedy-Fraser. Air collected by Frances Tolmie in N. Uist.

				Reference and Title			Ascriptions	
		Tolmie						
No.	T.J.	G.App.	P.B.		Ref.	Kennedy-Fraser	Tolmie	Kennedy-Fraser
15	103	—	—	Fàill ill o-bo-ro Example 6	SH,II,42	The island herdmaid ("Sa choill ud thall')	A memory from Eigg, revived at Bracadale Manse, Skye, 1860.	Gaelic words and air collected in Eigg by Frances Tolmie.
16	74	53	—	Oran arabbaig (A song of strife)	SH,III,xiii	Oran arabbaig	Sung by Margaret Gillies (cottar), Ebost, Bracadale, Skye. 1863.	From Skye (Reaping Song).
17	66	—	11	Hill-ean is ó bug ù (The cattle are lowing in the pasture)	SH,III,36	Uist cattle croon ('Cronan cuallaich')	Sung by Mary Ross, from Killmaluag, Skye, 1901.	Air noted by Frances Tolmie from Mary Ross, Killmaluag, Skye. Words . . . by permission from Dr Carmichael's Carmina Gadelica.
18	54	...	—	Hó ró, lail ó	SH,III,84	The return from the fairy hill	Sung by Mary Ross, from Killmaluag, Skye, 1901.	Tune from Frances Tolmie, Skye.

	Reference and Title					Ascriptions	
			Tolmie		Kennedy-Fraser		
No.	T.J.	G.App.	P.B.	Ref.		Tolmie	Kennedy-Fraser
19	50 (ii)	—	44	*Bean Mhic a' mhaoir* (The wife of the son of the maor [or bailiff]) *Example 30*	SH,III,98	A Barra love lilt	Mrs Hector Mackenzie, Dunvegan, Skye, 1862.	Two airs alternate, one noted by Frances Tolmie, the other (as also the Gaelic words) by M. Kennedy-Fraser, in Barra.
20	No number P. 228	—	—	*Hó, fream, forum* (A song for tightening the cloth)	SH,III,xxi and 126	Birds at the fairy fulling	[Two-bar fragment, quoted in an annotation.]	Air noted by Frances Tolmie in Bracadale, Skye. (Gaelic words collected by Kenneth MacLeod.)
21	90	—	—	*Am bròn binn,—aisling Rìgh Bhreatainn* (The melodious sorrow,—the dream of the King of Britain)	SH,III,175	The sea-quest or The harp-sorrow ('Am Bròn Binn')	Sung by Margaret MacLeod (cottar), Portree, Isle of Skye, 1870.	The melodies collected by Miss Frances Tolmie, Skye and Miss Annie Johnson, Barra. Words collected and collated by Kenneth MacLeod.

		Reference and Title			Ascriptions	
	Tolmie			Kennedy-Fraser		
No.	T.J.	G.App.	P.B.	Ref.		Tolmie	Kennedy-Fraser

No.	T.J.	G.App.	P.B.	Title	Ref.	Kennedy-Fraser	Tolmie	Kennedy-Fraser
22	59	—		*Hó leib-a chall ó*	FTH, 114	The uncanny manniken of the cattle fold ('Ho leiba chall o')	Sung by Mary Ross, from Killmaluag, Skye, 1899.	Noted by Frances Tolmie from Mary Ross, Killmaluag, Skye.
23	57	‥		*Hé, mannd'thu* (Ay, bashful thou)	FTH, 70	To Iona	Sung by Mrs Hector Mackenzie, Dunvegan, Skye, 1864.*	A processional by Kenneth MacLeod set to an ancient Skye Air noted by Frances Tolmie. [English words only.]
24	63	—		*Chaidh na fir a Sgathabhaig* (The men have gone to Scavaig) *Example 2*	FTH, 74	The Seal-hunters o' Scavaig ('Chaidh na Fir a Sgathabhaig')	Remembered from childhood in Minginish, Skye, 1852.	Heard by Frances Tolmie in Minginish in 1852, and by M. F. K. at Skeabost in 1922.

* See note 2 to Appendix A, p. 179

		Tolmie			Reference and Title		Ascriptions	
No.	T.J.	G.App.	P.B.	Ref.	Title	Kennedy-Fraser	Tolmie	Kennedy-Fraser
25	61	—	45	FTH,110	*Oran mu'n Ghruagaich-mhara* (A song about the mermaid) *Example 10*	The seal-maiden ('Gruagach-Mhara')	Sung by Mrs Hector M'Kenzie, Dunvegan, Skye, 1862.	Two airs, the first from Barra, the second from Frances Tolmie, Skye.
26	36	—	—	MSH,30	*Eòghann Bàn* (Eoghan the fair-haired)	Till I return (Gon an Till Mi Nall)	Sung by Mrs Arch. MacDonald, Cleadale, Eigg, 1902.	Air from Cleadale, Eigg.

APPENDIX C

Different Versions of
A' Bhean Eudach, 'The Jealous Woman',
or
Bean Mhic a' Mhaoir, 'The Wife of the Bailiff's Son'

The first of these two titles is the one by which the song is generally known. Miss Tolmie uses the second in the *Journal*; the first is used in *Puirt-a-Beul*. The text in the *Journal* is substantially the same as that quoted here from *Puirt-a-Beul* (reprinted from the second printing, 1931, by permission of Gairm Publications, Glasgow). The tonic sol-fa tunes given there above the text are here transcribed into staff as *Examples 28* and *29*. *Example 30* is from the *Journal*. Miss Tolmie notes on the music MS of the last-named, 'This air suggests the swinging of a Bell'.

A' Bhean Eudach
(The Jealous Woman)
Waulking Song

Eilidh Chailein! o ho hi ri!	Eile Challain, o ho hi ri!
Cha b'é'n ainfhios,	It was not ignorance,
O ho, hi ri!	O ho hi ri!
Thug dh'an tràigh mi,	That took me to the shore,
Cha b'è, cha b'è,	It was not! It was not!
Ach an t-ailgheas,	But inclination;
'S è 'n duiliosg donn	It was the brown dulse
'Rinn mo thàladh,	That did my alluring,
Thug gu sgeir mi	That led me to a rock
Nach dean tràghadh.	Which will not ebb.
'S a' bhean ud thall	O woman yonder,
'N cois na tràghad,	Above the strand!
Nach truagh leat fhéin	Is it not grievous to thee,
Bean 'ga bàthadh!	A woman drowning?
Cha truagh! Cha truagh!	Not grievous, not grievous!
'S beag do chàs diom!	Small is thy pity for me!
Sìn do chas bhuat,	Stretch forth thy foot,
Thoir do làmh dhomh	Give me thy hand,
Feuch an dean mi	That I may try to
Buille shnàmhadh!	Swim a stroke;

No sgòd dhe d'bhreacain
Ma's è 's àill leat!

Or a corner of thy **plaid**,
If thou prefer it.

  Theirig dhachaidh,
    Hùg O!
  Innis tràth è,
    Hùg O!
  Ceil è, ceil è,
    O hi ri o ro,
  Air mo mhàthair,
    Hùg O!

  Hasten home,
    Hùg O!
  Tell it early,
    Hùg O!
  Hide it, hide it,
    O hi ri o ro,
  From my mother,
    Hùg O!

Gus an éirich
Grian am màireach,
Mo thruaigh an nochd,
Mo thriùir phàisdean!
Fear dhiu bliadhna,
Fear a dhà dhiu,
'S fear beag eile
Dh'aois a thàladh.

Till shall arise,
To-morrow the sun!
Woe's me to-night,
My infants three!
One of them a year,
And one of them two,
Another little one of
Age to be cradled.

The same with different chorus.

  U bhil, a bhil,
Thig a' churach,
O ho rin o, ro hug éile,
  U bhil, a bhil!
'n so am màireach
Bithidh m' athair ann,
'S mo thriùir bhràthair,
Bithidh mac a' Mhaoir ann
Air ràmh bràghaid,
Fleasgach donn a'
Mhiog-shùil tlàthar,
Beul an t-sùgraidh,
  'S beul a' mhàrain,
'S gheibh iad mis' an
Déighs mo bhàthadh,
Mo chòta gorm air
Bharr an t-sàile,
'S mo chuailein donn
Air dhroch càradh,
'S mo bhràisd airgid
Air creig làimh-rium,

  U vil, a vil!
The coracle will come—(or boat),
O ho rin o, ro hug éile,
  U vil a vil.
Tomorrow hither,
My father will be there,
And my brethren three,
The son of the Lord, or Judge, will be there.
At the chief oar (ràmh bràghaid)
The handsome brown-haired young man,
Of tender, glancing mirthful eyes,
Of the mouth of merriment
  and melody,
And they will find me,
After being drowned
My blue skirt on
The surface of the brine,
My brown coil of hair
In disorder,
And my silver brooch
On a crag beside me,

'S mo fhaidirean ann	And my Beads
Lag mo bhràghaid!	In the hollow of my throat!
'S buidhe dh' an té	Fortunate for her
'Théid 'nam àite,	Who will take my place,
Gheibh i modh is	She will find respect there,
Ciall is nàire,	Good sense and modesty;
Gheibh i gobhair	She will have goats
Bhios air àrd-bheann,	That are on high hills,
Gheibh i caoraich	She will get sheep
Mhaola bhàna,	White without horns,
Is crodh-laoigh a	And calving cows that
Ruith mu'n àiridh,	Run around the shealing,
U bhil, a bhil!	U vil, a vil!

The jealous woman enticed the other woman to the shore at low water, as if to gather dulse, and then left her on a rock to drown with the return of the tide. In the course of time she married the husband of her victim. She was singing the tragic event one day, in the above words, when the husband overheard her, and was so horror-struck that he immediately put her away.

There are three tunes to this song with different forms of chorus. (Other tunes to this song are still heard. See chapter 13.)

Example 28   Eigg Tune

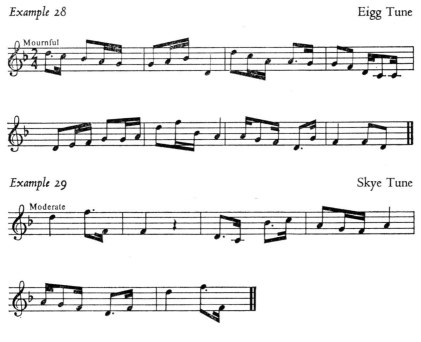

Example 29   Skye Tune

Example 30

Bean Mhic a'Mhaoir
(The Wife of the Son of the Maor [or Bailiff])

Sung by Mrs Hector Mackenzie,
Dunvegan, Skye, 1862

Eil - e chall - ain, O ho hi rì.————1.Cha b'e'n ain-nis! O ho hi rì.

APPENDIX D

Reminiscences
of Miss Frances Tolmie
MS on ten sheets of exercise paper among Miss Lucy Broadwood's papers in
Cecil Sharp House.

Let me remark to my kind and so remarkable interesting and pleasant Friend
Miss Lucy Broadwood that whatever I have done through my comparatively
long life has been attained in a tentative and intermittent manner amid the
interlacing of seemingly accidental circumstances; while under all, Aspiration
sought expression of what was best in every possible form.

I remember my first Prayer perfectly when a very little creature, and believe
that it has stood as my sole spiritual action through all these years, though
saying words many a time. My Mother was undressing me, and speaking in a
whisper, as my Father was lying asleep, and dying, behind the curtain on which
was a gay pattern of birds in a tree, much admired by me. It was a great uplift
to me to hear that I was now to kneel, at her knee, and repeat a Prayer. I was
in real earnest, and am not wiser or better to-day than I was at that moment.
'Gun sireadh, gun iarraidh' (without seeking, without asking), as a great
surprise, has each change taken place ever since, down to the day in 1908,
when Miss Winifred Parker, whose name I had never heard before, called on
me and mentioned the name of Miss Broadwood in connection with the
Collection which I had committed to the care of Dr. G. Henderson. I had
always hoped to give these remains of a bygone time to a true Musician, and
had not found one duly qualified by natural gift, and training, and gladly
accepted this suggestion of their being offered to the Folk-Song-Soc. subject
to Miss Broadwood's selection of the most suitable. Some of the Lullabies
[*Marginal note*, Uiginish] I remembered from the grand era when I was a
wandering and wondering spirit between Heaven and Earth, and my brother
Alan was in his cradle. I remember one day, it was in early Summer, when I
was in our nursery, he being fed with a spoon, and I with a large egg before
me, and a 'piece'. In a complaining voice I exclaimed that I did not like a
Duck's egg. O! said the nurse, What! not like the egg which thy own pretty
Cock laid! I was then bound in honour to do what was respectful, and ate the
egg, which however, tasted very like that of a duck.

At *Rudh' n-dùnain*, over in Minginish, there used to be waulkings at intervals,
accompanied by loud singing of many voices in Chorus; and we children used
to listen with pleasure; acting the scene afterwards in our own playground, a
hollow near the river, and outside the garden wall. We had a series of plays
for the 'Slochd' or in the nursery and Staircase, on longer winter evenings—

197

such as Macleod of Macleod and his party riding down the glen; Johnny's dead; a lamentation on our brother John, after his departure for College at Aberdeen; a waulking; a preaching, after a visit from our minister Mr. Neil Mackinnon. [*Marginal note*, deep groaning among the audience—exclamations of *Och*—Ochan—Ochan.] The expulsion of Adam & Eve from Eden was also a favourite and very noisy performance. In the early evening hours before candles were lighted, our eldest sister Jeanie, well instructed ere I began to go around, used to sing, & play on our table-shaped Piano, and I would often go and sit beneath it to hear the wonderful vibration. But the finest musical strains were from an iron gate on which we swung when waiting to welcome home members of the family & friends riding in a cavalcade down the glen. These musical sounds were afterwards recalled when I heard the Sonatas of Beethoven in Edinburgh. I have never enjoyed Music but in an irregular way, thus coming & going like the wind, echoing here—there—or as the expression of the soul of home & from the bothy in which abode Oighrig Ross in Bracadale, to the sunny abode, the 'Grianan' where I found great gladness one night in London. My knowledge of the old songs was in those days that of a careless child.

1854. My mother moved to Strontian in Ardnamurchan to keep house for our brother John who was parish Minister, and Alan & I went also. A young lady came from Edinburgh to finish my education while Alan attended the parish school. We bought a 'Collard' which had been owned by our brother's predecessor, and I was hearing all sorts of 'pieces' of music; but no more Gaelic singing was heard in the house; though a Gaelic-speaking parish. There were several Lowlanders in the community. At the end of two years we returned to Skye, John succeeding Mr. Neil in Bracadale (the surnames of ministers were never said in those days). It was then that I began to learn the songs my mother sang in her youth—that I heard John singing from the Sàr Obair to Mr. MacIntyre the School-master. Miss Whyte's mother died,—she had to leave. (Utterly un-Gaelic, she is my good friend to this day.)

Then came Miss Matilda Wrench to our parish, who knew Miss Macleod of Macleod in London. She invited me to spend a winter with her in Edinburgh, and with my Mother's consent, I went away with her in Oct. 1857. I was attending an English class every day,—taking lessons in Music from a Miss Yanewiz—a Polish lady, I believe. Mr Thomas Constable directed me to her: Mr. C. was friendly with Miss Wrench,—and arranged that I should go to church with his family on Sunday—my dear friend having a seat in a Church where the ministers would certainly be beyond a young girl's comprehension. Miss Y. should have played herself, and awaked my enthusiasm, which would then rise like a tide over all difficulties. I was not equal to my music lessons, & had no gladness in them.

On returning home to Bracadale, my spirit was always going behind the present day, and then when walking over the moors escorted by Effie Ross, I learned her songs, as the music I ought to have. And then Miss Wrench came again and I accompanied her a second time to Edinburgh—suffering much mentally. I am now a thoughtless child compared with what I then was—the music was in dire confusion—the religious opinions of the time difficult to adjust. In the interval we used to correspond regularly, & she gave me exercises to do in French and Italian. It was then that Mrs. Thomas Constable asked me to come by-&-by to stay with her, when two young daughters would be under my care. It was while with this dear family that some kind of order came into my conflicting ideas regarding the Ancient and Modern times. It was an illuminating atmosphere, from rare sympathy, social intercourse, and varied reading. I found there the 'Book of the Dean of Lismore' which I read aloud to my German Master—Herr Weisse—and with that the West Highland Tales of Campbell of Islay. In German I read Sophocles and Aeschylus—and a beautiful Hindu legend, the story of Savitri—I had music lessons too from Madame Weisse. [*Marginal note.* To which I was not equal, partly from near-sightedness (unconscious) which made reading difficult while the ear was too quick.] It was never forgotten where I came from and occasionally I might be asked to sing a Gaelic song—when my choice usually was the 'Lament for young Raasay,'—the Song about the Gruagach; and Ailein, Ailein! It was at a later period that on hearing 'Tall Margaret' Macleod sing, and Herrot in Uist, I immediately recognised what in childhood had not come to my knowledge. Afterwards came the deep slumber in England; when I was living in the bosom of goodness for many years; but never forgetting my early aspiration to be *efficient*,—in which aim I have failed—but not inconsolably so. Excuse this scribble dear Miss Broadwood—it all bears on the songs—and how I came by them, and how proud I am to think that they are considered worthy to find a place among the records of the Folk Song Society.

I had not touched a piano for more than 20 years on returning to Scotland from England, but began to recall favourite airs then, & to note down tunes when friends wanted any; first at Oban where I was 10 years, & now in Edinburgh; never forgetting the earlier period when I was like one burdened & old, who am now young with one foot on the gangway ready to sail away—away into the Unknown.

APPENDIX E

Frances Tolmie's story, 'Oirig and Gormul'

'Oirig and Gormul' was written by Frances Tolmie at the request of the Rev. Alfred Brown, minister of St Columba's, Oban from 1896 to 1905, for his church magazine. It appeared in six monthly parts, from January to June 1904.

Oirig and Gormul:
A Fireside Tale of the Eighteenth
Century

PART I

These two, Oirig and Gormul, were bosom friends, and dwelt together for many years at Tor-uaine, a hamlet in Glen-Colum-Kill, a deep, dark valley opening towards the Western sea, in an island of the Hebrides. The friendship began when Gormul, an orphan, scarcely a year old, was carried home to her own abode by Oirig, the weaveress, who was living alone, and filled with compassion for the hapless babe. Oirig was elderly, tall, and spare in figure: her hair was grey, and braided under a linen cap; about her shoulders she wore a tartan scarf fastened with an old silver brooch of Norse design. She was a very quiet person, but not therefore reserved, though still in manner, for she had always a pleasant smile, and wonderful brown eyes streaming forth glances of kindness and intelligence, which conveyed the meaning of the words she was slow to utter, and immediately inspired the child with confidence. Gormul (signifying 'Blue Eye'), was named after her young mother, and throve under Oirig's watchful care, whose goat supplied abundant nourishment for the little one during her infancy, which was a varied dream of happy events, rarely disturbed by awaking touches from the Life of Reality, in which, nevertheless, her own influence was powerfully felt.

Gormul and her young associates at Tor-uaine had full enjoyment of their time of genuine childhood, and were never dull, or at a loss for amusement at home, on the shore, the moor, and hillside. They wandered over the strand gathering strange things from afar, pretty stones and shells, or played with the advancing wave; there was free and unrestrained 'oarin'' in an old boat, high and dry above reach of the tide; they rolled themselves down a fragrant flower-clad brae into a grassy hollow where no harm could come to them, and often paddled in the burn trying to take eels and trout with their hands; on a pool they sailed adventurous fleets of tiny boats, made from the long flat leaves of the wild Iris; in sheltered nooks, while some would be intent for hours over the game of the 'Five Whelk-shells' or Pebbles, acquiring extra-ordinary dexterity in tossing them up and catching them ere they fell to the ground, others would sit patiently making necklaces of flowers. But there was always a vein of seriousness in the proceedings of these little people. Houses were constructed on a spacious, if somewhat straggling, plan, where they imitated the deportment of their seniors at a marriage feast, a preaching, or baptism; but a favourite subject of representation would be a funeral, a drowning, or the departure of the brave, with swords and helmets of rushes skilfully plaited, accompanied by a proud piper, to follow their Chief to war, when the attendant harrowing circumstances, the lamentations of women, would be acted with befitting enthusiasm and noise.

On one occasion, however, the feeling which gave opportunity for dramatic entertainment was of a joyful nature, in remembrance of the day—a day of the days—when the Chief, on an otter-hunting expedition, landed from his galley to see his people in this remote corner of a wide domain. It was with rapture the visit was ever after mentioned by them—a surprise which found them all ready with becoming speech of well-chosen words, and dignity of behaviour, to receive their august visitor. Courteously they went forth, the inhabitants of Tor-uaine to bid their Chief welcome with every sign of reverence and love, to which he responded in the ancient language of their country with equal consideration and respect. Behold! there was he in their midst, their very own, to whom they were 'sib', in varying degrees by birth and fosterage; stately, magnanimous, and kind, their hereditary Ruler and best Friend, who could stand for them before the King—the impersonation of a hero, for whom they would willingly give their lives. This pride in their chief, too deep for utterance, was quickly and surely apprehended by the young, and embodied in a play which they brought out with subdued earnestness and decorum. Sometimes their demeanour changed from that of gracious hosts and guests to an air expressive of stern denunciation, when they acted the Repulse of the Traitor, who was never to be permitted to enter a house at Tor-uaine, but to be repelled with horror. The 'bad man' was a log set on end, which they pelted with clods and stones, and addressed in terms of execration and contempt. As the closing scene of this performance, Gormul would advance with several flat stones in her hands, and be Oirig, offering bannocks and cheese to the unhappy wretch, with words of pity ere he fled to the wilderness whence he had dared to venture in search of food.

At these meetings Gormul often carried about as her doll, hushing and lulling it to sleep with a song, a round stone from the shore wrapped in a plaid (quite an armful), the weight of which was suggestive of a heavy child needing special care lest it should fall. This object of solicitude was named the 'Cagaran' (or darling), and lent itself easily to any sort of treatment. It was frequently scoured in the burn, or rolled down a steep slope that it might learn to walk, and at the fireside it endured any degree of heat without complaint. About the doors on frosty evenings they would be merry and warm playing the primitive game of 'Sgiobag', with the Man-in-the-Moon occasionally looking down on them; or they would be out and in, wondering after a long period of cloud and gloom at the brilliancy of the sky, penetrated to their inmost soul by the effulgent gaze of the Evening Star gliding down into the West. All they beheld was cause for wonder, not without fear, when at sunset there was the appearance of a great conflagration over the sea, and when the 'Tremblers' came and went over the shoulder of the mountains, shivering, changing, their pale hue sometimes turning to crimson of deepest dye. Old Muldonach the Shepherd, would point to the Plough and other constellations—'The King of Mengan's Daughter (Orion), her Gillie and Dog' and the 'Grioglachan' (Pleiades), from the position of which men knew the time, and when they should be going to sleep. Within doors the pastimes, though different, were not less interesting. There was much pathos in the Lullaby of the slumbering Sheep-mother to her Lambs, one on each side, while the Fox comes stealthily and carries them away, and she, unconscious of her loss, goes on singing to them. 'How many horns has the goat?' with forfeits, usually led to some excitement, and the 'Dance of the Ducks' to hearty laughter over the awkward movements of the dancers. Fairy tales might be repeated, and dancing songs with quaint and absurd words, which frequently affect the aged as memories of a higher and better life.

> 'My eyes are dim with childish tears,
>   My heart is idly stirred,
> For the same sound is in my ears
>   That in those days I heard.'

And may be all that they can remember of native 'verse', such as 'Mhórag an tu, tu?' 'Mhórag an tu bh' ann?' 'An cual thu gu'n robh snaoisean 's Mhuileann Duibh, 's Mhuileann Duibh?' Old Muldònich sang many a one of these to little Gormul sitting on his knee. Thus were the children unconsciously teaching themselves at these games, and learning to take part some day in the work of the world. Nor were they without receiving historical impressions, giving them a sort of perspective in their view of the past—the vast depths, the mystery of the times of old, the days of other years. A green mound rose above the hamlet from which it derived its name of Tor-uaine, where their pagan forefathers had been laid to rest, but where no Christian had ever been interred. On a cliff above the sea a ruined tower or dun was conspicuous, erected beyond the dawn of local tradition. On the moor near a lake a subterranean dwelling had been discovered by the roof suddenly falling in, which was straightway regarded by the youthful observers as most certainly the den of unknown and terrible wild beasts and hobgoblins, such as the 'Water-Kelpie'. On a smooth level spot half way up the declivity behind Tor-uaine stood an erect memorial stone, twelve feet in height, in memory of one Una, of whose existence there was no other record. Near this monument greetings and challenges might be offered to an echo, a 'MacTalla', or 'son of the ground', which had a marvellously articulate tongue and clear voice. Up in a corrie above the glen was a deep cavern where wandering outlaws would be incarcerated and securely closed in with heavy blocks of stone till duly delivered to the officers of the law. With awe and pity was the solitary grave regarded of a wicked woman, who, long, long ago had been buried alive there for the crime of milking her neighbours' cows at night. The Prophecies of Kenneth the Sallow-faced were also known to Gormul and her playmates, which gave them an equally solemn forecast of what was yet to be, some day upon the earth. Thus was the age of play merging gradually into that of earnest and continual toil, which would often be illumined in after years by memories of innocent childhood. Oirig, though absorbed by her occupation, which gave scope for abstracting trains of ideas besides was, nevertheless, not always absent from these youthful entertainments, for she kept a wakeful ear to the changing tones of voice, whether of grief and pain, or of joy and mirth, of her little friend, responding to her in silence when she came home, by a glance from the beautiful eyes, which would console the child in sorrow, restrain undue impetuosity of feeling and direct the growing nature to turn from its natural bent if in error, and follow the better way. When the lightning flashed and darted through every crevice, followed by terrifying peals of thunder, and danger seemed very near, a look at Oirig was enough for Gormul; there was protection from every form of evil, common, or mysterious and rare.

PART II

In thus recalling some of the amusements of infancy, and the significance of these, in the development of the children of Tor-uaine, it must not be supposed that they had not been receiving any religious instruction, for they were brought up on the natural and reasonable plan of following in the footsteps of their parents, whose belief they imbibed from their earliest days, through the unconscious influence of example, by correction, and listening to whatever was talked about at the fireside; thus receiving impressions on right and wrong, never to be effaced. A feeling of family reverence was strong then, and one of the most effectual of religious influences, when each child was usually named after an ancestor or near relation, ever deeply mourned, whose memory was in this manner to be preserved, and always held up as a portrait of the ideal man or woman to the young living representative in the community, towards whom a special regard would be manifested and passionately cherished by some devoted grandmother, looking far before and able to see far behind;

earnestly resolving that the heavenly ray which once illuminated this sequestered vale should never be extinguished upon the earth, but, like a vestal lamp, be always burning, down through the ages to come. When the young men and maidens went forth into the world, the single exhortation they received would be: 'Remember those from whom you have come', words implying all that was hallowed in every home; and they succeeded, or they failed, as they obeyed, or gave no heed to the warning voice of love. Those who remembered, and did not turn this glorious principle into a cause for absurd vanity, indicated their claim to being of good descent by one quality above every other, that of Fidelity, and generally won the confidence, unsought, of all with whom they came in contact. From the imperative desire of showing respect to the beloved dead, it often happened that two in a family must bear the same name, followed by distinctive adjectives, such as dark, brown, fair, young, tall.

At night, in the long winter season, it was the custom of the inhabitants of Tor-uaine to meet at one or more of their dwellings for a 'Ceilidh, or friendly discussion of everything under the sun', from affairs of Church and State down to their own personal concerns, which often gave rise to anxious uneasiness when rumours of threatened famine came to their ears, or of a deadly fever passing through the glen. By common consent the abode of Oirig was preferred to any other; her silent look of welcome was remarkably cordial, and the peace which there was felt on turning in from the roar of the sea, the wind, and the torrent foaming down in the deep gorge, was for ever after a sacred memory with those who often went there, and returned to their homes refreshed and the better for having been in her presence. There was no rattling, no clatter, no sound of hail on the kindly thatch overhead. With a bright fire of peats on the hearth in the middle of the floor, and open above to the glistening black rafters, the apartment was warm and well ventilated, the smoke being directed by management of a current of air, to go straight up through an aperture in the roof. Oirig would leave the loom in the evening and be seated at her spinningwheel, and Gormul near her on a low stool, would diligently be carding the wool and preparing it for her to spin. The friends coming in, one by one and saying 'Fàilt oirbh' ('Hail to you'), would find places on a long settle, chairs, and stools, some sitting on the well-swept earthen floor or on a few peats put together, the 'sunnag', or straw easy chair being reserved for the principal guest of the evening, who was generally Patrick the Fair (Pàdruig Bàn), the genial Catechist of Glen Columkill. In addition to the light from the fire, a 'crusie', well supplied with seal or fish oil and a rush wick was always hung near the dresser where 'cogues', wooden bowls, crocks of clay, a wooden platter, and horn spoons would be neatly arranged, with large shells from tropical seas adorning the ends of the shelves. There was also near the lamp a small bookcase fastened to the wall, containing some old, well-thumbed volumes, chiefly Latin, such as the Vulgate, a Psalter, the 'Imitation', by Thomas-a-Kempis, Virgil, and others, bound in parchment, and an Irish Bible. Though never opened, these books were regarded with great veneration as monuments of a bygone time. Beneath stood a large girnel containing the household store of meal, ground in a quern by Torquil and Christian, a brother and sister living near. In a corner of the room was an ancient cupboard, where a few relics were preserved, and where Oirig kept a flagon containing a special cordial, extracted from various herbs, which she administered to those who were in need of rousing and encouragement, and in danger of sinking into a state of apathy and despair. A battle-axe, a rusty claymore, and a shepherd's crook were hanging on the same side. Above the loom a quantity of yarn was suspended ready for immediate use, and laid along the beams supporting the roof, were long fishing rods convenient to be taken down when wanted. There must always have been a wise cat presiding on Oirig's hearth or perched upon the loom, having seemingly intelligent appreciation of the activity of movement manifested by her mistress, and admiration of the deftness with which she played the 'game of the shuttle', looking on with the air of a connoisseur.

The Ceilidh was not an occasion for idleness, though some had nothing in their hands, being more in need of recreation and rest after a day of toil in the mountain or on the sea. The women would knit or twine thread with a spindle; and ready-witted men would weave the bent grass into matting, much used in all operations of winnowing, roasting, and grinding grain, and also for curtains and screens; make baskets of willow twigs, or mend nets while joining in the conversation; or someone would recite a legend, word for word, as originally composed; or sing the heroic deeds of the 'Feinn' to a monotonous chant, with a chorus, in which all sang together. The bagpipe would vary the entertainment, or a wandering fiddler might be invited to play, who would change the course of their thoughts by the exquisite strains of some Lowland airs which they had never heard before, or a new song would be mentioned and sung, which, delighted with its wit, or pathos and melody, all must learn. The packman, who supplied many needs, was always a welcome arrival with his fluent speech, pleasant anecdotes, and unrivalled knowledge of the world. A sailor often appeared after a long absence, or a soldier, who had thrilling tales of adventure to relate. Some nights the Catechist, appointed by the General Assembly to assist the minister in his wide parish, where there were few roads or bridges over streams, would address the company on some points of doctrine and Scripture history, and then question every person, old and young, as to what he or she remembered and understood on the subject, the children, too, being admonished, to be always true and kind in thought, word, and deed. He was also in the habit of repeating the Psalms aloud, so that they might fix them in their recollection, and be able to sing when moved to join in praise, without embarrassing hesitation. This exercise of the memory was much needed then, when the Irish version of the Bible had become unintelligible to the people of 'Albainn', or Scotland, and had not yet been translated into their own dialect, which in the course of time had been undergoing a fundamental change. When the company departed on nights of profound gloom, and no faint light was visible above or around, a very quaint effect was produced by specks of fire receding in different directions from peats burning at one end, and held in their hands as torches, by those who had to find their way home over the pasture, beyond the cluster of dwellings forming the centre of the hamlet.

PART III

The Sundays were observed with great reverence and intelligent delight at Tor-uaine. It was at the Catechist's own house the people assembled in their best clothes on the Lord's Day. Public worship would be conducted with grave and intense enjoyment. There were no books in their hands—the Precentor chanting each line of a verse ere it was sung by the congregation— all could take part in the singing without difficulty. This good man, Pàdruig Bàn was of great assistance to the revered minister, Mr Calum, who came round on horseback to attend to his people as often as he was able, expressing a hope of meeting many of them, sometime, at the solemn celebration of the Lord's Supper, held at the Parish Church, once a year. At public worship they sang the Psalms only, but there were many beautiful old hymns which had never been collected or written, throughout the country, of which Oirig knew the greater number, such as the 'Song of Pity', 'The Song of Forgiveness', the 'Song of Hope', and often sang softly to herself when sitting at the loom. Of her own accord Gormul learned every one of them—though not fully understanding their meaning—purely for the sake of doing whatever seemed to give pleasure to her elderly friend, who, moreover, would be murmuring them to herself when lying awake in the silence of night, and never failed to share her delight in some favourite lay with the suffering and the infirm, to whom she was true 'Anam-chara' (soul-friend) in times of loneliness and sorrow.

Perhaps Gormul could not read very well, and had no knowledge of the English language, but was not therefore rude and vulgar. On the contrary, she was well versed in poetry, proverbs, legendary and historical lore, and could, like Oirig, express herself in her native tongue with absolute correctness and elegance. Though no scholar, she was daily learning much and becoming wise, by simple attention to the duties that devolved upon her on ceasing to be a child, and being left to the exercise of her own discretion. Her daily round might be in the following order: she would rise early, knowing the time by the sun and the crowing of the cock, or by the tides, and let out the fowls, and milk the goats or cow; then rouse the slumbering embers on the hearth and make a bright fire; prepare the morning meal (tea was as yet unknown in the Glen but in the tales of sailors returned from China); arrange the house; assist Oirig at the work of preparing wool for spinning, washing, dyeing, greasing, carding, and so on; run on a message to the shieling or beyond the glen, barefooted, but sometimes wearing brogues made by Muldonich the shepherd ('no fleeter was the mountain roe'), and promptly convey a reply relating to a web of kelt, drugget, or flannel; have an eye to the cow and the fowls lest they might stray into the corn-lands; and guarding chickens and ducklings from the approach of birds of prey; sitting or sauntering along, holding a distaff and diligently twirling a spindle to make the best use of the time, while listening to the piping of the birds on the strand, such as St. Bride's Gillie, and others, to the warbling of the lark from the moor, and to the repeated notes of the mavis—'illy-ri-vig! illy-ri-vig! illy-ri-vig!'—from the crags of the burnside; or hasten away to St. Colm's Well to fetch a reviving draught of coldest water for a feverish sufferer: or wander at certain seasons along the shore, the pastures, and base of the mountain, in search of lichens and roots for Oirig's use in dyeing wool; or gathering Simples for Catriona Beaton, of the celebrated race of doctors, who inherited a knowledge of the medical properties of plants; 'St. Colum's plant' would be among them, 'St. Patrick's Cup', 'St. Bridget's herb', also those named in remembrance of the 'King of Britain's son', and of the renewed 'Cù-chulain'. There would often be dulse and shellfish to get, which, prepared with meal, made very wholesome articles of food, and in autumn small fish in abundance might be taken by youths and maidens with rods at high tide. Washing was of frequent occurrence, and mending of clothes, with new things to make. When work was finished, Gormul often went to engage women in the glen for a great 'waulking', and would deliver a special invitation to the best singers. Besides all these details of domestic duty, she took her turn like other women, at the outdoor work of the hamlet, when for the general good they wrought collectively. In spring they cut seaware for the enrichment of the soil, working rapidly at low tide with calm sea; in early summer there was the same need of promptness in cutting and drying the peats, and in having them conveyed to the hamlet and stacked near the houses. When there was grass to cut and make into hay, every other occupation would be laid aside for a few days, and all would take advantage of dry weather, and be equally zealous in autumn in reaping and getting in the corn. Gormul was one of the most skilful in the use of the sickle, and when the reapers divided themselves into rival bands, singing words of mutual defiance with a chorus, she was often the leader on the victorious side.

Among the neighbours Gormul had devoted friends, such as the old shepherd, who every spring never failed to carry a motherless lamb down from the hill in the pouch of his plaid for her to rear from Maiseag's milk; and Calum 'Buachaille', the herd, who was always pleased when she went by, over the moor, to visit his blind mother and Annag, his sister; while Faicill, his wary dog, would greet her with a bark of welcome, when, to all appearance, absorbed by the care of his excitable charge, so easily put into a state of dangerous panic by any unusual sight or sound. Her heart's delight when at leisure was to gather the little children about her, the toddling things and 'wee tots', remembering the sainted Colum's injunction 'to give the love that was greatest to the foot that was least', signifying childhood still in the infant stage. On New Year's Day (old style) she would run races with them on the sands, and have thick little bannocks ready for each child, and sometimes be able to prepare a bowl of 'stapag' (cream mixed with meal), of which they would partake with horn spoons, sitting in a circle in some sheltered nook. At Easter she would hide eggs in tufts of grass and in corners behind rocks and walls, where the little ones could easily find them, believing that, by permission granted only at this season, they were stealing them cleverly, to roast them afterwards at a fire of their own, at a safe distance from the houses. Then, at mid-summer and Hallowe'en she helped them to make bonfires of sticks gathered on the shore. Nor was Gormul forgetful of the aged and infirm, running when she thought of them, or Oirig made a remark, to stir up their fires, or to carry in water from the well. One summer a duck, whose hatching somehow had gone wrong—the nest had been scattered by a sudden flood in a rivulet near which it was situated—concentrated all the strength of her maternal affection on Gormul, and followed her about anywhere, finally waddling into Oirig's fireside, to the surprise and indignation of Béusag, the cat, with the evident intention of establishing herself there as 'house pet'. The cat, too wise to make a scene, would spring lightly to the top of the girnel, surveying the droll intruder from that elevation with ironical glances, and mocking movements of head and tail; the duck preening her feathers near the fire, turning herself round as if to get the benefit of the warmth, would look up into Gormul's face as she sat spinning or carding, and seem to say 'Am I not your own real favourite among all the creatures? Fàg, fàg! fàg, fàg!' Béusag would afterwards be loudly applauded when the new pet retired, for her admirable behaviour on such trying occasions, and receive much caressing with a bit of fish or drop of cream. So sensitive was Béusag, that words had to be softened in sound so as not to jar upon her, especially those in which the letter R was prominent, and this forbearance of hers was a most remarkable instance of her good sense and power of self-control.

Thus did this community live in peace and friendship for many years, poor but orderly, never idle nor overtasked either, till Gormul had grown into a tall maiden, fair to behold—strong, gentle, and good. Her eyes were dark blue, and her hair, which she now began to roll into a coil at the back of her head, was brown. Oirig was always with her spiritually at her work, as she had been during the early period of imaginative play, in the Fairyland of childhood. When she came in weary from some task needing arduous endeavour, she was met by a far-seeing glance, commanding consolation and rest, from the radiant eyes which soon were to be veiled with tears, and Gormul suddenly gone for ever.

PART IV

One morning Gormul rose at dawn to fetch water from St Colum's Well, which was at some distance away, round a headland, near the shore, for her friend Muldonich, who was ill, and asked for nothing better in this world than a refreshing drink from the consecrated spring. To the grief of Oirig, and the consternation of the community, she never returned home, nor was she seen at Tor-uaine any more. Careful search was made in every direction, in caves, caverns, and deep rifts in the rocks; the tide went far out, and came in again, but there was no trace of the missing one. There were many conjectures as to the cause of her disappearance; some believed that she must have tripped and fallen over a precipice into the surge below, or been swept away in a moment by an awful wave running in on the land; others thought that she might have been kidnapped by the lawless crew of a passing vessel, recollecting that a ship of most sinister aspect had recently been descried on the coast by a keen-sighted shepherd. Calum Buachaill knew by Faicill's signs of uneasiness that strangers were in the neighbourhood, but satisfied that with advancing day, no harm would come to the cattle from anyone with marauding intent, gave no further heed to the circumstance. True sympathy with Oirig was manifested by the other good women of the hamlet, but no one could give her any comfort. At night, the children wept sore for 'Goilamuil', and imagined her cold, weary, and forlorn in the Unknown, beset by terrifying phantoms and monsters; and ere long, were enacting the sad event in a succession of vivid scenes ending with a tremendous commotion, when the 'Muileartach Mhór' (the wild woman of the sea) came rushing in, and defying all resistance, bore the unfortunate maiden down into the depths of the ocean. Like their seniors, the little ones too, did not forget to raise a 'Lament for Gormul' at their play-waulkings. The bereaved Oirig was in deep distress, but seldom made allusion to the change in her daily life; not repining, when according to the ancient saying: 'On her the two days were come,' but continually missing the gladsome, girlish voice calling in the fowls, the kid, the calf, to be fed at stated intervals, and Maiseag, the cow, to be milked.

Others offered their assistance, but the tones of their voices had not the expression, cadence, and meaning of Gormul's as she called out 'díug!' 'díug' to the hens, 'big!' 'big!' to the chickens, 'minnean!' 'minnean!' plaintively to the kid, and 'saogan!' 'saogan!' to the calf, in a freer manner. Though unable to talk, Oirig could pray, and when sitting alone at the loom, used to let her thoughts flow into a measured form, which she would adopt to a simple melody and chant in an undertone. It had always been her habit, and was now a relief to her feelings thus to sing or 'croon' over her work. Sometimes she would wander along the shore and address the sea, if the waves were rolling in after a storm: 'Where hast thou hidden her, thou Raving One?' And then from the tumultuous roar reverberating on every side, an answer seemed to come: 'By Command—for Gormul's sake—I spared the wicked, who deserved, a hundred times, to drown!' When the ocean was calm, and gulls and terns were rejoicing with mournful cries, she would again remonstrate with the mighty Power: 'Why wail thy Birds as if in sorrow for the lost? where is my Gormul lying?' and in a gentle murmur as the wave sank sobbing at her feet, these words of promise to her fancy came: 'Thy Gormul is not desolate, and even now is sending forth her thoughts to thee'. Then she would return home strengthened, and resume her work. One dark and stormy day, she was much reassured, on turning inland from the shore, by the spectacle of a magnificent rainbow spanning the glen, and shining against the ominous gloom behind. Her feelings fluctuated according to the signs that struck her imagination in sleep or in the waking dreams of day. When the men came in from fishing in the early morning, singing a slow 'Iorram', 'On Saturday I had great sorrow, Iùriv o-hì, iùriv o-hù', because their boat was well-laden, and heavy to pull, she would exclaim: 'Thus might a dirge for Gormul sound'.

One of the songs she composed and sang, ran in the following manner in Gaelic assonant rhyme:

The Song of Oirig—and of Gormul

Chorus.

> Art thou gone away for ever?
> All the day I long for thee;
> Art thou gone for ever, Gormul?
> 'Art thou waking, art thou sleeping;
> Is thy resting place the sea?

> 'Art thou in the Heaven high, while
> I remain on earth to grieve?

> 'Sitting lonely at the loom,
> Remembering and missing thee.

> 'To the Father I commit thee,
> Blessing thee from morn till eve.'

Seated on a bench at the end of her dwelling, whence there was a view of the horizon, resting and meditating according to her wont, at the close of day, till the stars appeared, Oirig sometimes heard the croak of the Raven, and the quivering of his wings, from the depth of the firmament, as he was returning at nightfall to his inaccessible retreat in the corrie above, and would sigh and say, looking upwards: 'O, thou Bird of foreknowledge and wisdom, fain would I be to understand what perhaps thou art telling me; like Fearchar, the great physician of old, to whom a raven, after announcing where there was urgent need of his presence, he would be far on his way thither ere met by the anxious messengers sent forth in quest of him. 'Hast thou not a message for me, also?' 'Hast thou heard or seen ought of Gormul?'

Though never sensible of feeling dull on their own ground, in the homes of their fathers, on whose hearthstones the sacred fire, once kindled, had not been allowed to 'go out' for many generations; not tempted to conceive the idea that their lot must be unfortunate because far from cities and the busy haunts of commerce, the folk of Tor-uaine were not indifferent to every variety of rumour and news, reaching them by land and sea; every incident having a certain significance, affecting them with a shock of surprise, and not seldom being regarded as the fulfilment of a dream. Thus it was with wonder and keen interest the tidings were received throughout the township on a wild day of wind and heavy rain in autumn, that a Calaman (a dove), apparently driven by the storm, had been discovered cowering in a hollow on the sheltered side of Oirig's peat-stack. The exhausted bird was taken into the warm dwelling, and being tenderly cherished, gradually regained its strength, but never attempted to fly away. It stayed all winter, becoming so tame that it would alight on Oirig's shoulder, who, bending her head towards it, in the attitude of St Gregory, when his Dove came breathing into his ear, a deep knowledge of the world's sorrow, that could not be expressed in human language, would earnestly say: 'O thou little Calaman, come to me from afar, hast thou seen Gormul? What if thou be Gormul herself come to comfort me? In spring, as if a slumbering recollection were awaking in it, the dove became restless, and went occasionally on long flights when the weather was fine, returning later each time, till one evening, when it did not come back as usual, and was seen no more. Oirig often sent her thoughts after the Calaman, and never lost the impression that as an emblem of the Divine Compassion, it had been sent to console her during a long and dreary winter. When the agitation attending her loss had in some degree subsided, she set herself resolutely to believe that all was well with Gormul, and that some day they would both meet again in this life; a hope entertained by her for several years, in the course of which many changes occurred at Tor-uaine. Having become somewhat frail, and no longer able to work as before, though still vigorous in mind, Oirig had given over her loom to a younger person. Seated in her 'Sunnag' one morning, near the fire, holding a piece of knitting, which was now her constant occupation, the Catechist entered, and said with emotion: 'Beloved of Women, hast thou heard the news? My son, Alan, has returned safe from a disastrous voyage.'

PART V

Alan followed, and related how his vessel had been wrecked in a hurricane on the Island of Monte Verde, north of Venezuela, in South America. Wandering about he came to the country house of the proprietor of the island, Senor Lorenzo de Monte Verde, where, though there was fierce hatred felt at that time towards Great Britain by the Spanish people, they treated him kindly, and he received permission to stay at this hospitable mansion till he should meet with a favourable opportunity of departing for a British seaport. While there, he was greatly astonished one evening, to overhear from an enclosed court, open to the sky, in the tones of a woman's voice, the names of places with which he was familiar at home, chanted slowly, and with earnest expression, thus:—

'Grùl is Brunal'—Grùl and Brunal.
'Dà Chnoc Sgarral'—The two hills of Sgarral.
'Cnoc nan Oigh'—The Maidens' Knoll.
'Airidh Mhic Leoid'—MacLeod's Shieling.
'Am chrò chaorach'—Time to fold the sheep.
'Aig ceann caol'—At the narrow end of
'Druim Orrail'—Druim Orrail.
'U' ulaidh, 's mo luaidh'—My treasure, my most-loved.
'Beinn Duagraich'—Is Beinn Duagraich.

Another day he heard a song from the same court, also in the language of his native glen, and on enquiry, was given to understand that it was the noble Senora herself who was singing. Hearing the name of Oirig, he listened with attention—the melody was one which Oirig used to chant, the following being some of the verses which fell upon his ear, while the singer was lulling a child to sleep:—

Chorus: Oirig, do not thou forget me,
                Though thou never see me more.
                O! do not forget me, Oirig!

                Without father, without mother,
                Fondly didst thou take me home.
                Oirig, etc.

At Colum's Well the wild men seized, and
Bore me from my native shore.
   Oirig, etc.

Far away, across the ocean
To a folk and land unknown
   Oirig, etc.

To the Father I commit thee,
Blessing thee from eve to morn.
   Oirig, etc.

He was now most desirous of being presented to the lady of the house, whom he had not yet seen, and when conducted into her presence as 'the British lad', 'the British sailor' immediately recognized in this handsome matron of most benevolent mien, Gormul, the long-lost playmate of his youth, who also remembered him, and enquired eagerly and anxiously about Oirig, his father, and all the old friends at Tor-uaine. In explanation of his having heard her chanting one evening, she said that it had always been her habit ere retiring to rest, to go out and repeat under the shining stars, words of prayer and remembrance, as Oirig used to do at home. Then she related the manner of her strange disappearance. Having gone early to St Colum's Well for fresh water to comfort the aged Muldonich, she was suddenly seized by fierce-looking men, who were filling casks from the spring, and rolled in a sail to stifle her cries, was swiftly rowed out to sea, and put on board a great ship, where she found a number of unfortunate youths and maidens, who had been kidnapped like herself, to be sold on the cotton and sugar plantations in America as criminals, under the ban of the law. Among the captives was a devoted mother from the west side of Lewis, who had contrived to get on board to share the weal or woe of an only son. Gormul used to sing Oirig's Songs of Consolation to this good woman, the others taking up the refrain, and on one occasion, the captain, who was listening, began to weep, and ever after was kind to them all, the sailors, also, seeming sorry for what they had done.

On arriving in port, they were marched to the slaves' market-place, where a Spanish gentleman, who was passing along, noticed Gormul, and divining what she really was, purchased her, believing she would be a pleasant-looking attendant, amid a retinue of black men and women, on his wife and daughter. Till he could send for her to his residence, on the island of Monte Verde, he placed her at a convent in this town, of which his own sister was the Mother Superior, where, in the care of the tender-hearted nuns, the mourning girl gradually recovered from a state of sorrow and dread, and was not long in acquiring a sufficient knowledge of the Spanish language, which enabled her to speak fluently when summoned by Senor Lorenzo to her new home on his beautiful and salubrious island, where she was received with every mark of kindness by his family. Her composed and modest demeanour; her willing obedience, her generosity of disposition, and disdain of meanness and falsehood, being rightly regarded as true signs of honourable descent, all were pleased, when eventually the Hebridean maiden became the wife of the eldest son. Then Alan produced the keepsakes she sent to Oirig—a miniature of herself, a necklace of sparkling precious stones, and a fine silken scarf, which he laid round her shoulders. 'Let me hear the "Song of Remembrance",' she said, and when Alan complied, that pleased her most of all. 'Now am I ready to depart,' she added calmly.

PART VI

More than a year after the departure of Alan, son of Patrick, on his next voyage, on a fine morning in the month of May, when the cuckoo, unseen, was calling on high from a bushy cleft, and the air was fragrant with primroses, and a peculiarly fresh odour awaking memory and hope, was emanating from the sea. [This ungrammatical sentence is given exactly as it is in the original. Probably the full-stop should be a comma. Editor.] Great astonishment was caused, succeeded by alarm, when a large vessel, displaying the flag of Spain, appeared round the headland, and sailing up the loch cast anchor at exactly the safest spot. A boat was then seen approaching, and skilfully directed to the best landing-place, the steersman of which shouted to the crowd assembled on the bank above the shore:—'Hail! ye men of Tor-uaine! Have ye no welcome for your friends to-day!' Recognizing the voice of Alan, son of Patrick, they hastened down, when he explained how it happened that the *Aguila* (Eagle), a Spanish privateer, should thus arrive under his guidance as pilot in their obscure harbour. The use of this vessel was granted by the Government to Señor Lorenzo de Monte Verde, in consideration of important services rendered by him to his country, and during a cessation in the frequent hostilities with Great Britain, at Gormul's entreaty, despatched, under the name of La Paloma, the Dove, with her two sons on board, and her favourite nurse, to convey Oirig, if so disposed; to her own island home in the far West. The sons of Gormul, dressed in the uniform of Naval Cadets, were then introduced and most cordially received; their gallant bearing being commented on with much admiration. The elder, Fernando, was of Spanish type, dark-haired, of grave countenance, and slender in figure. Donaldo, the younger, in marked contrast, was remarkably fair, of more robust frame, with fearless, flashing blue eyes. 'O! how he resembles Donald, son of Tormod, son of Magnus, his grandfather, who fell in battle,' they exclaimed, and gave him their hearts there and then. Oirig met her welcome visitors at the door of her dwelling, when each youth, bowing reverently and holding his cap in his hand, said: 'Fàilt' oirbh, Oirig!' but she embraced them with many ejaculations of wonder and praise. 'Will you come with us?' they said; 'Our mother is longing for you, and has prepared a house, thatched and furnished like this, near our own home, for you to dwell in, when Serafina, our old nurse, and Merla, her daughter, will be your attendants.' Oirig responded with much feeling, declaring her willingness to traverse the wildest seas to be once more with Gormul. Preparations were immediately made for her departure, and soon completed, as she had already made all her important worldly arrangements. An attached kinswoman, Raonuild Ruadh (Ranhilda the red-haired) offered to accompany her on the voyage, and remain with her in the new home, and in the meanwhile packed up what effects were necessary to take, such as the 'Sunnag', the Distaff, and a chest of Plaids and Blankets with her clothing. The Spanish youths occupied the interval of time in visiting the places associated with their mother's happy childhood, the incidents of which she was wont to relate to them with all the charm of a romance or fairy tale. Gormul had always been the favourite playmate of her children, while wisely instructing them in the language and best traditions of her fathers, and no sons could surpass Fernando and Donaldo in their single-hearted devotion and loyalty to her. First of all, followed by a band of children, they repaired to St Colum's Well, where they recalled their tender mother's overwhelming terror, when carried away by the Pirates; then they climbed the hill and made the Echo talk volubly and vociferously in Gaelic, Spanish, and the lisping Negro dialect; nor did they forget the remnant of primeval forest further on, where, with a feeling of awe, as if entering a holy fane, the children of Tor-uaine went nutting in Autumn; they roamed round by the lake in the moor, and bade defiance to the Water-kelpie supposed to be lurking under the 'Dhuilleag bhàite' (leaves of Water Lily) floating on the surface; they sailed boats of Flag-leaves there, and caught trout with their hands in the burn; they were at the pretty water-fall above the pool where the webs used to be washed, and linen bleached on the lovely sward forming the verdant margin; they rolled down the flowery braes, shouting with joy, and ran races with their numerous escort on the sands. Able to talk Gaelic fluently, they were at ease wherever they went, and were too well-bred ever to be indifferent or scornful of the customs of a community living in more primitive conditions than themselves, where some souls, great and simple, spiritually aspiring amid many sorrows and perplexities, attained a freedom, transcendent and untrammelled by ties that bind the heart too closely to the world. On the day of her departure, friends gathered from far and near to bid Oirig farewell; Mr Calum was among them, and speaking words of loving appreciation for all, was enabled by his genial and tactful manner to help them in maintaining an attitude of composure on this most affecting occasion. When they were assembling, a trusty messenger, the 'Gillie ruith' (the runner) arrived from the Chief with a benediction, and his own silver-mounted staff to support her steps in advancing age, which Oirig acknowledged with her fervid blessing in return; then, replying to the Minister's address, she endeavoured to say what she hoped might sustain and comfort those whom she was leaving, never to meet again. Each person present accepted these utterances as especially suited to his or her own case, for times of great trouble and anguish were drawing near; war was imminent; much distress would follow, and the changes predicted by Kenneth, the Seer—'Ships would be seen sailing up the Great Glen on the Mainland', 'roads would run everywhere', and 'bridges be erected over streams', and the people begin to move away to new lands beyond the Western Sea. At the sound of a bell on board the ship, the Cadets, followed by Ranhilda and Alan, stepped forward to conduct their venerable friend to the boat which was waiting for her. The sun was setting, and a gorgeous purple glow, paling to crimson and rose, came over the mountain range; the Cuckoo might be heard from a distant cove, and the Corn-crake from a leafy hollow; the innocent Mavis, without concern, was warbling its evening song from a pinnacle above the hamlet; the Plover was whistling and the Snipe bleating from the moor, whence the Curlew also was sending forth a signal cry. When the boat was moving off on the full tide, with gently splashing oars, there arose into the still air a strange and solemn sound of quavering, plaintive, and strong deep voices combined, singing one of Oirig's favourite hymns, led by the minister, who 'gave out the line' in melodious and sonorous tones. This hymn was composed by Mr Calum himself in his youth, and bore some resemblance to the following verses from a collection published in England about the same time by an English Divine:—

> A thousand ages in Thy sight
>   Are like an evening gone;
> Short as the watch that ends the night
>   Before the rising sun.
> Time, like an ever-flowing stream,
>   Bears all its sons away;
> They fly forgotten, as a dream
>   Dies at the opening day.
> O God! our help in ages past,
>   Our hope for years to come;
> Be Thou our guard while troubles last,
>   And our eternal home.

No one lay down to sleep at Tor-uaine on that eventful night. All watched to see the departure of the Paloma, as spreading her wings out wide, she went gliding slowly round the headland, and vanished soon after dawn. It was long ere tidings came of the departed ones; not till Alan returned again, who described the meeting of Gormul with her sons and Oirig more by gestures, with tears in his eyes, than by ordinary words.

The conclusion of this tale—once related at the minister's fireside by little Morag of Oransay to entertain him when ailing—is, that Oirig, regaining strength in the gladness of a renewed relation with Gormul, in whose generous and beneficent manner of living there was ample room for her, reached to a very advanced age; her lustrous eyes had not become dim, nor had her mental faculties failed when the hour of her departure came. The two friends were sitting hand in hand at eventide, with their faces turned towards the expanse of sea extending northwards, conversing on the times to come and the careers of the children, when the Angelus sounded from a chapel standing apart on a promontory above the bay; Oirig listening with rapt attention, exclaimed that she was hearing loving voices, long silent, calling to her, with the cadence of the lonely bells—what the Bells of Perth once said to Ruari of the Hills—in these words:—

'Thig dhachaidh!	'Come home, thou:
Thig dhachaidh!	come home thou!
Gu d'leaba,	To thy rest,
Bhith-bhuan:	Eternal!
Bhith-bhuan!'	Eternal!'

and leaning back, with an expression of joy suffusing her countenance, gently passed away. Gormul did not mourn as for one dead and gone; Oirig, as in the early state of separation, became a cherished memory, and influence ever present with her. The names of Oirig and Gormul may still be found among the different branches of the highly esteemed family of Monte Verde, over-sea.

At Tor-uaine there are only moss-covered walls to be seen where the hamlet once stood; and the glen, where no roads have ever been made, is now almost forgotten and unknown.

F.T.

INDEX OF SONG TITLES

ENGLISH TITLES

Bold figures show the page on which the song is reproduced.

GAELIC TITLES

Bold figures show the page on which the song is reproduced. The Gaelic spelling is that of the Tolmie *Journal*, pp. 273f. Editor.

INDEX TO PERSONS

To prevent duplication the appendices are excluded.